P9-CRN-339

Love in a World of Sorrow

A Teenage Girl's Holocaust Memoirs

Fanya Gottesfeld Heller

DEVORA PUBLISHING
JERUSALEM ◆ NEW YORK

LONGWOOD PUBLIC LIBRARY

Love in a World of Sorrow
A Teenage Girl's Holocaust Memoirs

Published by DEVORA PUBLISHING COMPANY

Text Copyright © 2005 Fanya Gottesfeld Heller
Editor: Fern Levitt

Cover and Inside Design: David Yaphe

All rights reserved. No part of this book may be reproduced or transmitted in any form or by any means, electronic or mechanical, including photo-copying, recording, or by any information storage and retrieval system, without permission in writing from the publisher.

Library of Congress Cataloging-in-Publication Data
Heller, Fanya Gottesfeld
Love in a World of Sorrow: A Teenage Girl's Holocaust memoirs / by Fanya Gottesfeld Heller
p. cm.
ISBN 1-932687-16-5 (hc : alk. paper) – ISBN 1-932687-17-3 (pbk : alk. paper)
1. Jews — Ukraine — Skala-Podol'skala — Biography. 2. Holocaust, Jewish (1939–1945) — Ukraine — Skala-Podol'skala — Personal narratives.
3. Jewish girls — Ukraine — Skala-Podol'skala — Biography. 4. Skala-Podol'skala (Ukraine) — Biography. I. Title.

Library of Congress Control Number: 2005920693

Cloth ISBN: 1-932687-16-5
Paper ISBN: 1-932687-17-3

*Dedicated to the
loving memory of my parents,*

Benjamin and Charlotte Gottesfeld.

"And You Shall Teach Them"
Letters of Appreciation

Students and educators who have heard Ms. Heller speak about her Holocaust experiences or who have read the first edition of her book have sent her many letters attesting to the impact that she has had on their lives. Here is a sampling from educators...

"Thank you for speaking to my class... Nothing we read in a book or see in a film can compare to meeting a survivor. The experience touched them in a very personal way and will certainly leave them with long-lasting impressions."

— Helen Bruno
teacher, The Calhoun School, New York

"The memoir is an extraordinary work by any standards. It was so vividly written that I could picture even the seemingly unimaginable. It was so honest and candid that I trusted your memory implicitly throughout. I was deeply moved from beginning to end."

— Christopher R. Browning
Institute for Advanced Studies, Princeton, New Jersey

"This group of students...most know little about the Holocaust (aside from reading The Diary of Ann Frank*) and your message was very important to raise their consciousness...Many of these students come from parochial schools and Holocaust studies were most certainly not stressed."*

— Rita Scher Dytell Ph.D.
Associate Professor of Psychology, Cooperative Program,
Department of Psychology, Manhattan College /
College of Mount St. Vincent, New York.

And from the students...

"... I am also impressed that you took what happened to you in the past to help the present, to better the future... I want you to know that I feel you are a good role model for me. I feel that from today on, you will always have an effect on the way I live my life."

— Sherri

"... I would like you to know that, even though I didn't experience your suffering, I felt what you went through. My mother grew up in South Carolina with discrimination and racial hatred. She always felt low and like she couldn't fit in. But your story of courage and hope helps me as a young black woman growing up and going out into the world. You have made me feel that anything can be accomplished."

— Samantha

"I am an exchange student from Germany...spending half a year in the United States. I read your book, Strange and Unexpected Love, *for my social studies class and I really enjoyed it...My grandparents lived during World War II, and I really cannot understand how something like the Holocaust could have happened. I asked my grandparents several times why they did not do anything against the Nazis, why the German population has not done anything against the concentration camps, for example. Their answer was incredible. They said that they did not know anything about what happened in these camps. How could six million Jews be killed without the Germans knowing about it??!...When I read the book I had a lot of different feelings. On one hand, being German makes me feel a little bit guilty, because all this happened in Germany and the Germans did these cruel things to the Jews. On the other side, I try to convince myself that I am not the scapegoat for all the cruel things that happened under the power of the Nazis and Hitler...I hope it will never, never happen again!*

I know that there are a lot of prejudices between different races. There is stereotyping all over the place. However, I cannot understand why people think that they are better than another race!? As long as there are prejudices in this world there cannot be real peace, but I hope that one day it will happen!"

— Michaela

Contents

Author's Preface
to the Second Edition

My original purposes in writing this book were to uncover the truth about the death of my father and to commit my story to writing for my children and grandchildren. Disturbing thoughts still possessed me from the days of the Holocaust. The waking nightmares, obsessive fears, and unanswered questions led me into psychoanalysis and a painful journey of discovery. My first session with a psychoanalyst in New York took place in January, 1969. I thought psychoanalysis would be the best way to start the New Year. It took two years in therapy before I mustered the courage to tell the psychoanalyst what I had faced during the war, beginning with the German invasion of Poland in 1939, and ending in 1944, when our area was liberated by the Red Army.

I was afraid but desperate to somehow discover what had happened to my father, who had disappeared just at the moment of joy when my mother, my brother and I were being liberated by the Russian Army in 1944. My father's body was never found, though we searched the battlefields. I still did not wish to believe that the man my family suspected had committed the crime. This was probably the main reason I chose to enter therapy. I wanted somehow to find out the truth.

And I came to understand the importance of my story both as family history and as a contribution to the Holocaust record.

Publication of my story was greeted with warm praise and expressions of compassion for which I will always be grateful. It would scarcely be accurate to report, however, that the responses were universally generous and understanding. The account of my romantic involvement with a Ukrainian militiaman was objectionable to some readers. The editor of a major Jewish women's magazine refused to publish a review. Certain members of my own synagogue turned a cold shoulder. Most devastating were the anonymous phone calls from a few angry survivors, who said that the revelations in my story were a desecration to the memories of those who perished.

Many of these indictments have been a source of distress. I can make no apologies for what I did to survive or for the candor of my account. The unrelenting fear of death and gnawing pain of hunger led to acts of desperation among many who survived; some stole, others lied and schemed. Still others took comfort in intimate relationships that might be considered illicit or misguided in ordinary times. It was not all pure and righteous, but it happened. Even though the story I told was not always what some might consider respectable, I felt it was my obligation to those who were no longer able to tell their stories to be honest and true. Let the judgments fall where they may.

My feelings have not changed and I have neither altered nor deleted any details of my account for this new edition.

As Rabbi Irving Greenberg pointed out in his Foreword to the first edition, my story was "unfinished," recounting little of my life or that of my family in the decades since the war. Many voices have urged me to share more of my story. A reunion with one of the blessed souls who helped save us, some news about others, and a perspective of more than fifty years all compelled me to compose an Epilogue at the end of the book. We have also renamed the book from its original title, which was *Strange and Unexpected Love* to the new title, *Love in a World of Sorrow*, because we think it more faithful to the themes and spirit of the work.

The writing of this book spanned a period of three years. During this time many people and experiences affected my life and the telling of this story. Republication affords the opportunity to reiterate my thanks to all those who supported my journey with love and encouragement, who assisted in the editorial and publication process, and who communicated their reactions to the first edition.

It was during a UJA Mission to Dachau in 1988, led by Erica Jesselson and her late husband Ludwig Jesselson, that I first began thinking about writing this book. Erica and Luddy's deep and abiding friendship has provided me with an important anchor in my life since the death of my dear husband, Joseph. They opened their hearts and their home to me and gave me the courage to pursue this endeavor.

I would like to express my appreciation to several people who offered me assistance, advice and unstinting encouragement. I am indebted to Rabbi Irving Greenberg, President Emeritus of CLAL, for his insightful, thought-provoking and reverent Foreword, and to his wife Blu for her special sensitivity; to Dr. Arnold Richards and his wife Arlene Kramer Richards for their unfailing perception; to Joan Rosenbaum, Director of The Jewish Museum, for her enduring support; and to Helen Nash for her friendship and poignant response to my story.

I offer special thanks to Rabbi Dr. Norman Lamm, Chancellor of Yeshiva University, and his wife Mindy for including me as a member of the family of this outstanding academic institution.

Dr. Philip Felig, a great humanitarian and my personal physician, and his wife, Florence, were constantly there for me during the process. Dr. Felig kept me going whenever my anxieties took over and began to manifest themselves in physical symptoms. He believed in this project and helped me through some very difficult times. His wife remains a dear friend and my biggest advocate.

I am indebted to those who helped shape the manuscript and bring the first and second editions to fruition. For the first edition, Anneliese

Wagner's enthusiasm, energy and editorial abilities were skillfully applied to molding the material; Nessa Rappaport, Aviva Cantor and Dr. Eva Fogelman provided relevant criticism and praise; Bernard Scharfstein, of KTAV Publishing House Inc., furnished the final tender touches to the birthing of the book; and Rochel and George Berman of Berman Associates went to great efforts to introduce the book to a wide readership. For this current edition, my public relations representatives, Zeesy Schnur and Amara Levine-Reich of Schnur Associates, have coordinated the updating of the book, as they so capably coordinate my volunteer efforts, working with Yaacov Peterseil and his staff at Devora Publishing, who have polished the book for its second edition (text edited by Fern Levitt, book designed by David Yaphe).

I wish to acknowledge the support and love of my children, Miriam, Benjamin and Jacqueline, my grandchildren, Natasha, Adam, Sophie, Shira, Joshua, Aliza, Sarah and Joseph, and the inspiration of my new great-grandchild, Simcha Meir. With this book they have joined me in a painful journey back to the past. I honor the memory of my mother, Charlotte Gottesfeld. Despite poverty and bereavement following my father's death, she made a life and home for my brother Arthur and for me.

Of course, I alone take full responsibility for my account and for the accuracy of my recollections. Since many of the people I describe did not survive, I can only hope I have recorded their actions fairly. I pray that their spirits will find solace in the knowledge that their experiences will become part of the history of our people. May their memories be blessed.

I renew the dedication of this book to the memory of my father and mother, Benjamin and Charlotte Gottesfeld.

Fanya Gottesfeld Heller
New York, NY
December 2004

Foreword

The Nazis laid down their arms and surrendered on May 9, 1945, but their process of inflicting pain and death on Jewry never ended. The continuing casualties can be seen in the higher mortality rates and shortened life spans of survivors everywhere. The pain is renewed in the isolation of people who face an old age of absolute loneliness or who sit *shiva* all alone because many of the relatives or friends who should be with them did not survive. The Holocaust lives on, inflicting wounds, in the nightmares of those who relive moments of painful separation and helpless humiliation. It strikes without warning in the day reveries which summon up moments of agony-filled flight with lungs bursting and heart wildly beating, or eternities of terror (that actually lasted days or hours or minutes) in which people sat, totally defenseless, watching as the heartless death-dealers came closer and closer.

The survivors are the unsung heroes of this relentless war which hatred and death wage against love and life. Since 1945, we have taken them for granted — a sin for which we shall all be held accountable when we get to the *olam ha-emet*, the world of truth.

There was no advance preparation for treating the survivors — so many died during liberation when, in an excess of mistaken good will, they were given too rich food, too much, too soon. There was no world consensus to help them — so many languished in DP camps or in Cyprus detention centers for years. There was no understanding — so many were greeted with devastating suspicion ("What are those numbers on your arm? Were you a criminal, imprisoned somewhere?") or with dismissive coldness ("Why do you *farshter* [disturb] our *simcha* with your terribly sad stories?").

Many survivors fell silent, never to speak again. Others did not tell their story until decades later, when the atmosphere changed, when they could finally trust society enough that it would listen respectfully, if not sympathetically. Yet, despite all this, the survivors went on living; therein lay their heroism and greatness.

Was there ever courage to match their daring plunge back into life? The survivors had to exhibit open-eyed bravery, knowing that no one act of sacrificial abandon, no brief charge into the jaws of hell, would win them victory or blessed surcease from sorrow. To decide to live was to commit to an endless twenty-four-hour-a-day, seven-day-a-week battle with demons of fear and pain who probed continuously for every weak spot to unravel their will to live. Who but the Eternal One can ever measure what prodigious efforts were needed to scale a wall of betrayal, cruelty, and apathy in order to trust another person enough to love again? What steadfastness did it take to grapple with the memories of evil and death that ceaselessly pull the survivor away from the living and back toward the grave? What extra measure of bravery did it take to keep the battle within, without dragging others into the line of fire, in order to live as if life were really normal? What elemental will-to-live did it take to wrestle all night — and then all day — with Esau's champion and not to yield? Jacob, the mother's boy and trickster, emerged from one night's wrestling grown into Israel, the one who struggles with God and human beings, and overcomes. Then what name can adequately describe the stature of the survivor who wrestles all his or her life, who grapples on after being exhausted? After being lamed?

Fanya Gottesfeld Heller, the author of this memoir, is such a heroine of life and love. As this book reveals, she lived with demons and memories, wounds and torments. Every step that she has taken over these decades has been shadowed by unresolved questions and torturing mysteries. Yet one never would have known this from the daily annals of her life. With her husband, Joseph, she created a new life in a new country. They put behind them the evil past, yet brought with them their background, their Jewish tradition, their commitment to family, their love of good deeds, their creativity, initiative, intelligence, judgment, and drive. Together they built a family with good Jewish and human values, a successful business run ethically and responsibly, a career of service and *tzedakah* for many Jewish causes. Fanya took up advanced study and serious analysis as well.

And when she suffered the untimely loss of her beloved Joseph, Fanya did not withdraw or grow disillusioned. She responded to her grief by stepping up her good deeds, her care for others, her generosity and helpfulness, her commitment to life. And now, she has taken up the task of witness and writer. The unfinished story of her remarkable second life is not told in this memoir. But I refer to it because I believe that Fanya and Joseph's life together deserves to be seen in all its heroic stature in the context of the story told here. The life that they lived so lovingly, so beautifully after all that they went through is more than we, or God, could ever have expected or deserved. No wonder the Talmud tells us that God puts on *tefillin*; in the divine phylacteries is written the praise: "Who can compare to your people, Israel? [They are] a people unique in the whole world!"

The tale that is told in this memoir is related in a quiet voice; the book speaks with discretion, understatement, restraint. But no one should underestimate the power and depth of its witness. Scene after scene lacerates our souls and breaks our hearts. Who can ever forget the description of the murderous *aktsia*, the frantic race to hide, the fetid air, choking, being unable to breathe in the hiding place, as the dogs

15

came closer? You will remember Grandfather Azriel Gottesfeld, the tall, straight soldier, marching in the front row of Jews, proudly wearing his Emperor Franz Joseph military medal, then being shoved into the box-car for Belzec. You will remember Zhenia, who asks to be sent to Belzec to bring an end to the suffering, but is sent to serve as a maid, who is taken by an SS man to be his mistress and seeks to play Queen Esther's role to help save Jews, who is ditched by that same man when he is found out, who is dumped by him in the village square as he shouts "whore" and curses at her; she runs to save her life but is shot down by him in cold blood. Afterwards, the townspeople tear all her clothes off and mutilate the body . . . You will remember the bystanders: how Stanislaus tears Chaya the Wig's baby apart . . . How Sidor, who was good enough to hide them, makes his move on the young teenage girl, Fanya . . . How the neighbors stand by laughing, cheering, screaming as the Germans, tipped off, search and dig out the barn in which Jews have hidden . . .

There is not a false note in the book. No vaseline is smeared on the lens of this camera which zeros in on all who are caught up in this world. It records unflinchingly: Grandfather Jakob caught by the Nazis, broken by the prospect of death, begging to save his life by turning in hiding Jews. He leads the killers to the place where his wife, among others, is hiding. The cruelty in this scene could only be topped by the final act. The Germans shoot Grandfather Jakob with the brutally cynical statement, "This is how we repay traitors."

Marynka, Sidor's wife, constantly rages against hiding the Gottesfeld family, constantly threatens to inform the Germans, then flirts with Fanya's father . . . who must not offend her, indeed must pacify her in his responses. Father and mother, trapped, struggling with despair, cut off from community and calendar. Not even knowing the date of Yom Kippur, Fanya's mother guesses at the date and fasts . . . Father does not.

Father and mother know that non-Jew Jan's love for their daughter has moved him to hide them, to feed them, to save them. In the unspoken interstices of relationship, understanding, judgment, need, they accept and communicate this to their daughter. They know (and keep silent) when the relationship turns physical and also resent (and keep silent) the embarrassment of a Jewish-Gentile relationship.

What are we to make of the account of the teenage girl and the family's savior? We can appreciate the delicacy and tact of the account; there is neither a haze of nostalgia nor retroactive whine of the victim. Jan is presented kindly, understandingly, but no roseate halo colors his picture. Can the emotions of gratitude, attraction, caring coexist within one person, side by side with anger, suspicion, resentment? Can a book capture such complex truths without resorting to breast-beating or to Grand Guignol scenes? Read this account and you will experience its integrity and truth and understated power.

Thousands of personal accounts from the Shoah have appeared, but our need to know is not sated. We need more books like this one. We need to know how people lived (and died) humanly during this inhuman period. We need to know more than the mass killings and general roundups. How did individuals adjust, struggle, work, shop, help their families, keep friendships, watch the sun rise? Every scene, every face, every name snatched from the maw of forgetfulness is a victory for memory over oblivion, which is to say, a victory for life and love over death and the void.

We need these victories, and not just to fight the Holocaust deniers and revisionists (The names of those pathetic liars will be erased by the very history they seek to twist and obliterate). We need these victories because it is part of our effort to restore the balance of life and memory that was so badly disrupted in the Holocaust. We need them because we are all called to witness. We have always been called to give testimony: "You are my witnesses, says the Lord" (Isaiah 43:10).

Perhaps some will nevertheless whisper: Why tear open old wounds? Why rattle skeletons in the closet? Let the Talmud respond: "Perhaps you [as potential witnesses] will say: who needs all this trouble? Your answer is already spoken [in Leviticus 5:I] 'if he is a witness — he saw or he knew — if he does not tell it, then he shall carry [the stain of] sin upon him' " (Babylonian Talmud, Sanhedrin 37a).

So sacred is the name of God that the *halachah* forbids us to treat it with any hint of disrespect. Thus, pages printed with God's name cannot be thrown away, even when worn out. Known as *shaymos* (names), these sheets are to be buried with respect.

So precious is the human being that he or she must never be treated with disrespect. One who dies must be handled and buried with the greatest of respect. The halachah goes so far as to rule that even articles of clothing or other items that are splashed with the blood of a dead or murdered person cannot be thrown away. They must be reverently buried. I believe that the halachah already forbids people to handle books like this one except with the greatest of respect. Someday it will be recognized that it is forbidden to throw one away. Even when its pages are worn out from countless readings and endless pondering, such books will have to be reverently buried, for they are written — and suffused — with people's blood.

Irving Greenberg
Jerusalem, Israel
September 21, 1993

I

The Aktsia

My Eighteenth Birthday: September 26–29, 1942

❖ 1 ❖

"They're coming!" Aunt Lolla shouted.

Trying to shake loose from my nightmare, I rolled deeper into the blanket on the floor of the attic. But footsteps clattering on the stairs shocked me awake.

"Run, get going!" echoed from every room, the panic reverberating through the walls of the stairwell. Doors slammed open as mothers searched in the dark for their sleeping children.

I peered out the window, which looked down on the main avenue of our *shtetl*, Skala. Through the early-morning haze I could make out figures in German uniforms two blocks away, jumping off a truck, its headlights dimmed; and closer, men with rifles and machine guns kicking in doors. Huge dogs barked, and several that were unleashed darted in all directions.

It was, I later found out, the beginning of the aktsia — the day and a half of September 26–27, 1942, when the Gestapo and the Ukrainian militia joined forces to stalk every one of Skala's Jews.

Our family of sixteen — my parents, younger brother, aunts, uncles, and cousins — had assembled the night before in the home of my mother's parents, Jakob and Miriam Wasserman, a large house with three huge windows from which we could watch for the Germans. After dinner in the living room, we had debated whether they would come for us during the night.

"Not on Succos," one aunt had said.

"That's what they expect us to think," my father said. "The Germans have their own ways of celebrating our holidays."

He insisted on a night-long vigil at the attic window. I thought this was an unnecessary precaution, but I also knew that my father's hunches about German actions had always been right. We took turns at the lookout post but, as the night wore on, my young cousins straggled off one by one to various bedrooms, and each hour after midnight saw another uncle and aunt give up the vigil and find beds.

At the first peek of dawn, only my mother's sister Aunt Lolla and I remained at the window, and I had fallen asleep. It was Lolla's total obedience to my father's instructions that saved us.

The thud of bodies colliding on the upstairs landing sounded in my ears as I raced out the door in my nightgown, without coat or shoes. My hair was in curlers, with a kerchief tied around my head, because after dinner the previous evening I had washed and set it in preparation for today's festivities: Succos and my eighteenth birthday.

I dashed toward the hiding place that my father and uncles had prepared for us. It was at the end of a vast yard five or six blocks long, owned by Grandfather Jakob, whose lumber business had once been the largest in Skala.

At the far end of the yard stood a beautiful villa built by Jakob for his eldest son, my uncle Wolf. The villa's two back rooms adjoined the warehouse that Uncle Wolf had rented out to an egg-exporting firm before the war. It had been taken over by the Germans, and a few Jews were doing forced labor there under guard.

My father, Benjamin Gottesfeld, was an engineer by profession. Working for weeks at night, he had broken into the warehouse through a closet in one of the villa's back rooms, removing the door and camouflaging the entrance with a false panel — an unremarkable-looking wall lined with shelves. Under the floor of the main workroom of the warehouse he had dug a cave in which we could hide. Night after night he had carried out the sacks of earth with care, leaving no telltale trace. He had covered the ground inside the hole with straw and, with the help of my uncles, Wolf, Munio, and Mottel, had buttressed the hole with logs.

Vaulting over boards of lumber in the yard and tumbling across a rolling barrel, I sprinted straight ahead amid the noise of screams and shots coming from just beyond the wooden fence. From only a block away, the sound of heavy battering was followed by a volley of gunfire. I felt a sudden pain in my shoulder: a bullet must have hit me! *Ignore it and run faster,* I told myself, but the lumberyard seemed to have gotten longer since the last time I had wandered through it.

Uncle Wolf, his wife and two daughters had slept in their villa that night and hadn't known what was happening until my father had pounded on their door to wake them. By the time I reached the villa, my father had gone to the back room — Wolf's room — and removed part of the panel covering the closet. He told me to squeeze through the opening. I crawled into the long, narrow workroom of the warehouse, which held tables covered with eggs, boxes, egg-candling devices — all the paraphernalia of an egg-exporting business. Then my father handed through my eight-year-old brother Arthur and my mother; and after her came Grandmother Miriam, aunts, uncles, and cousins. Only Grandfather Jakob remained in the villa.

Peeking through the camouflage of clothes in the closet, I heard my father shout at Jakob. Tugging at his gray beard and squaring his sturdy shoulders, my grandfather shook his head in an emphatic "No!" My father gestured at the entry and finally shoved Grandfather toward it. I steadied him as he came through but he brushed my hand away. What had appeared to be an old man's trembling was instead the bristling of fury.

Standing in the middle of the warehouse floor that was covered with straw and sawdust, we were startled by a series of sharp raps on the false panel. For a long minute my father stood rigid, his eyes blinking rapidly. Who knew about the hiding place? Then we heard the voices of a neighbor and her daughter who called to us from the back room of the villa, insisting on being taken in. They had somehow learned that we had a place to hide. Knowing we couldn't risk leaving someone outside who knew where we were hiding, my father opened the panel to let them into the warehouse.

• • • • •

At the far end of the room, my father pried a square cutout from the wooden floor and motioned us, one by one, down a ladder into our hiding place. The hole was packed so tight that our shoulders overlapped as we crouched. I rubbed my eyes: I thought I had gone blind. No, it was simply so dark that I couldn't see my hand when I raised it. My heart, still racing from my sprint across the lumberyard, clanked and hammered against my ribs and seemed to speed toward a crash. My father whispered that we must not speak.

My Aunt Malcia stopped a few rungs down the ladder and held up her arms. Her husband, Uncle Wolf, placed their fever-flushed five-year-old daughter into her arms.

"Diphtheria," my mother whispered. The sick little girl began to whimper.

"Sleep," her mother crooned, "go to sleep."

I don't know how long it was until we heard footsteps above, the unmistakable tread of heavy boots mixed with lighter footwear. Aunt Malcia put a gag in the child's mouth as we held our breath. I worried that they would see the outline of the trapdoor of our hideout in the sawdust as they scoured the place, but somehow my father had managed to disguise it with straw. I listened for the crack and splinter of breaking wood, but it did not come. The Germans had orders not to destroy the warehouse, which had become German booty.

"No Jews here," I heard someone call out, and another voice echoed his report.

"Bring a dog," someone ordered. I held my breath as I heard a barking beast rampage above my head. But the smell of broken eggs must have confused him. Eventually, the Germans and Ukrainians gave up. A few curses at Jews and they left.

Someone needed a chamber pot. Suddenly we all seemed to need one, but there was none. My father had barely finished digging out the hiding place and hadn't had time to enlarge it or stock water and food. This was its trial run. No pot, no water, not even a candle, and hardly any air.

Despite the hot squeeze of bodies dripping perspiration from running, from crowding, from fear, I began to shiver. Only the damp, compacted clay I felt when I stretched my hands above my head calmed me, reassured me. I did the only thing I could think of to do: I began unrolling the curlers from my hair. I didn't want to be caught with curlers in my hair when they came back to drag us out.

I had often tormented myself by imagining the scene of my last moments. What would I do? Beg them not to shoot? Would I cry, wet myself as I was doing right now?

They wouldn't shoot us in the yard, I kept assuring myself, *not in my grandparents' yard.* I knew that if I cursed them to their faces they would. And I had heard shots as I ran. Where would they take us? To the cemetery?

At that moment I heard a train whistle. A train had come for Skala's Jews.

When he heard the train whistle, my father climbed out of our hole and up to the attic of the warehouse to see what was going on. It looked quiet, but he decided we should wait another day underground to be sure the immediate danger had passed.

In the crush of the cellar, gasping for air, with the feverish child's moans a steady accompaniment, suppressing as long as possible the need to relieve myself again, I wished for one moment that they would come, find me, drag me out and get it over with. And then, seeing how selfish that thought was — it meant that seventeen other people would die too — I took back the wish.

In the jumbled hours and minutes of that day and the endless night that followed, only specific moments marked the time passing: the release of a leg from its cramped twist or the shift to hold Arthur on my lap to relieve my mother. Arthur, though small for an eight-year-old, squirmed a lot and had to be soothed to sleep. Feeble snores told me the sick child was still breathing. Efforts to breathe rasped all around me. We sucked the same fetid air into our lungs and pushed it out again. Once in a while, when someone fainted, my father tilted the cover up for a few moments and the person was held up for some breaths of fresh air, but the risk was great. If a looter was rummaging about, he would surely betray us.

I slept through most of the second day.

• • • • •

My father went up to the attic to check again. He seemed to be gone for ages.

"All quiet," he reported upon returning. He knelt at the edge of the hole and held out his hand toward us. "It's over."

We sat there. After a while I climbed out and helped my father pull the others out of the darkness. I tried to steady them against the light. My grandparents sprawled on the floor of the warehouse, and the children jumped around, happy to be able to move again.

We crawled back through the closet into Wolf's villa and walked into the front room.

The door swung open. On the doorstep stood a six-foot-tall young Ukrainian militiaman with an armband and rifle. There was a moment of terror.

Then we saw he was "our Jan," the man who had befriended my

parents, brother, and me in the past year of the German occupation, who had brought food and news to our home almost every day, the man my father had trusted with the knowledge of our hiding place. Our Jan, who was called "Jewish uncle" by his compatriots, a derogatory and insulting epithet meaning "Jew-lover."

Still holding his rifle, Jan hugged and kissed me, Arthur, my mother and father, and we hugged and kissed him back.

"It's over," he said again and again, "it's over." Jan had been hanging around the villa for hours, waiting for us to come out. He was afraid to go in, fearing to be spotted and followed by a passing militiaman. All of them knew how he had protected us in the past, and they scorned him for it.

My mother began to cry, and seeing her, I felt in danger of breaking down myself.

No, I thought, *I'm alive, why cry?* I kissed my Grandmother Miriam, and she squeezed me lightly. Her usual strong bear hug had weakened. Grandfather Jakob stood near her, his body taut, and I tried to take his hand but his fingers remained rigid and I released them.

The family split up. Wolf and Malcia and their daughters stayed in the villa. My grandparents went home with Uncle Munio and Aunt Suza, who lived with them. Accompanied by Jan, the four of us, Aunt Lolla, her husband and two sons, set out for the house we shared.

What we saw on the way was a scene out of Dante's Inferno. Dead and dying people were strewn all over the street. Children were running around looking for their parents, and parents were looking for their children. Houses stood empty as if a cosmic cyclone had sucked their occupants to another planet. Dead bodies sprawled on beds and floors. Doors and windows were smashed open, and everything was gone — clothes, furniture, all the occupants' possessions had been taken either by the Germans, the Ukrainian militia, or Polish and Ukrainian looters.

The doors of our own house were broken in and the glass from the windows lay shattered on the ground. Everything in the house was gone, except the few photographs strewn over the floor, where they had been thrown when their frames were emptied and stolen. There was no food left; the secret place where we had hidden it behind a wooden panel in the entrance hall had been discovered.

Jan brought a bit of food for us, and milk for Arthur and Lolla's boys, and stayed with us the rest of that day and all that night. We wanted to wash but we were afraid to go out to fetch water.

He told us about the aktsia — how doors had been smashed with poles and axes, Jews routed from their houses, bunkers and hiding places, beaten and humiliated, and stripped of any valuables they carried or had hidden in their clothing. Those who did not instantly obey German commands were murdered on the spot. The sick and mentally retarded were shot. The others, shoved, clubbed, their heads cracked open, were herded to the *Umschlagplatz*, the assembly-point in what had once been the Polish officers' garrison on the main avenue, and from there to the barracks once used by the Polish border guards, now fenced-in with barbed-wire.

When the Nazi's count of the prisoners, taken at noon on the second day, fell short of the required 700 dead or captured, several members of the *Judenrat*, the Jewish Council, and the *Ordnungsdienst*, the Jewish auxiliary police unit that enforced its decisions, were added to the complement of prisoners. Only one was able to buy his way out.

Jan reported that a conductor on the train had told him that the young and able-bodied men had been taken to the Janowska camp in Lvov. A man who had jumped off the train reported the destination of the elderly, the women, and the children: the Belzec death camp.

❖ 2 ❖

The day after the aktsia, posters went up in Skala ordering the town's seven hundred remaining Jews to report to the ghetto in Borszczów, fifteen kilometers away. My parents hired a man with a wagon to take them, our Wasserman grandparents, and Uncle Wolf and his family to Borszczów. The drivers who had already returned reported that Jews from several towns were crammed together in designated houses, ten or fifteen to a room. Only a few Jews managed to stay on to work for the Germans in Skala. The town was now officially rid of its Jews — at least as far as anyone could see.

"So where are *your* Jews?" someone had asked Jan on the street.

Arthur and I hid in our house until nightfall, when Jan came by to take us to the barn adjoining his family's house, a ten-minute walk from our home. There we climbed up the ladder to the attic. Anticipating our need of a hideout, Jan had spent many nights in the barn's attic, building a false wall that was indistinguishable from the real one. In the narrow space between the false wall and the real one he had put a straw stool, an all-purpose hook, and a shelf, and hollowed out a place in the hay to serve as our bed. There was a chamber pot in the corner.

Jan sat at the small triangular window, really just an air-hole since it had no glass, watching for activity from the house. His mother, sister, and brother-in-law, who lived there with him, though sound sleepers, might have caught a glimpse of our arrival. His mother had forbidden him to bring us onto her property, and his sister and brother-in-law had taken him aside to tell him that if they found us on the premises, they would turn him in, along with us.

Jan told me that my paternal grandfather, Azriel Gottesfeld, had been shoved into a boxcar on the train bound for Belzec.

"I didn't have the heart to tell this to your father," he said. "There's time tomorrow."

I loved Grandfather Azriel, who had bought me chocolates and other treats at the Cukernia café when I brought home A's from school. In his youth, when Azriel had been a soldier in the Austro-Hungarian army, his height, carriage and handsome beard had so distinguished him as a model of manhood that he had been chosen to stand in the front rank when Emperor Franz Joseph reviewed the troops. Now someone had betrayed to the Germans the hiding place he had built for his son Leo, Leo's wife Laura, their daughter Micia and himself; Azriel had walked to the train in polished boots, as well-groomed and proud as if he were still a young soldier. He took with him only his *tallis*, his prayer-shawl.

Seated on fresh straw in the attic hideaway of Jan's barn that night, I burst into tears. With Jan there, I felt safe; my weeping was for the warmth of the blanket, the sweet aftertaste of bread in my mouth, the hay that still carried the scent of a summer meadow, the news about my beloved Grandfather Azriel, and my exhaustion from two days below ground expecting to be discovered at any moment.

"It was my eighteenth birthday and we were eighteen people in there," I said. "What do you think it means?"

"It means you're alive and so are they."

I moved closer to him.

"For a while down there I didn't know if I was alive or dead. I was sure I had been shot while running in the lumberyard. Ever since then it feels like a bullet is poking into my shoulder-blade like a giant needle."

Jan ran his hands over my skin for signs of a bullet hole. His fingers combed through my hair searching for evidence that my scalp had been grazed.

"Nothing," he said.

"But I felt the bullet enter my back as I ran. It's in there. I can feel it."

He searched me again. "Don't think about it now." He said nothing more and stroked my hair, over and over, with his hand. Then he leaned back and pulled the brim of his cap down over his eyes.

That night it seemed as if I couldn't get enough of the moonlight, and I fell into a dream of gentle winter snowfall, with snow blanketing the world until it was as white as the moon.

II

Growing Up in Skala

Birth to Age 15: 1924–1939

❖ 3 ❖

Skala, the shtetl where I was born on the holiday of Sukkos, which fell that year on October 14, 1924, means "rock"; the old city was built on a rocky hill surrounded by a small forest on the shore of the river Zbrucz. The surroundings were so beautiful that there was talk of developing the area into a resort.

Before World War I, Skala had been part of the Austro-Hungarian Empire. After it was ceded to Poland in 1919, the river became the border with the Soviet Union and Skala became a garrison town, with several officers and about fifteen soldiers quartered near the marketplace. They rode about on horses and spent most of their time drinking, playing cards, and womanizing.

The town had 5,500 inhabitants. About 3,000 were Greek Orthodox Ukrainians; 1,000 were Catholic Poles; and 1,500 were Jews, the vast majority of whom, including my family, were religiously observant.

Our relationships with the Poles and Ukrainians were always strained. The peasants were superstitious and still believed in the blood libel; the priests often told them in church that the Jews had killed Jesus. Sometimes when they drank too much after returning from church, they threw stones at Jews or beat them, so we always closed our windows when we saw them coming up the street.

We knew little about the gentiles; they lived their lives and we lived ours. Business was the main contact between us. There was a marketplace on the main avenue facing my Wasserman grandparents' house. At least twice a week, the Ukrainian peasants would bring their produce — eggs, beans, grain — to sell to Jewish merchants, who exported these commodities to Western Europe and elsewhere. After the market the peasants would go to a *kretchma*, an inn, to drink. When the peasants would come out of the inn, Jewish shopkeepers would be standing, one after another, outside their little stores in the front rooms of their homes along the avenue. The peasants would buy kerosene, salt, sugar — which was expensive and sold in lumps — fabric and clothing, leather, hardware and farm tools.

There were also occasional fairs where the Jewish merchants sold the peasants suits and clothing, boots, shoes, and quilts. Our only other contact with the Ukrainian peasants was when we needed them to be *shabbas goyim*, to light the stoves and ovens on the Sabbath.

Once a year, on New Year's Eve, the Polish officers held an elegant ball at their garrison, inviting only the "fine Jews" — my father, my mother, and her beautiful younger sister Suza among them.

The Jews in Skala knew one another so well that they spoke of each other not by name but by nickname — the *shtumeh* (the one who didn't speak), the *krumeh*, (the one who didn't stand up straight), the *sauer* (the sour one who was always depressed); the *sheitl* (the woman who had lost her hair and wore a bright red wig).

Our rich social and cultural life revolved around our two-story *Beit Am*, or community center. Lectures and concerts were held in its large auditorium, as were the performances of our amateur theatre troupe. There we celebrated Purim and Chanukah and other holidays. The Beit Am housed a library with 5,000 books; a reading room; and an excellent school, from kindergarten to the eighth grade, belonging to the *Tarbut*

Hebrew cultural movement.

The situation in Poland after the First World War was difficult for Jews, but it deteriorated even further after the death in 1935 of Marshal Pilsudski, a Socialist whom the Jews had looked to as their protector. The Jews cried bitterly when he died — they knew what was coming — and shortly after, the Fascists took over and implemented official anti-Semitic policies, hoping to forbid ritual slaughter, thereby preventing the production of kosher meat, and instituting an economic boycott of Jewish enterprises.

Jews felt they had no future in Poland and many — including one of my second cousins — became Communists or Zionists. We had active chapters of Jabotinsky's Revisionists, religious Zionists, and other pioneering movements that sent young people on *hachshara* to training farms where they prepared for *aliyah* (immigration) to *kibbutzim* (communal farms) in the Land of Israel. Hashomer Hatzair, Beitar, Hanoar Hatzioni — all these youth groups met in the Beit Am.

❖ 4 ❖

My father, Benjamin, was his father's favorite. He was the third of the nine children who survived out of the thirteen born to his parents, Azriel and Hinda Gottesfeld.

Azriel came from a very poor family and worked as a glazier: he had golden hands. He built a hothouse for the wife of a Polish count who liked him, and later he built his own family a beautiful two-story house on a main street across from the Polish garrison. He had tenants in the upstairs story and in the basement.

Azriel was tall, proud, and good-looking and he carried himself like the soldier he had been. He was also the kindest imaginable human being, good-natured and sweet. He and my extremely intelligent Grandmother Hinda were devoted to each other; they always ate from the same bowl, and he helped her bake the bread when she was pregnant or nursing and busy with children.

Mendel was their oldest child, and after him came Esther. She married a fellow named Mendel Gottfried, who had started a business in Paris importing eggs from Skala. His business flourished, and he came back to Skala to find a bride. He married Esther, and they brought five of her brothers and sisters — Mendel, Usher, Krenia, Brana, and Tuvia — to work with them in Paris. Esther and the others sent money to their parents, and Azriel used some of it to set up a small hardware store. He never forgot that he had been poor, and every Friday gave needy Jews potatoes, flour and bread; on Passover he gave them matza.

Esther and the other Paris relatives came home to visit in style and their annual summer visit was always a major event for us. Every year Esther took her parents to a spa. From Paris they brought grapefruit, oranges, chocolates, and the best sardines. They hired a cook for their summer visits and gave dinner parties, and left us their clothes when they returned to Paris at the end of the summer. My mother was proud of her wardrobe of the finest Parisian fashions.

Grandmother Hinda didn't like my mother; she thought my mother made demands on my father for a higher standard of living than he could afford. The only time we were invited to my grandparents' home was for a slice of cake when the aunts and uncles came from Paris for their annual visit. We never ate meals with the family, and I never slept at their house or had a relationship with my grandmother.

Azriel and Hinda's three other children — Leo (Leibish), Sophia, and my father — remained in Poland. Leo became a wealthy and successful businessman in Lvov, and lived there during the Russian occupation, but returned to Skala after the German invasion.

Sophia was an intellectual who knew *Tanach* (the Hebrew Bible) and quoted Bialik's poetry by heart. But she was not considered marriageable because she was not attractive in the fashion of the era. In those days, the conventional standard of beauty for a woman was to be fair, pink, and plump, with beautiful hair and full breasts, and Sophia did not possess these qualities. She reached the advanced old age of twenty-four before she married. Her mother was very worried about her. But the money sent by Esther and the others to their parents provided enough of a dowry for Sophia to marry a doctor or lawyer, at the then-going rate of about $1,800. She married Zygmunt (Zisha) Zimmerman when she was twenty-four and they had a son, Dolek.

Grandmother Hinda never forgot, to the end of her days, how worried she had been about Sophia. Even when she no longer had daughters to marry off, she was jealous of other parents whose girls married young.

"Nu, some people have luck," she would sigh to my father.

My father would reply, "Mama, you've married Sophia off already, why are you still jealous?"

• • • • •

My mother, Szencia (Charlotte), was the daughter of Jakob and Miriam Wasserman.

Rich from a young age thanks to his successful lumber business, my grandfather Jakob could afford to marry Miriam Horowitz, a blue-eyed Bukovinian beauty with no dowry. Miriam was good-natured and resourceful. Jakob provided her with a lavish lifestyle — many servants and a *drozhky*, a carriage with horses to take her to market. She wore lovely Victorian-style suits.

They lived in a magnificent house on the main avenue of Skala: it had a long flight of stairs at the entrance, large windows, beautiful furniture, and heavy velvet drapes of dark green and red. Grandmother Miriam had a large garden where she grew flowers, fruits and vegetables — tomatoes, strawberries, raspberries, and cucumbers. We drank coffee and cold drinks on summer Shabbat afternoons in the gazebo in the garden.

None of our homes had electricity, and the rooms were heated with coal stoves. Our drinking water came from a well, via pail and rope, in the Wassermans' garden. Water was also delivered from the pump-well down a rocky hill where the non-Jews lived — near the Jewish cemetery, the bathhouse where the men went to *shvitz* on Friday, and the *mikvah* (ritual bath) — by water carriers who sold it to their customers. Once a week, on Thursday nights, we heated the water on the stove and brought the bathtub into the kitchen to bathe. Sometimes I bathed with my mother in a tub in one of the little cubicles in the mikvah before she went downstairs to immerse herself in the pool, and I would wait for her until she came upstairs.

But my grandmother had a special bathhouse with a large bathtub which Grandfather Jakob had built for her in the garden. She also had an elegant outhouse that boasted special paper, a step up from the cut-up newspapers with which the rest of us managed.

Fortunes, though, can also take a turn for the worse. Jakob's lumber business prospered until the Depression, when he lost everything and was left with stacks of IOU's. He used to take me up to the attic to show me the sacks of Polish money, now devalued and worthless. My grandparents were able to keep their house but had to let the servants go. Jakob was an angry and depressed man, and when I watched the way he drank his tea in the kitchen, elegant pinkie extended, stirring it with a rough twist of the wrist that spilled some into the saucer, I sensed something troubled and brooding about him. Grandmother Miriam's loyalty, her uncomplaining adjustment to the decline in their fortunes, struck me as a better model of conduct than Jakob's brusque, impatient manner.

Although we lived one house down the avenue from my maternal grandparents, and as their oldest grandchild I spent a great deal of time in their home, I never saw a smile from Grandfather Jakob, and he never inquired how I was or what I was doing. He often came striding to our door to ask me to write business letters for him to his creditors — he liked my handwriting — because he couldn't afford a secretary. At Christmastime, he instructed me to deliver gifts, including the cakes Grandmother Miriam had baked, to his non-Jewish creditors. I treated him the way he treated me: as an honorable business acquaintance. Grandmother Miriam indulged me sufficiently to make up for any lapses of warmth on his part.

My mother was the second of their five children. Wolf was her older brother, and Lolla and Suza were her two younger sisters. Her youngest brother, Bubcio, had died of tuberculosis, then called "galloping consumption," when he was twenty-one. Grandmother Miriam had taken him from one sanitarium to another and to doctors in Vienna, to no avail. I remember Miriam crying, sitting on a stool, while I kept asking what had happened — I was four years old and they didn't tell me until much later. My grandmother never recovered from Bubcio's death and always dressed in black after that. Her deep mourning for her favorite child was seen by some as exemplary piety and by others as unhealthy. Her great show of grief was balanced by Jakob's stoicism.

Wolf was the apple of my grandmother's eye. He was the intellectual; he had studied in a Polish *gymnasium* (high school) which had a quota for Jews and was extremely expensive; later he attended universi-

Fanya with her Mother's Family, the Wassermans. (*Front row*) Bubcio, Fanya's mother's youngest brother; (*Middle row, seated*) Fanya between her maternal grandparents, Miriam and Jakob Wasserman; (*Back row, L to R*) Suza, Fanya's mother's younger sister; Wolf and Malcia, Fanya's mother's older brother and his wife; Fanya's parents Szencia (Charlotte) and Benjamin Gottesfeld; Lolla, Fanya's mother's sister.

ty. He was very religious, he recited poetry, he could give nice speeches; but he had no profession and couldn't make a living, so Grandfather Jakob had to support him. Then he married Malcia, a rich girl from another shtetl near Stanislaw, about 70 kilometers from Skala. Jakob built a small villa in the yard for Wolf and his family. Malcia was a little older than Wolf but she had a dowry, on which they lived. She also ran her own little business out of their home, crocheting lace curtains. Wolf and Malcia had two daughters.

My mother's younger sister Lolla was beautiful, with her light eyes, curly reddish-brown hair and fashionably full figure. She was also very vain; I remember her often looking at herself in her hand-mirror. She was a popular young woman who liked to dance, sing, and go to parties. Lolla had another side too: she was quite an intellectual and loved to read. But although she had graduated from the Polish teachers' semi-

Fanya's Extended Family. Taken in front of Uncle Wolf's villa, where the family hid during the first aktsia. (*Front row, L to R*) Benjamin Gottesfeld, Fanya's father; a cousin; Wolf and Malcia, Fanya's aunt and uncle; Szencia (Charlotte) Gottesfeld, Fanya's mother; Fanya as a little girl; Lolla, her mother's sister; and Lolla's husband, Mottel. (*On stairs*) Many of Fanya's cousins. Suza, Fanya's mother's sister, is in the black dress and the bead necklace directly in the center of the back row. Bubcio, her mother's brother, is toward the right with the open shirt and handkerchief in the pocket.

nary, she never wanted a career.

Lolla married Mottel Feingold, a successful businessman who sold shoes, bags, and sweaters; he was on friendly terms with the few Polish noble families in town. They had two sons: Julek, with his flaming red hair, was a good boy and tried hard to please his mother, but she favored her younger son David, who had beautiful blond hair and blue eyes. David was sickly, and Lolla took him from doctor to doctor to seek out a cure.

My mother's youngest sister was Suza, blond, blue-eyed and very tall; statuesque in her long gowns. She had a beautiful voice and was a singer in the amateur Hebrew and Yiddish theatre troupe which performed at the Beit Am. All the Polish officers chased after her, and it was Suza who attended their New Year's ball in a long evening dress.

By the time Suza reached the marriageable age of eighteen, Jakob had already lost his money, and she knew she wouldn't have a dowry. She decided to learn a profession so she could support herself. She went to Cracow, where Grandmother Miriam had a sister who was well-off, and attended a trade school to learn how to make corsets and bras. She opened an elegant little studio in her parents' home, where she made all the corsets for the officers' wives and the noble ladies of the town.

Suza loved Munio, a dentist from Czortkow, about 40 kilometers away, and everyone knew about their romance. One evening I found them lying together under a blanket on the living-room sofa at our Wasserman grandparents. This kind of behavior was considered improper in our rather prim family — but it intrigued me. It seemed to me that an exciting episode in one of the novels I had been reading had come to life.

❖ 5 ❖

My father was very handsome; he had gray eyes and black hair, and was generous and kind like Grandfather Azriel. A good man with a good heart, he would often send some poor person to my mother and instruct him to tell her, "Your husband said to give me a coat."

Although the family was poor when he was growing up, my father went away to study at a Polish gymnasium. He didn't have much to eat and his parents would send him food packages containing food that could last, like crackers, but he was so hungry that, by the time he returned to his room from the post office with the package, he had eaten up all the crackers. He earned a little money by tutoring other students at the gymnasium.

After graduating, he studied engineering at the university in Czernowitz. When he came back to Skala, there were no jobs for a civil engineer. He started a little hardware store which went bankrupt because he let customers buy on credit.

My father courted my mother Szencia for five years. She was beautiful, with her dark eyes, black hair, and beautiful white teeth. Although she had attended a business school in Czortkow, my mother wasn't really interested in her studies and, unlike her sister Suza, never tried her hand at a career. When her parents had to let their servants go, she took over the family housekeeping. My mother called herself "Cinderella" because she did all the chores, including cleaning up after her sister Lolla.

My mother chose to believe that her father had been cheated by a junior partner rather than to accept that the state of the economy and her father's inability to cope with it had caused the loss of his fortune. Despite having lost all his money, Jakob opposed my mother's marrying my father because he came from a poor family. My father threatened suicide, and my mother's parents finally gave in, but Grandfather Jakob refused to give my mother a dowry because she married my father

40

against his wishes.

Grandfather Jakob bullied my father to give him the little money that remained after my father closed his hardware store, and my father became his partner in the lumber business. He lost everything and there was a falling-out between the two men, which accounted for the surplus lumber which lay, for years, piled in our yard. My father took the blame for the failure of the partnership, saying he was not a businessman, and steered clear of his father-in-law. Later he started a small lumber business in his own yard, where I used to hide and read my books.

My father was right — he had no head for business. He was a scholar, a man of the *Haskalah* (Enlightenment movement), a believer in education who loved literature and *Yiddishkeit* (Jewish culture). He was part of the small circle of intelligentsia in Skala whose members gathered at our house to play chess and cards and discuss politics and current affairs. They included the commander of the Polish garrison; the postmaster; the manager of the estate of our local Polish nobleman, Count Golochowski; the principal of the Polish elementary school (a rabid anti-Semite); a rich landowner who often asked my father for advice; Ulanowski, a member of the Polish *Szlachta* (gentry); and Moizesevich, an Armenian, who owned the only pharmacy in town — a beautiful old store with its dogwood, jars and scales, and fantastic smells.

Our home was full of books in many languages — French, Russian, German, Polish, Hebrew, and Yiddish. When I was a little girl, I would use my finger to trace the words in the book my father held as he read to me. Sometimes the book had no pictures, but I didn't care. His voice, its resonance vibrating in my back, my hair, my ears, filled me with comfort, and sometimes I stopped listening to the words and was just mesmerized by its sound.

My father wanted me to have a good education, but my mother didn't care about that. Her passion was being a *balabusta*, a meticulous housekeeper with the reputation for having the cleanest home in Skala. She wanted me to get married, and worried that I wouldn't because

41

there was no money for a dowry.

•　•　•　•　•

I received my primary education at the Pulaski School, a Polish institution, every day until 1:30 pm. The school was free, but it was not obligatory, and many of the peasants' children didn't go to school at all. Classes were held on Saturday, the Jewish Sabbath, but the Jews didn't attend school that day and the Polish pupils would tell us the homework assignments. I remember winning first prize for an essay I wrote (with Uncle Wolf's help) for a contest sponsored by a savings bank. The topic was, "Why People Should Save Money." I knew a lot about that topic from my own family's experience.

Each ethnic group in the school had religious instruction once a week with its own special teacher. The Catholic priest taught the Poles; Father Derewienko, the Orthodox priest, taught the Ukrainians; and Mr. Bouk instructed the Jews. Mr. Bouk was an old bachelor who lived with his two unmarried sisters. We didn't take him seriously and used to play, eat, and write letters during class. I would read my Polish books.

One of my fellow pupils was the grandson of the manager of the count's estate, which was his summer residence, located near the railway station and a small forest, about a 20-minute walk from the center of town. As children, this boy and I played hide-and-seek in the estate's vast park, which boasted beautiful lawns, statues, lakes, tall graceful trees, and a lovely garden. His family would invite me at Christmas to see the tree, and I was enchanted by the glass balls, the lights, and the angel on top. But, typical of our relationship with the gentiles, we never invited them to our home for Chanukah.

After my daily studies at the Pulaski School, I went to Hebrew school from 3:00 to 6:30 four afternoons a week and all day Sunday. On Sundays in the summer, Hebrew school classes would often go to the little forest near the train station for lessons and a picnic.

The school, with its Zionist orientation, was part of the Tarbut movement, and our dedicated teachers had been educated in the movement's seminary. All subjects — Jewish poetry, literature, and Bible with commentaries by Rashi, the famous medieval French commentator — were studied in Hebrew, and it was also the language used for projects and plays. I loved Hebrew school, particularly its library.

One of my distant cousins, Choneh Gottesfeld, who had become a writer in America, returned to Skala to visit his parents. We were sure

Fanya's Hebrew School class. Fanya is in the third row from the front, the fifth student in from the right. Only Fanya and one other student survived the Holocaust.

he was a very famous writer, and the Hebrew school held an assembly in his honor where he spoke to us and asked us questions; we sang songs and recited poems. I was chosen to deliver a paper I had written in Hebrew on the Marranos, Jews who lived as Christians to avoid persecution in fifteenth century Portugal and Spain. (When Choneh returned to America, he wrote a book in Yiddish about his visit to Poland.)

For an hour in the late afternoon after Hebrew school we went to the home of Sluwa Kassierer to do homework under her supervision. Sluwa and her two sisters, all of them seamstresses, supported their old parents and lived in two small rooms. They were close to thirty, and their unmarried state was considered a *shanda*, an embarrassment. Every family who could afford a few pennies considered it proper to send their children to the Kassierers to do their homework. Actually, we didn't do much there — we usually ate apples and socialized.

After eighth grade, I wanted to go to high school, but there was none in Skala. Fifteen kilometers away, in Borszczów, there was a state high school, with a quota for Jews, and an expensive private school. There was also a Hebrew high school in Stanislaw, but this didn't work out. So a lawyer manqué named Lachmann rented a room and organized a school of twelve students in Skala. We covered the first two years of the high school curriculum — on the strength of his brilliance as a teacher of math, history, geography, and literature — in the mornings, and I continued at the Tarbut school in the afternoons.

The money for my school tuition, which was high, came from my father's father, Grandfather Azriel, who was interested in my education. I was close with my grandfather. He would come to our house every Saturday afternoon with a gift of chocolate, and we would chat about whichever book I was currently reading. Whether Polish or Hebrew, I would tell him the story or recite a poem for him. I went to him first whenever I got good grades and, as a reward for being a good student, Grandpa Azriel would take me to the Cukernia, a coffee house, for currant drinks and ice cream with waffle-wafers.

Once in a while I stayed overnight at my mother's parents' house — usually on a Sunday night. I engineered the sleepovers when I was engrossed in a particularly wonderful long novel — Dickens or Tolstoy — so I could read all night long and stay in bed with the book Monday morning instead of going to school. Sometimes, when I was reading at night by the light of a candle, Grandfather Jakob would catch me.

"You're going to go blind or crazy from too much reading!" he would warn me.

In the morning Grandmother Miriam would bring me hot chocolate and sit on the bed holding the tray.

"Reading is bad for the eyes, and who's going to marry a girl who wears glasses?" she would say. "Let me remind you, you won't have much of a dowry." There it was again, that ever-present concern about girls catching a husband with their dowries or their looks.

"I'm not interested in marriage," I would tell her.

"Ah ha!" she said. "That's all the more reason you should forget about these books. Leave school and apprentice yourself to a seamstress."

My two grandmothers, who differed on just about everything else, were in agreement that I should earn my livelihood by sewing — and the sooner the better. In Grandmother Hinda's view, advanced schooling was a waste of time and money for a girl and had the potential to make her crazy. I was willing to take the risk.

My father was delighted that I loved books and school. As a man who loved learning, he centered all his hopes on me and my education. He encouraged me to pursue the dream I'd had since I was a little girl: to study medicine.

•　•　•　•　•

Lotka and Zhenia were my two best friends from our days in elementary school. Lotka and I were second cousins; her grandmother and Grandfather Jakob were brother and sister. We lived next-door to each other, with our house on one side of hers and my Wasserman grandparents' on the other, separated by a little garden.

Lotka's parents, Mottel and Szencia Sternberg, were among the few Jews in Skala who did not keep a kosher home.

"Our cook prepares ham for us and fries pork chops in butter," Lotka once told me.

In the 1930's, Mottel had lived in Prague. Upon returning to Skala, he married Szencia, and in the large front room of their house they opened a fancy grocery store, patronized by the Polish officers and the town intelligentsia. I used to be entranced by the chocolates, jams and fancy cakes, and sometimes Lotka shared a package of French butter cookies with me.

"Even if you weren't my cousin," Lotka said when we were little, "I would have chosen you as my friend."

Lotka was beautiful, with brown hair, green eyes, and heavy, dark eyebrows like her father's; and she played the violin. I always thought myself ugly in comparison to Lotka and was jealous because the boys I liked ran after her instead of me.

I had a crush on our big, husky classmate Rubcio, but he preferred Lotka. He liked me as a friend with whom he could discuss books and issues, but it was Lotka he wanted to hold hands with and kiss. Lotka's parents considered him an inappropriate boyfriend for her because Rubcio's parents owned a kretchma, where country people — people who would never dream of shopping at the Sternbergs' fancy store — stopped for a drink when they came to town.

Rubcio lived with his whole family — his mother, his father, an old-maid aunt who washed laundry for a living, and two orphaned cousins — in one dark room of a house on the main avenue. His mother was always peeling onions to add to the herring they served to their peasant customers in the other three rooms of the building, which housed the kretchma.

Lotka's mother, Szencia, wanted me to be a good influence on Lotka. "Encourage her to read and study," she would say. "Help her with her homework." I was happy to oblige. I admired Szencia for her cosmopolitan tastes; she was well-read, sensitive and easy to talk to.

Szencia was the first person who ever told me, when I was in high school, that I had beautiful eyes. I had never heard such a compliment from my father, who always told me I was smart, nor from my mother, who had never admitted to my having any good features, except that I had inherited my father's intensity and ingenuity. So, when Lotka's mother told me that I had beautiful eyes, it rather went to my head. For a while I saw Lotka as my rival for her mother's praise.

Zhenia was my closest friend. She was radiantly beautiful; she looked like an angel. Years later I saw a perfect copy of her face in a reproduction of a Fra Angelico painting, and it dawned on me that I had always based my standard for good looks on her fair skin, bright blue eyes, curly hair, and rosy cheeks. As we entered our early teens, her body filled out and mine simply elongated, making me feel awkward and lanky as I walked while Zhenia glided as though she were dancing.

Zhenia's mother was a widow; her husband had died of a heart attack when he was still young. Zhenia and her mother lived with her grandmother and uncle. Her grandmother, like Rubcio's parents, supported her family by running her own kretchma.

An only child, Zhenia had a sense of herself as selected for special privileges. When she managed to advance from grade to grade without any effort, she took it as her due. I never saw her read a book in all our years together in Polish and Hebrew school. She didn't care about her studies and was a vivacious, happy-go-lucky type.

Zhenia seemed to live a charmed life. If she stole a handful of cherries or apples from a neighbor's tree or tomatoes from a garden, no one noticed; but if I so much as reached out to pick one, the owner would throw a stone at me. Zhenia and I devised many carefree activities, such as the times we climbed, always in unsuitable shoes, up the sheer rocks for a view of the river from the Turkish Tower. These ruins of a thirteenth-century castle were mysterious and romantic, especially by moonlight. We young people went to the Tower for the freedom to run around among the ruined halls.

I used to walk up to the Tower with Lotka, too, and with my first boyfriend, Izio. I met Izio on the beach by the river where we used to sunbathe and swim. I was impressed with him because he was ten years older than me, had served in the Polish Army, smoked cigarettes, and looked like a non-Jew.

"What does an older guy like him want from a young girl like you?" asked my parents and Aunt Suza pointedly.

"He says I impress him," I informed them, "because I speak beautifully."

We used to meet secretly on the promenade above the river and stroll there on Sunday afternoons. He held my hand, he wrote me letters, and we even kissed.

In September 1939, Izio was called up to the army. I went with him to say good-bye at the train station. War had broken out.

III

Education Under the Russians

Age 15-16: September 1939–Spring 1941

❖ 6 ❖

The Red Army marched into Skala in mid-September 1939. The Polish soldiers and officers were taken by surprise and tried to run away, clad only in their underwear, but were caught and taken prisoner.

Some of the rich Poles in town managed to escape, among them Count Golochowski, who simply drove off in his car to Romania, later lived in Palestine and finally settled in England. The Russians occupied his estate and turned it into a hospital. Some well-to-do Jews also ran away, fearing they would be sent to Siberia because they were "capitalists", of whom the Communist Russians did not approve. Lotka's parents fled with her to Lvov, where they hoped to blend in and live unnoticed; this would have been impossible in a small shtetl like Skala, where they were well known. Many Jews from German-occupied western Poland also streamed into Lvov and other cities in the eastern part of Poland which had been taken over by the Soviets.

The Jewish Communists in Skala embraced the Soviets the same way the Ukrainians later welcomed the Nazis — with exhilaration. One of my father's cousins, a leader of the underground Communist party, had been imprisoned by the Polish government and tortured — his fingernails torn off — in Bereza-Kartuska, the infamous prison for political prisoners. When the Russians invaded eastern Poland, he was freed. He returned to Skala a hero and became an important official in the Russian administration.

It was a benign occupation at first. Polish, Russian, and Ukrainian are related Slavic languages so, though we spoke no Russian, we and the Russians could understand each other. The Russian soldiers had been instructed to propagandize among us. They boasted that their factories could produce anything.

"Do you have lemons?" asked one girl.

"Of course, our factories make lemons!" answered a soldier.

Then the Russians closed all the stores and warehouses. The peasants robbed and looted them. The Jewish merchants and storekeepers lost everything and became poor overnight. Every man became an employee of the state, working in agriculture, the stone quarries, or on road and rail construction gangs.

My father, assigned to work as an engineer, was put in charge of repairing the bridge over the Zbrucz River, which had been damaged in the early days of the war. I often brought him a hot lunch at the bridge.

It was during this time that he met Sidor, whose full name was Izydor Sokolowski, a Polish peasant who worked in the labor brigade on the bridge and who was to play a crucial role in our lives three years later. On one occasion, when Sidor had not fulfilled his work quota and was accused of sabotage, my father, who was known for treating the workers fairly, intervened on his behalf and saved him from punishment. Sidor never forgot this act of decency.

My father also did some trading on the black market with some of the Russians, selling them leather hides for which they paid in gold coins. They sent the hides home to be made into boots. My father and other Jews in town had saved and hidden some of the hides they had acquired before the war, and these later came in handy to barter for food and other necessities and for bribery during the German occupation.

One of the Russian officers who bought my father's hides used to visit us frequently. Only after a few months did he admit that he was a Jew and show us his passport to prove it. Stationed in Skala among Ukrainians and Poles, he had seen enough of what happened to Jews — even Jews who wore a Russian uniform — to make him wary. He would drink vodka from a large glass and sometimes, when he was drinking, he would cry. He once spoke of the Bolsheviks who — unlike the Mensheviks — he said, were not against the Jews, and how the Jews had joined their ranks.

One Friday night, my mother served him tea in a glass with a silver holder. That was a signal that he was a special person, someone to be nice to. She offered him some of her cherry preserves and cake. While he ate, he cried. I can still see his streaming tears flowing into his mouth as he took one bite after another. The peaches and cherries my mother had preserved in brandy reminded him of his family, the times of plenty and then the times of killing and dispersion. All of his family had been transported to Siberia.

Crying and eating, the sugar and salt mingling, he looked up and said, "You don't know how good you have it, such a good life." He grasped a large glass of vodka and, without spilling a drop, swept his arm to take in the room, furniture, food, and the four of us. Then, with one lift of his elbow, he downed the whole glass. Realizing perhaps that he had gone too far, he looked around the room as if totally sober at that moment, then took another piece of cake, stopped crying, and began to sing.

• • • • •

Unlike the Poles, the Russians had no objections to Jewish students attending state high school. Since Skala had no high school, I took the entrance exams so I could attend the one in Borszczów. My mother paid for my room and board with a Jewish family — Mrs. Bradler, her daughter Rose, and Rose's husband.

I was fifteen, and it was my first time away from home. I remember sitting on the bed in my rented room before the semester began, preparing my school uniform. I was sewing the school insignia onto the breast pocket of the jacket I was to wear over a navy jumper. The insignia had an eagle and a motto about a mighty mind and a lofty soul.

As I knotted the final thread I thought how little of myself I revealed to others, how my book-world often seemed the ultimate reality, and how I was eager to take on more challenge than that available in my small town. Sitting with the blazer on my lap, I ran my hand over the lettering and the eagle, as a tingle of fear mingled with the lure of the unknown.

Most of the students in school were Jewish but there were a few peasant youths, plus the sons and daughters of Russian officers. The Russian students knew little of the outside world. Once, when we were discussing art, someone mentioned the Louvre.

"The Louvre — is that in Borszczów?" asked a Russian student.

I concentrated my full attention on school work and on trying to fit in with my classmates.

The Russians had taken down the pictures of Jesus and the Madonna and Child that had once hung in the classrooms and replaced them with portraits of Stalin. They had also fired all the Polish teachers and brought in Russian replacements. World history was dropped, replaced by the geography of the Soviet Union and the history of the Russian Revolution. Latin was also excised from the curriculum.

All subjects, including Marx and Lenin's writings, were taught in Russian, the official language. We were forbidden to speak Polish or Hebrew. Many works of world literature and of Polish literature were forbidden as well. We did a lot of physical activities and calisthenics; military training with rifle practice was taught by a handsome Russian officer on whom all the girls had a crush.

The teachers frequently demanded that we write our autobiographies. When describing my family, I mentioned only Grandfather

Azriel, who was a glazier. I did not mention Grandfather Jakob since he had once been a well-to-do merchant. I struggled with myself over omitting Jakob, but I could think of no way to protect him other than to deny his existence.

The teachers started to make young Komsomols of us. I came to believe the socialist principle that by working together people could produce what was needed and would receive an equal share of what was produced. Being a Komsomol meant attending frequent meetings, trying to earn medals for achievements, and contributing one day of labor a week. On Saturdays, to earn medals, I shoveled snow, worked in the fields, or taught peasants who were brought to the school how to read and write Russian. We also worked in a public health clinic where we talked to peasants and held their hands while they were being vaccinated. On my first working Saturday I feared that God would punish me for breaking the Sabbath, even that He would take off my hand, but He didn't seem to notice.

One of the literature teachers, a tough woman commissar, wore the usual uniform of a collarless blouse, long skirt, high boots, and no make-up. Her hair, the same color as her wan skin, was combed tight against her head and anchored down. Ten medals rode over her restless bosom. She never allowed a lesson to pass without commenting on my hair, which I wore in a pageboy that glanced off my shoulders as I walked.

"Long hair," she said, "takes time away from study and from useful work. How can you be a Komsomol if you spend so much time on your hair?"

Eventually, I simply pinned it under. To be more precise, Stasiek, a Polish boy who sat behind me, would fold and secure the thick coil until it resembled a strap of black leather. The touch of his fingers as they grazed my neck tingled in a way that made me simultaneously look forward to and dread that class.

Since she could no longer pick on me for my hair, the teacher found other ways in which to ridicule me. She gave frequent oral exams. To spite her I didn't do the homework and, when she called on me, I spouted answers written on my hand. Heat rose to my cheeks and up through my head so that at the roots of my hair I felt the consequences of sin.

It was this teacher who called me in and wanted me to denounce Grandfather Jakob, whom they knew all about.

"He was rich," she said. "Who is he? Does he have servants?"

How could I denounce my grandfather?

"I don't know anything about him," I said, "I don't have any relationship with him."

The principal told us it was our duty to reveal the names of members, of an organization at school, who were "enemies of Russia." This was a group of Ukrainian students my own age who had secretly banded together. They wanted a free Ukraine, independent of Russian control. After they were caught and forced to "confess," they were shipped off to Siberia. None ever returned. Their faces haunted me.

Once all the students were ordered to watch the public execution of a black marketeer in the market square. The man was already starved and beaten to death when they brought him there in a truck with a sign around his neck reading, "I'm a Traitor." All the stores were closed — as if for a holiday — and the workers and students were made to watch the noose being placed around his neck. When he was hanging, we were told to applaud. One of my girlfriends almost fainted, and I had to hold her up. We applauded, and the man was left hanging there for four days.

After that, when I had to pass the square on the way to and from school, I was terrified.

❖ 7 ❖

Though budding young Komsomols, my friends and I practiced minor deceptions. My friend Shimek (Samson) would give us passages from outlawed Polish books, which we circulated and discussed among ourselves. And we laughed when Galsworthy's works were forbidden but Gogol's were not.

Sweet, brilliant Shimek Bosek had been my friend since I was a young girl in Skala. Our fathers were best friends and had studied together at the university in Czernowitz. Mr. Bosek came from a fine family, some of whose members had settled in Paris, and his brother, Mendel, was a violinist. Shimek's father was a Zionist who had settled in Palestine in the 1930's, but a bout with malaria and the unsettled conditions had so disillusioned him that he had returned to Skala, married and opened a little store. Shimek was an only child.

Shimek and I had gone to Polish and Hebrew elementary school together, but he was two years older than I. When I was still at Lachmann's school, he was already attending the high school in Borszczów. By the time I entered the lower grades of the Borszczów high school, which required a blue emblem on our uniforms, he had advanced to the higher grades, where the insignia was red; it was his old blue emblem that I had sewn onto my blue jacket.

In the winter of that year of high school, when we returned home on visits, we held gloved hands while dragging our sleds up the hill — each the other's consolation on the hill of adolescence — and then descended the slope, sitting upright or belly-down. In the spring, when the weather was fine, Shimek and I often sat in my parents' garden discussing an absorbing book. Brilliant Shimek! How I admired his ease with languages! To dazzle me he would switch from English to German to Latin to Hebrew in the same sentence.

At dances, though, Shimek was of no help at all; he didn't like to dance. I did. I would scan the room for a partner. In fact, I recall that looking for a dancing partner was my most absorbing interest at the time, almost completely eclipsing the rumors that somewhere west of Skala our enemies were preparing an invasion.

Shimek and I were offered the opportunity to study Russian in Leningrad and become interpreters. We were thrilled at the prospect. But our fathers so feared that two young Jews in a big foreign city would end up in Siberia that, the night I discussed it with my father, he suffered a violent ulcer attack. That settled it for me. Shimek decided that, if I was not going, neither would he.

Life in Skala did not stand still while I was away at school. On one of my visits home I discovered that Grandmother Hinda had died; on another, that Suza and Munio had married. They had gone to a rabbi in Czortkow, 45 kilometers away, rather than have their wedding in Skala, and they had not invited her parents or sisters. When they came back from Czortkow, Grandmother Miriam hosted a little party for them. On another visit I learned that the Soviets had closed the synagogues and the Hebrew school, and had confiscated most of the books in the library. Several Jews had been deported to Siberia.

I remember endless journeys in the winter darkness, from Skala to Borszczów and back, squeezed between Russian soldiers in a public sled. There was always one who had the "illness" my girlfriends referred to as Roaming Fingers. The fierce cold stung my face while waves of heat seared my body under the heavy traveling rugs. I protested the liberties they took.

"I wasn't doing anything — it's just your wishful thinking," they laughed at me.

"Freckles! A girl with freckles! What man would want you? Why don't you buy some cream and get rid of them?" sputtered one soldier as I insisted that he remove his hand.

Another said, "With your figure, you should wear trousers," and his friend stuffed a cigar in my mouth.

The sled drivers, who were Jews, ignored me. I never mentioned any of this to my parents, but in bed at night I would vow to report my tormentors, only to lose my resolve by morning. The next time it happened I froze and burned as usual.

In the last year of high school I kept my curiosity about love and sex to myself, indulging in daydreams, shy crushes on boys, and puppy love for our military training officer. I was still seeing Izio, who wrote to me at school and once in a while visited me there. I thought my dark navy jumper brought out the midnight-blue tints of my hair to advantage. Since my body had barely begun to find its curves, I had to count on my coloring — black hair, pale skin and faintly Oriental gray eyes — for the promise of good looks.

I was confused about how to relate to my looks. When I had asked my mother whether I was pretty, she said, "You have the look of a smart girl." But Grandmother Miriam had warned me, "Don't look too serious, it's unbecoming in a girl."

People did respond to something in me, a type of gumption that was variously described as "joie de vivre" or "naiveté" but which I assumed naturally as the perky openness of adolescence.

It never occurred to me then that Jan, ten years my senior, noticed me as I returned home from Borszczów one day and then watched for me on numerous other occasions. I only found out afterwards that he had particularly noticed the insignia on my school uniform. He would describe the eagle in detail, years later, while he held me in his arms for hours on end to soothe my fear of the guns beyond the door.

IV

Under the German Boot

Age 16–17: Summer 1941–September, 1942

❖ 8 ❖

June, 1941. I had finished two years of high school in Borszczów and was home for summer vacation when we heard that the Germans had marched into Soviet-occupied Eastern Poland. The Soviets abandoned Skala, and its warehouses and stores were again looted by criminals and Ukrainian peasants. My Communist cousin fled to Russia with his comrades, leaving his wife and child behind.

Two weeks later — on July 8, 1941 — Skala was occupied by the Hungarians, then allies of Nazi Germany. The Hungarians descended on us like locusts — raping, pillaging and stealing. Even the loaf of bread my mother had in the oven was stolen as they swept through town.

In the last week of July, Hungary expelled the Jews from the Trans-Carpathian region of Ruthenia, which it had annexed in 1938 when Czechoslovakia was dismembered. The Jews were driven without mercy across the Zbrucz River toward the Soviet Ukraine. For hours and hours one day, 3,000 weary, hungry Hungarian Jews of all ages stumbled through Skala, dressed in their best clothes and laden down with bundles.

I felt helpless when I saw a guard beat an old woman with a club until she bled — it would have been suicidal to try to help her. Another guard stood there swigging from a bottle and pointing his rifle at her. Finally, two passing men dragged her along with them.

Later I heard about a boy from Ruthenia who had appealed to the soldiers for food and rest. He was hung upside down in the town square. Every time he fainted, water was thrown over him to revive him. A Skala rabbi came to pray at the scene until the soldiers beat him cruelly. Finally the boy's sister, a girl I knew from Lachmann's school, managed to bribe the soldiers to stop the torture.

The Jews of Skala collected food and clothing for the Hungarian Jews and bribed the soldiers to allow them a brief rest in town. They brought hot food for all, and medicine for those beaten by the guards and Ukrainian peasants, and rented wagons to take the Jews the rest of the twenty or thirty kilometers to the Ukrainian border.

Jews who had fled east in 1939, just a step ahead of the Germans after they invaded western Poland, had told us their horror stories of internment, confiscation of property, brutality and murder.

"Exaggerations," most of us preferred to believe when we heard these tales.

"The Germans have a tradition of enlightenment," my father had said. He counted on this tradition to mediate the ruthless impulses of the conquering army. This is how well denial worked even if we had read *Mein Kampf*.

For a while we said, "If the army arrives."

Soon we were saying, "When it arrives."

One brutally hot day, at the end of July, we heard the motorcycles and trucks of the approaching German Army and ran to hide in Grandfather Jakob's cellar. Peeking through the little barred window, we saw the Germans pitch their tents in the lumberyard. They jumped from their motorcycles and sidecars and shed their jackets as they lounged against my grandfather's stacks of lumber. After gulping from a jug of milk, one German began to sing a ditty and the rest picked up the refrain. A large jar of tanning cream passed from hand to hand and they slathered it onto their exposed skin. The grease glistened on their faces and arms as they angled them toward the sun for optimum bronzing. Their buttons, buckles, visors, glasses, shiny boots, even their hair and fingernails took on a dazzling sparkle with thousands of prisms reflecting the light of Hades' fire. I knew this glitter spelled night and death.

While they bantered and bellowed, their guns and gear spread over our property, I knew I wanted to see them grovel for mercy in the dirt of the yard, their faces glistening with the sweat of fear.

From the cellar window, we could see the Ukrainians — who hoped for an independent state and believed the Germans would give it to them — welcoming the conquerors with blue-and-yellow Ukrainian flags and swastika armbands. Father Derewienko, the Greek Orthodox priest, greeted the Germans with the traditional gift of bread and salt.

The entire night before the Germans arrived, our dachshund, Ralf, had howled and cried pitifully. We couldn't find him when we ran to hide in the cellar. When we came out, we found him lying dead in the garden. He had not been killed — he had just lay down and died.

We buried him among the flower beds in my grandmother's garden.

• • • • •

The Germans set up the headquarters of their civil administration in the beautiful house on the count's estate. The Ukrainians formed a militia which the Germans — who had no intention of allowing an independent Ukrainian state — used for their dirty work, which the militia did willingly.

The militiamen were peasant boys who found it glamorous to carry a rifle, put on an armband, lord over the Jews, loot at will, and then get drunk and sleep it off. It gave them satisfaction to thrash people, including children, and make them cower on the ground before dragging them to headquarters. Many times they shot fugitives on the spot.

Primitif, a popular word in everyone's lexicon, referred to Ukrainians. Even before the Germans' arrival, some young Ukrainians had, on a whim, tossed a grenade into the home of David and Rosa Herscher. Rosa was killed. The few Ukrainians who were members of the town intelligentsia were not known as friends of the Jews.

It was the Ukrainians who supplied the Germans with the list of fifteen Jewish leaders, who were ordered to meet and choose a seven-man *Judenrat* (Jewish Council), whose unenviable job it was to announce and carry out the German decrees. The Judenrat was located in the home of Rabbi Yehuda Drimmer on the main avenue. His half-sister was a good friend of mine from Hebrew school.

The Judenrat was forced to establish an *Ordnungsdienst*, an auxiliary police force, armed only with clubs, which compiled lists of people and property and enforced orders. My Uncle Zygmunt, Sophia's husband, was a member of the Ordnungsdienst. How my father managed to avoid conscription to these bodies, I never knew. He was a loner; perhaps he convinced them he could do more good in an unofficial capacity via his vast network of gentile acquaintances.

One of the Germans' first decrees was that Jews had to wear a white arm band with a blue Jewish star. Within a few days, the Germans ordered the Jews to turn in their radios. Then they demanded Jews deliver up all their valuables — furniture, linens and china that the Germans used for their headquarters — and jewelry.

My father hid all the silver from our dining room cabinet — a set of tea-glass holders, a few cups for Shabbat wine, our six schnapps cups, our candlesticks, the box where we kept the precious lumps of sugar under lock and key, and some cutlery. He buried these objects near a tree by our outhouse in the garden. Most of the silver cutlery remained in the house in a strongbox hidden under the false bottom of the bedroom armoire.

Frequently I had to deliver a donation of linen, china, kitchen utensils or furniture — and once the nightstand from my parents' bedroom bumping in a wheelbarrow — to the Judenrat in fulfillment of a German demand. Later, in the dead of a brutally cold winter, a call came down through the Judenrat to bring in all fur articles. I delivered the lining of my father's coat, my cow-skin muff and Arthur's earmuffs. To disobey was punishable by death. Nevertheless we hid my mother's Persian lamb coat, hoping to barter it for food.

Sometimes the Germans took hostages to make sure their demands for goods and provisions were carried out. If delivery did not occur within the designated time — two hours, for example — the hostages were shot. Three members of a Judenrat committee figured out each family's financial ability so that a tax could be collected and the proceeds used when the Germans demanded blackmail money.

The Judenrat was forced to register all Jewish men between the ages of sixteen and sixty and supply a certain number to report every day for repairing the bridge over the Zbrucz River, which the Russians had blown up as they retreated, and to work on the count's estate and in slave labor camps outside town. Uncle Wolf, assigned to work in the fields of Count Golochowski's huge estate, told us that almost all the German guards behaved in a barbaric manner towards Jews and only a handful showed humane inclinations. Major Braun, for example, invited Shimek's Uncle Mendel to play violin duets, and did not mistreat him, but he never restrained any of his men from beating other Jews.

Daytime hours, when my father was in danger of disappearing in a forced labor round-up, now posed a menace. For a while he and other men evaded the daily workgroups to avoid the brutality of the guards, but it meant that the members of the Judenrat and the Ordnungsdienst bore the brunt of retaliatory beatings.

The Judenrat was trapped between the community's distrust of their decisions and the orders of the Germans.

Once, when a group of fifty men conscripted to go to Czortkow encountered a returning group, and learned about the back-breaking work accompanied by beatings, half of them fled. The Judenrat, though warned by the Gestapo that hostages would be killed if it didn't produce the escapees, ignored the warning and on that one occasion nothing further happened.

• • • • •

Each morning felt like a starting line on an obstacle course — no one knew what hurdles the day would present as we stood poised, and waiting, calculating how to dodge the whack of clubs and the bite of bullets.

The worst day of the week for me was Thursdays, when I had to lug buckets of water to fill the bathtub for the week's baths. We had to lug water ourselves, since the Russians had abolished the water carrier trade and the Germans had conscripted the Jewish water carriers to perform forced labor. The pump well designated for use by Jews was a twenty minute walk away and, besides lugging the full pails home, pumping the handle called for well-muscled shoulders. On winter days, when the water froze in the pipes and I came home with empty buckets, my mother's disappointed shrug hurt me more than the weight of full buckets would have.

My mother seemed to sense that we would not be living in our home much longer and insisted, while she was still the mistress of the house, that the house look its best. She polished and scrubbed, swept and beat the rugs with renewed energy, and folded and refolded the one spare sheet we had. She brushed the few items of clothing we still owned, then hung them at measured intervals along the closet bar.

Even before the German invasion my mother had banished my father's books to the attic, calling them "dust collectors." I had been delighted with this arrangement, since it was a joy to find a fragrant nook for myself up there with Heine in hand and apples just an arm's length away, each one laid out separately on rows of pans so no rotten fruit would infect another. Now the apples were gone and the books collected their dust, undisturbed by my father or me.

One day the front door burst open. The inner door handle banged into the chest beside it, fell off, and spun on the floor. Standing in the doorway was Engel, a German officer who liked to be recognized as the lord of the town, the owner of each person and object. You could hear

63

Engel coming because his dog barked and snarled at people as they made their way down the street, causing them to scream and him to curse.

My mother saw how intently Engel stared at me while the dog strained toward her. Even daring to address him before he spoke could risk a bullet. She began pulling a chair towards herself as a shield. He shoved the chair at her with enough force to knock her down. The dog looked ravenous. He bucked and sprang into the air, his leash still wrapped around Engel's hand.

"Very clean," Engel said. With extended finger he tested an upper shelf.

"Clean Jews," he said as if he had discovered a blue rose.

Engel studied the contents of the highboy, as if he might consent to ship the highboy and selected items in it home to Juterborg. The dog growled louder by the minute.

I stood there desperate for something to appease the thrashing dog when Engel dropped the leash, but the dog sprang at me and his fangs penetrated my side. Engel called him back with words of praise and they left.

My mother tore my blouse off and began washing the wound. She didn't say a word, didn't even ask if I was in pain, didn't hug me or kiss me as she usually did when I was hurt. Neither of us were the same people we had been half an hour before.

Finally, as she tied a clean dishtowel around my midriff, she asked his name.

"Engel, Engel," she repeated, not saying a name, nor the German word but "angel" in Yiddish.

"Angel, angel, an angel came for a visit."

❖ 9 ❖

The Germans forbade the peasants to sell food to Jews, and it was practically unobtainable as the winter wore on. Once in a while, when I heard a rumor that a farmer had slaughtered one of his animals, I would take some item from the house in hope of trading it for some meat.

I consoled myself when I failed. *Tomorrow I'll find a way to get some flour; I'll buy it or barter for it — or steal it if I can just figure out how.*

Each day the scramble for a little food occupied me totally. I ran all the errands because my father had to stay off the street, lest he be dragged off to a slave labor camp, and my mother certainly couldn't trust seven-year-old Arthur to ferret out food. She stayed home out of fear that if Engel made another surprise appearance at the house, Arthur would fall under his boot.

On one of my errands I caught a glimpse of Izio — he was, I learned, living in a small village about ten kilometers from Skala — passing on Aryan papers. Other times I would see my old schoolmate, the estate manager's grandson, on the street. Whenever he saw me he would walk away without speaking. He gazed at the ground so he wouldn't have to look me in the eye.

Running errands was dangerous. One day I managed to slither past Captain Hera, Major Braun's deputy, just as he was poised to strike me. Instead he grabbed an old man by the beard and beat him with his pistol butt. Another day a different officer, Feiffer, stopped me as I was delivering a pair of shoes to one of my aunts. He took the shoes. He didn't strike me, but he cursed me on seeing that the shoes were all I was carrying.

Arthur was small for his age and unable to tag along when I left the house or wander about outdoors. He created a place for himself under the kitchen table and became his own best companion. He played war games and naval battles with pots, pans and crockery. My mother's insistence on neatness surrendered to his games.

I never observed him long enough to determine if the Jews, the Poles, the Russians or Germans were winning. Sometimes the French joined the fray, because France was where we most wanted to be — in Paris with Aunt Esther.

Arthur was intrigued by his name, which he associated not only with the port at the end of the Trans-Siberian railroad but also with the fortress-like synagogue in Skala called "Port Arthur," built during the Russo-Japanese War.

One of my friends, who had been pressed into working for the Germans, told him, "I made up a package of food from Engel to send to his family in Germany, and his first name is Arthur too."

"No, it's not," Arthur said.

"It truly is," she insisted. But Arthur shook his head and pounded the meat mallet on the overturned coal bucket to simulate an aerial attack until we retreated to the yard.

"Oh, go read a book," I hissed at Arthur when one of his incessant mock battles tangled him around my ankles as I crossed the floor.

"I don't know how," he said.

I stopped for a moment and tried to think what that must mean for him. I had read books and discussed them, had consumed knowledge like bread portioned out by my father along with the daily soup. But Arthur had only completed first and second grade in the Russian school before the German invasion and he could barely read. I resolved to teach him at the earliest opportunity.

Arthur was playing on the floor the time Captain Hera and his men burst in to look over our things. Hera ignored us and simply pointed to a credenza here or a vase there, which his underling noted in a little book.

Hera commented to one of the soldiers, "Clean, very clean. Reminds me of my mother's house. You could eat off her floor." The other man nodded appreciatively.

The men carted boxes of my father's books down from the attic and spilled them over the kitchen floor. Hera's anger at seeing volumes of German poets and a set of Nietzsche in a Jew's library drove him to a fit of frenzy. He trampled the pages underfoot, ripped the covers apart and ordered the books destroyed. My mother faded backwards toward the wall but my father, tears running down his face, stepped forward to retrieve a book. Hera battered him repeatedly with one heavy, torn volume, the jagged edge cutting into my father's cheeks and forehead.

"Jew-pig," he said, "now it's losing your books that makes you cry, soon it will be your children."

Suddenly Arthur piped up, "Fi, fi, fight him."

One of the soldiers aimed his gun and I sprang in front of Arthur.

Hera pointed to the things he wanted his men to carry out. When only one bed, a table and a few chairs remained, he shouted, "Now give this place a real cleaning," and cracked his baton across a dish to demonstrate what he meant.

After they left, while my mother washed the blood off my father's head and I salvaged the loose pages left behind from the books, Arthur asked my father, "Why didn't you hit him back?" None of us were in the mood to remind him of the guns.

From that day on, Arthur stopped playing war games.

❖ 10 ❖

We hoarded the little bread we'd obtained through barter, and every scrap was divided and assigned by size before we put it into our mouths.

Hunger made us desperate. Some nights my father or I would sneak into the fields of wealthy peasants outside town to root for potatoes, beets or cucumbers, or to steal rotten pears or apples — anything to stave off our hunger pangs. Sometimes I chewed the stems of the rotten fruit just for a taste resembling food.

One day we heard a rumor that some peasants had delivered cucumbers to the market. We'd had nothing to eat for breakfast or lunch and I couldn't remember when I had last eaten my fill.

I rushed off to the market with my school satchel and wedged myself into the stampede of people trying to get near the sacks on the peasants' wagons. I tried to press through the crowd by turning sideways and leading with my elbow, but I slipped on the slime of the trampled vegetables that looked more like over-ripe squash than cucumbers.

As the sour smell of rot wafted toward me, I heard a woman pushing her way out of the melee say, "It's not worth getting killed for. They're spoiled. The peasants wouldn't feed them to starving cattle." The vegetables were so rotten that the peasants had taken a chance on disobeying German orders not to sell food to the Jews.

With my satchel high on my shoulder, I forced my way between two men. One gave me a sideways kick that made me buckle at the knees. I pushed on, not caring that the cucumbers were no good. My mother would pare away the bad parts. I wished they were potatoes, but cucumbers would have to do.

"Hey, you with the school satchel..." A tall man with a rifle, wearing the armband of the Ukrainian militia, came towards me.

I was intent not to lose my place in line and tried to think of anything I could say to distract him. But for some reason I just held out my open hand to give him my coins. He closed my hand back over the coins and took my satchel. I noticed that his ring and pinkie fingers were missing. He had two forlorn knobs where the knuckles and fingertips should have been.

"Go home," he said in a voice used to giving orders. Then he smiled and I saw that he had even, white teeth. "Go home," he said again, but this time his voice had softened.

At home, an hour later, my mother glanced out the window and saw a man coming up the walk. When he knocked, her expression said, "I'm not going to open up." Another knock, louder this time.

I rose from my reading to open the door but my mother's trembling hand turned the handle first.

"Here are your cucumbers," the man said. "I'll bring better ones another time."

My mother held out a coin to him but he waved her away.

"My name is Jan," he said, as if that explained everything. He used his handkerchief to wipe off the cucumber slime smeared on my satchel.

"That's meant for notebooks," he said.

He looked at me and saw my finger stuck between the pages of a book. "Is it a good story?"

"Yes, it's very good."

As he left, he promised to bring eggs in a basket, not rolling around the bottom of a satchel.

"You have a plucky daughter," he said to my mother. "Bye, Blacky," he called to me, referring to the color of my hair.

"Do you know him?" asked my mother, as her fingers felt the yellowed cucumbers to find edible firm parts. She was too absorbed to see me shake my head. They were lousy cucumbers, ones that had lain in the September field too long: flaccid, bloated things, with parts nibbled away by field creatures or rotted by rain. In better days, my mother would have thrown them in the garbage. She used to sort through cucumbers and used only the small unblemished ones to make pickles.

"I thought you said there were no cucumbers," she said.

"No, I said I couldn't get any," I replied. "I guess I did after all."

W hen my father heard about our windfall he nodded.

"I know the man. A big man, right? Black hair and eyes? I sold him some lumber a while back. He stopped me on the street the other day. He's a militiaman so it scared me half to death. I thought he was going to take me to join a forced labor gang," said my father. "It turns out that he's engaged to be married and he wants to barter food for some linen and cutlery — maybe the Persian lamb coat. I told him to come any time."

We didn't have to wait long. One evening, soon after that, Jan came by our house with his fiancée, the daughter of a wealthy Ukrainian peasant named Dzsisiak. She had blond braids pinned to the top of her head and a tightly-wrapped full bosom. Though I had just begun to "round out nicely," as one of my aunts put it, I yearned for a figure more like that of the buxom bride-to-be.

"This is my wife Szencia, this is my daughter Fancia, and this is my son Arthur," my father introduced us.

My father went to the bedroom and took our silver cutlery out of the strongbox. My mother carried the silver knives and forks swathed in tissue paper to the table and unwrapped them, lingering as she cradled the handles, rubbing the ornate monograms with her thumb. The bride-to-be weighed each piece in her hand. The wrong initials didn't dismay her, but a missing fork did.

Jan sat down next to me.

"So, Blacky, do you miss school? What do you want to do after you finish school?" he asked, looking straight into my eyes.

"Medicine," I told him, "I'm going to Paris to study medicine after the war. My father promised me."

Jan seemed pleased. "Yes," he said, "Yes, Paris."

My father came back at that moment and repeated, "Paris," and then a soft, drawn-out "Paris." In a time of hunger and perpetual menace, at the far rim of Europe, each of us carried a Paris of our own in our imagination.

My father steered Jan to the corner of the sideboard and poured our last drop of schnapps for him.

After the engaged couple left we sat at the kitchen table drinking blackberry tea made from leaves I had gathered in the forest

"I don't trust him," my mother said. "He's a *goniff*, a thief like all the Ukrainians. He saw what we had left and he'll come back with a gang of militia who will help themselves and take us away."

"No," my father mused, "this one is different. I have a hunch he's a decent fellow."

My father's hunches were always right, but this time I too doubted him. To me, Jan looked like all the other Ukrainian policemen carrying their rifles that could kill us on a whim.

❖ 11 ❖

My parents, uncles and aunts held family meetings around our kitchen table. Each one had a tale of woe to report. When I appeared, they would gesture with an elbow, a tilt of the head, as if to say, "not in front of the child." Some horrors were whispered when I was out of earshot. Soon even that pretense fell away.

I was no longer a child. I was seventeen, a fact that did not escape notice. My figure had rounded out in the right places. Jan came to the house several times a week now. My mother baked special cakes for him from the flour he brought us.

"Be nice to Jan," my father said to me.

"I'm nice to Jan, as I am to all our guests," I said.

"Be nice to him," my father said again. When he said it several more times I began to wonder what he meant.

Dollars and gold coins suddenly began to surface in town. My father managed to convert whatever goods we had left into two hundred and fifty American dollars in fives, tens, and singles, and some gold coins. The American bills were tattered and torn, so he used a pot of glue to piece them together and pressed them smooth with the old iron which he heated on top of the stove in the corner of the kitchen.

We began to notice Ukrainian peasants walking around town in fancy clothes, high-fashion jackets and coats in the Western European style.

Three Hungarian Jewish boys, the last survivors of the unfortunates who had been herded through town in July, turned up in Skala. They reported to the Judenrat, that the three thousand Hungarian Jews had been held by the Germans at Orynin. The Germans told them they would be sent home, but then took them to a field and mowed them down with machine-guns. The Ukrainian militia had assisted the Germans and were in the front rank of the looters. The Hungarian boys had wormed their way out from under layers of bodies to escape.

The community arranged to help them. One family gave them a place to sleep, and they ate meals every day with a different family. A boy ate with us one day a week. He was so scared, he hardly said a word. The Judenrat eventually got the boys false papers and arranged their escape to Hungary. I heard years later that they had all survived the war.

While we were still trying to digest our shock, horror, and disbelief at the disaster that had befallen the Hungarian Jews, Jan came to visit us. I was "nice" to him, as my father had asked. I sat down next to him and complimented him on his new jacket. Its elegant wool fabric and fashionable cut looked odd over his baggy pants.

"Which tailor sewed your new jacket?" I asked sociably.

"I bought it from a friend," he said, and changed the subject.

One day, a peasant came to my father with an American hundred-dollar bill to ask where he could exchange it. We had never seen such a large bill before.

Jan offered to go to Czortkow to try to break the bill. He returned with zlotys for the peasant and a sack of cornmeal for us. My father invited him to share our meal. Jan took the chair beside mine, and from then on his place at the table was next to me.

I found out that he came from a long line of farmers, that some of his relatives still worked on farms and others had moved to town. He had worked for a shoemaker because he hadn't wanted to own his own business.

"How did you pick shoemaking?" I asked him.

"I like the smell of leather. I have a keen nose," he said. "From you, I detect the scent of a blossoming lemon tree."

I laughed. "You've never even smelled a lemon tree!"

"Maybe not, but I know how they smell from the taste of lemons," he said. "And you have the same flavor."

"Just as sour," I teased.

"No, just as shapely," he teased me back. "Anyway, I like working with my hands," he said. "It frees the mind. And besides, I can hammer my anger away. Give me leather, nails, and a hammer, and I'm happy."

"What are you so angry about?" I asked.

"I wanted to study, but it wasn't up to me. I had to leave school after the eighth grade, when my father died, to support my mother and sister and keep up the family farm. It's not the life I would have chosen for myself."

My respect for Jan grew. It was clear that he had the intelligence and skills to be more than a shoemaker. He was certainly not born to be a policeman for the Germans.

He watched over us every waking moment.

• • • • •

That cold winter, coal was scarce, kerosene for the lamp down to a trickle, the food shortage severe. My mother's Persian lamb coat had been bartered to Jan's fiancée for potatoes.

Jan had become a permanent fixture in our house. He always arrived with something: a bit of sugar or flour for my mother, eggs for Arthur and me. Any ordinary need — a burlap sack to cover a broken window, a warm coat, aspirin for a fever or medicine for my father's ulcer from Moizesevich (who continued to supply us, though he had been forbidden to sell medicine to Jews) — became a crisis that necessitated devious machinations, always involving Jan.

One night Suza's husband Munio had severe stomach pains and thought his appendix was about to burst. Dr. Meir Steuerman, our family doctor, was away, and the other Jewish doctors were in hiding. We sent someone to call the one Ukrainian doctor in town, a woman, but she refused to come because Munio was a Jew.

Jan volunteered to go to Borszczów for a doctor. He brought back a Jewish doctor he knew — the best one in town — in a horse and carriage. The doctor examined Munio, told him it was probably just an intestinal blockage, and gave him something for the pain. Then Jan took the doctor back to Borszczów. All of us were stunned that he had done this for us. And he refused to accept any payment, not even to cover the hay for his horse.

One day a large quantity of "milk" was made available to Jews in a shop near our house. My mother pressed two jars into my arms and told me to run. On the way, I suddenly realized that I didn't have any money. Nonetheless I joined the line, which was so long that I had little hope of getting to the front before the milk ran out.

"They call it milk," the man ahead of me said, "but it's only blue water left after the good milk is skimmed off."

"So get out of line, I'll be happy to take your portion," the woman behind me told him.

I felt someone tugging at my jars.

"Give them to me." It was Jan. "My cousin works here."

He shifted his rifle to his other arm. Looking up at him, I suddenly felt his height as he towered over me, almost half again as tall as I was. And his broad shoulders. If I hadn't seen him around our house so much, hadn't seen my father brighten when he walked in the door and my mother stop her perpetual cleaning and sit down to chat when he came to visit, I would have trembled in fear. Yet this man had a way of saying "Give them to me" that made it sound as though I were giving him a gift.

"One jar is for my grandmother," I told him. He led me to the front of the line, gave me one full jar of the whitish liquid from the butter-churning machine, and sent me home.

The next day Grandmother Miriam reported, "I almost fainted when I saw a brute of a militiaman walking up to my door! He gave me a jar of milk and touched his cap. Imagine, he touched his cap to an old Jewish woman!"

We trusted Jan so completely that my mother gave him some precious items for safekeeping: a suitcase full of her exquisite clothes from Paris, a feather quilt and two blankets.

"These are too good to give to the Germans, and someday we will need them. Please take good care of them for us," she said.

A month or so later, Shimek and I were sharing the garden bench on a day whose soft breezes made me impatient for spring. I couldn't concentrate on reading lately, but Shimek immersed himself more than ever in the few books he could find. Today it was a biography of Leonardo Da Vinci.

The book slipped off Shimek's lap as he reached for my hand. He retrieved the book. His hands were long, nicely shaped, and didn't seem to belong on his knobby red wrists. I didn't let him hold my hand but he settled for linking pinkies with me. I looked straight ahead. I was afraid that, if I turned my face toward him, he might think I would let him kiss me. We swung our pinkie-linked hands and then Shimek dropped the book again.

"Who is that guy?" Shimek was looking toward the kitchen window, where my father was lighting Jan's cigarette. I had been watching their little mime: Jan offered my father a cigarette, forgetting he didn't smoke, and my father, to show that he didn't oppose other people smoking, struck a match while Jan tucked the tobacco pouch and papers back into his pocket. The smoke billowed out the window.

I told Shimek about Jan — how he came often, how he had bought things from us and mostly did us favors.

"A Ukrainian gives nothing for nothing. This one is like the others: never without his rifle. He's got the same no-nonsense expression of all policemen," Shimek said. "Just wait. He's probably putting it on the bill."

• • • • •

Girls were ordered to work as live-in maids for the Germans, and we all knew what that really meant. For a bribe of three gold ducats, my father had arranged a compromise with the Judenrat: I would work for an officer in a job that would permit me to live at home. Since I had a knack for knitting, I became the personal knitter of sweaters for the Nazi chief manager of the count's estate, a swarthy *Volksdeutscher* (the

German ethnic minority in Poland) who was anything but the Nazi's ideal Aryan type.

My school friend Pepa's job was to be his full-time mistress.

"He has a habit of carrying a whip — and he enjoys using it," she said. "And you would shudder if you saw the night-time 'fun and games' at the estate parties to which the Judenrat has to deliver beautiful women from the finest families."

I asked what the rifle shots were that we heard all the way from the middle of town, after the cacophony of songs and breaking glass and screams.

"Oh, they do target practice on champagne bottles," Pepa said. "Full ones."

Turtlenecks were the style of sweater the manager fancied, and he wore them with riding breeches and boots. Boots were an important part of the Nazi uniform, and the Germans demanded them constantly from the Judenrat. To get the leather, the Judenrat granted exemptions from forced labor to the sons of the merchants who had hidden it to use as bribes. The Judenrat had Jewish shoemakers produce boots in black or brown.

The Judenrat also supplied me with wool that had been hidden by merchants. I picked up the wool at Judenrat headquarters. After I knitted the sweater sections at home, I took them to the estate for fittings.

As I approached the gates of the estate, I lectured myself, "He's a low-life, a vain bully, don't let him see you're scared," but I couldn't stop my hands from trembling as I opened the package containing the sweater front and back.

Without a word, the man stripped to the waist and stood stiffly in front of me in his black patent-leather boots. He was very tall, and I had to stand on a stool to pin the sections together. I tried to avoid touching him, but I could hear his breath accelerating, though he didn't move while I worked.

In the pidgin Polish of a Volksdeutscher, he asked, "What other colors of wool does your Judenrat have on hand? Though this off-white goes best with tan jodhpurs, don't you think?"

I assured him it did by polite-sounding grunts, my mouth full of pins.

"Make me the next one in a cable stitch," he said. Then he reached out and fondled my breasts. "I bet you're good at more than knitting," he leered.

I backed away and began folding up the sections. "It will be ready the day after tomorrow." If I worked all day and half the night, I would have the sleeves knit, and the entire sweater sewn, ironed, and finished by then.

"Don't leave so quickly," he said. He spread his hands on my buttocks and pressed me to him.

I pushed him away. One powerful arm pinned me to him again as he reached under my dress to touch me. I began to cry.

He pushed me down onto the bed. "The next thing you're going to tell me is you're a virgin." Anchoring me down with one arm, he allowed his free hand to roam under my dress.

"I am." I wanted to distract him but could hardly get any words out. I felt the sharp tear of his nails as he reached under my panties with jabbing fingers.

"Unpin your hair and shake it out."

I had to sit up to undo my hair. I carefully placed each hairpin in a pile on my lap. Tears fell on my hands.

"I am a virgin," I said again. "Is that so strange?"

"Not if you were my sister." As his two hands were wedging my knees apart, the hairpins rattled to the floor. A sob shook me. I fell on my knees and begged him to let me leave.

"Go, get out of here," he said, thrusting me away with both arms, "your runny nose is ugly. Make sure you bring the sweater by noon on Thursday."

The next day, a peasant pulled up in front of our house in a horse-drawn wagon and delivered a sack of potatoes from the Volksdeutscher, enough for us to live on for a few days. My parents didn't believe that he had given them to me without taking something more than a sweater in return, and people in town began talking.

But I held my ground. Every time I went to the estate after that I was terribly frightened. I kept telling myself, "At worst, if I rebuff him too much or too often, I'll end up in Czortkow prison, and my father will somehow find the money to bribe me out. Or if I'm sent to a labor camp, Jan will find a way to spring me from the train."

I reassured myself again and again as I walked to the estate, but could not shake off my fears. Sometimes my hands trembled so much when I was pinning the sweater sections on him that I couldn't put the pins in straight. But luckily, he never touched me again.

❖ 12 ❖

Jan brought us news about what was happening, rumors about what was to come, and, most important, advance word of forced-labor roundups. He only told me much later what this cost him; how much his fellow militiamen resented the "important business" which he used as an excuse to get out of joining in the roundups so that he could warn us and stay with us until they were over.

They all knew about his relationship with me.

"Are you better than the rest of us?" they would ask him. A good friend of his told him point-blank, "A Jewish girl isn't worth it." But they didn't report him. Maybe they were afraid of him; maybe he had something on them and they thought it wiser to leave him alone.

That February, slave labor was demanded for the Borki-Wielki camp near Tarnopol, and no one showed up — by this time everyone knew what awaited them there. The Ukrainian militia rounded up men off the street and searched people's homes until the quota was filled. Among the men they picked up was my father. For some reason, neither Jan's efforts nor a bribe to the militia could get him out of it.

Packed in a train under armed guard, my father managed to escape in transit. When he arrived home late the next night, he looked broken, as if he had long suffered under the whip. A further edict for additional slave laborers was issued. My father remained free by constantly sleeping at different relatives' houses, returning home for visits but rarely staying the night.

In April, on the first day of Passover, all men between the ages of twelve and sixty were ordered to report to Borszczów to be sent off to the Borki-Wielki labor camp. My father, Uncle Wolf, and Lolla's husband, Mottel, were among them. Zygmunt didn't have to go because he was still in the Ordnungsdienst.

Skała was plunged into gloom. Only women, older people, children, and the sick were left in town, consumed with worry about what was happening to the men. Uncle Zygmunt's sister ran all the way to Borszczów to find out, and upon her return she reported that the men were being held at a concentration point where a selection was going to be made. Some would be working as shoemakers, carpenters, and at other skilled work, but many would be sent to the stone quarries and the slave-labor camps.

Hoping to be sent home to work, my father claimed to be an egg-packer employed in the warehouse on Grandfather Jakob's property, where eggs were packed for export to the Reich. He urged Uncle Wolf and Uncle Mottel to say that they, too, were egg-packers. In any case, somehow my father, Mottel, and Wolf managed to escape, and they snuck home at night.

Some of the other men who had escaped were recaptured and sent to the Gestapo prison in Czortkow. Reports of barbarities had leaked from the prison, of brutal SS beatings, of men forced to work until they dropped, of dogs urged by their masters to attack the prisoners' faces, and of whip-wielding demons in boots stomping prisoners to death. A friend of my father's who had been ransomed from the prison with an enormous bribe told us of 120 Russian POW's, forced to walk in a circle for ten hours a day with their hands in the air. Within a few weeks they were all dead.

We began to hear rumors that children, the sick, and the elderly would soon be taken away in a full-scale raid. But taken where? And to do what? Children and the old and sick couldn't work on farms or in quarries or factories. Where would they be "taken"?

• • • • •

The children had no school to attend and nothing else to occupy their time. I had tried to sit down at the kitchen table with Arthur, Aunt Lolla's boys and Uncle Wolf's daughters to go over with them the bits of writing and arithmetic they had learned and were fast forgetting, but visitors or chores had always interrupted. I decided to start a school for

Arthur, my cousins, and six or seven other children. Looking at the curtains hanging on the line in the corner of the yard, at their lace panels which would require slow hours of ironing before I could try to sell them, I decided to make time for teaching by doing my chores in the morning before everyone got up. I proposed the idea to Shimek.

The children, who were seven and eight years old, came to my house, and Shimek and I shared with them as much knowledge as we could — a little reading, a little writing, some arithmetic. Sometimes Shimek brought an old book to read to them. We had no food to give the children to eat, and adjourned for the day when they got too hungry to concentrate or when their mothers heard rumors of a roundup and came to bundle them off home.

Arthur wasn't happy to have other kids around, interfering with his solitary play, but he liked to do sums and liked even more to wipe the chalk from the small slate we used to demonstrate penmanship. He would lick the chalk dust off his fingers to satisfy his growling stomach.

During the period our little school was in session, I enjoyed it hugely. I had discovered my own talent for dealing with children. I encouraged them to tell me what was on their minds and spent afternoons with one or another of them, interceding with a once-friend-turned-enemy or just holding a child on my lap and singing.

"You remind me of a St. Bernard," Shimek said to me.

On mornings when it was too cold, or when there was an alarm of an impending roundup, no children came and it was just as well. Those mornings I wanted only to go to my little hiding place in the far corner of the yard, where my father kept bits and pieces of lumber, and lie there as if it were a life raft. The idea had come to me from a book I had read about a person forced to abandon ship and float on a little boat on the wide, calm water. I didn't know how to swim, but on my raft I glided on waves under an open sky, oblivious to my mother's call. This kept me from drowning in the sea of rumor around me.

My wish to hide like a child coexisted with the other part of me, the part that drove a hard bargain and procured a whole box of candles in exchange for our lace curtains. Skala, the house, and the yard represented my childhood, and I wasn't yet ready for it to end.

❖ 13 ❖

With random roundups of Jews becoming more frequent, it was increasingly dangerous to venture out into the street. Now I faced an additional hazard. A Wehrmacht non-commissioned officer in his late twenties, Gottschalk by name, had developed a crush on me.

I could feel someone watching me even before he hovered behind or beside me, swathed in a huge black rain cape, or darted out in front of me and gripped my arm hard.

"Those Mongol eyes, where did you get those Mongol eyes?" he would say. "We must have a rendezvous, you and I." He thrust his fleshy face up close to me, and his brandy breath almost knocked me out. Gottschalk blocked my way, and I didn't dare push past him until he'd had enough of staring at me. One time, grinning with glee, he jostled me so that I dropped the beets I had gathered. He stood over me as I scrambled to pick them up before they rolled away down the gutter. He knew I spoke German and tried to pry a response out of me.

"Guten Morgen, Herr Feldisebel" was all I gave him.

Fear of being caught consorting with a member of a "polluted race" kept Gottschalk in check, except on rainy nights, when he would come to the house to look for me. On those nights, I slept in Uncle Wolfe's villa at the end of the lumberyard.

One rainy night he and another soldier arrived at our door, pistols in hand. I wasn't home. He put his gun against my mother's head and demanded, "Where's your daughter?"

"I don't know," she replied and told them to search the house if they didn't believe her. His pal slapped her, threw her against the stove, and beat her with the broom handle while Gottschalk stood there egging him on.

"He's from Vienna, a backwater town. Beating is second nature to him," Gottschalk said. "I myself am from Berlin."

My mother repeated this remark several times during the month she spent in bed recovering from the beating. "From Berlin," she said, "a superior type from Berlin."

Not finding me at home, Gottschalk and his henchman left and went looking for me at the home of one of my aunts. When I wasn't there either, they raped my aunt and forced her husband to watch. The rape had to be kept secret because, had the Gestapo found out, they would have killed her immediately: Germans were forbidden to "fraternize" with "subhuman" Jews. My aunt told a few members of the family but they didn't believe her — they didn't want to hear or know about it. She never told her children.

The parents of my friend and cousin, Lotka, had a hiding place in their cellar. Like my Uncle Leo's family, the Sternberg family had returned from Lvov, where they had been living during the Russian occupation, when the Germans invaded eastern Poland. The Sternberg's hideout was a crawlspace meant for a few hours' sanctuary — a narrow passage behind a false stone wall. The entrance was a hole in the wall concealed by shelves full of jars.

For two nights after the rape, Lotka and I spent the night in this hideout. We didn't sleep because we were so cramped; anyway, we were too nervous to fall asleep. The wintry drafts that penetrated through the wall gave us some air. We lay crammed in the space between the walls on a blanket, her feet serving as a pillow for my head until we switched places. We ate boiled turnips and bread. Actually it was a feast to us, since my mother had smeared some goose grease on the bread.

We told each other stories to pass the time, and laughed out of shared anxiety. Then we heard a clomp, clomp from above: a signal to remain quiet. What's the use of hiding, the sound reminded us, *if you're going to giggle and give yourselves away?*

❖ 14 ❖

One night, when he heard the rumor of an impending raid, Jan brought me to his home to spend the night in his room. When his mother saw that he had brought in a girl who was not his fiancée, and one who looked so obviously Jewish, she ran out of the house. His sister and her husband also saw me; they didn't say a word, but Jan could see how upset they were.

His room was immaculately clean, and his bed had goose-down pillows and an embroidered comforter. I lay rigid on the bed, terribly frightened. Jan sat by my side all night, watching me like a faithful dog. Early the next morning, he gave me a jar of honey and sent me home.

Later that afternoon, Jan came to the entrance hall of our house to make sure I had arrived home safely.

"I've made a decision," he said. "I've broken off my engagement. I'm not going to marry her."

This was the last thing I was expecting. "But you already announced the wedding date in church!" I said.

"Yes, her father swears he's going to avenge the insult," Jan said.

He took my hand. "I love you. I would do anything to save your life, to make sure that they don't get you. I would grab you away from the Umschlagplatz or pull you off the train. Wherever you are during an aktsia I'll get to you and not let them take you away, even if I have to murder someone." Then he kissed me, for the first time, lightly.

Jan's declaration of love came as a surprise. But it calmed me, gave me a sense that I was protected, acted as a kind of shield around me as I navigated in an increasingly hostile and stormy sea.

In June, the order came down for seventy-five girls to report for duty in a labor camp, but only six showed up. News of a night raid instigated by Hera filtered down to Jan, and he came to pick me up — this time waiting until his mother, sister, and brother-in-law were already asleep.

It was the first time he had brought me to the hiding place behind the false wall he had built in the hayloft of his barn. The sloping roof was so low that I hit my head as I made my way to the "bed," a pile of hay. Jan warned me that I was not to make a sound if he saw anyone in the yard.

Jan moved a bale of hay into position by the triangular window opening, sat down on it, and lit a cigarette.

I lay down but heard my heart beat so loudly that I sat up.

"Don't be afraid," he said. "No one will hurt you tonight."

"What's going to happen?"

"They're taking the girls to the work camp near Jagelnica. But only the single ones." He paused, then smiled. "Is that a good enough reason to rush into marriage?"

We laughed, each for our own reasons. He pulled a hunk of bread out of his pocket for me. "Watch the crumbs — mice, you know."

When Jan was sure that the transport of girls had left, he told me I could go home. I saw that each Jewish house had a Star of David either painted on its wall or hung in the window.

My parents believed I had been caught in the roundup. For a minute they stood frozen after I entered, then they both rushed toward me.

"Father, why don't we have a Jewish star on the house?" I asked.

"Jan will tell us when to hang it out," he said.

Barely credible stories began to float around, told by distraught escapees from different shtetls and by malicious peasants, about Jews forced to dig their own graves before they were shot.

My father, who had come to realize that the Germans in Skala were not the Germans of his beloved poetry, began to prepare hiding places for the family, not only the four of us, but my grandparents, aunts, uncles, and cousins as well. Jan procured the materials from which my father built the hideouts, and my father showed him where they were.

All the hiding places were on Grandfather Jakob's property. My father built no hideouts at our house, anticipating that the Ukrainians would come to look for him there and then would find the rest of us, too. The first hideout he built was under the tub in my grandmother's bathhouse, which had an earth floor. A camouflaged square cutout could be pulled up to allow us to descend into the hole via a tiny stepladder.

We had a few practice drills at night to learn to hide quickly and, though Arthur was awakened abruptly, he was never cranky. He treated the whole thing as a spy adventure. Perhaps he welcomed the change of expression on my parents' faces since afterwards, when we sat in the kitchen drinking our ersatz tea, the furrows between my father's eyes eased and my mother's hands, for a change, lay folded in her lap.

By August, when all houses had to be marked with a Jewish star, we were spending our nights — sleeplessly — in this hole in the ground.

Meanwhile my father, with the help of my uncles, began the back-breaking task of building the larger hideout under the floor of the egg warehouse. This was the hiding place which was to save the lives of six-teen members of our family and two neighbors during the aktsia.

By this time, all of our jewelry but two rings and my mother's heart pendant had been bartered for provisions. I accompanied my father one day when he brought the diamond ring, for safekeeping, to Father Derewienko, who now acted as chaplain to the Ukrainian militia. The priest took the little leather pouch containing the ring and put it in a large cabinet in his living room.

My father told me, as we left the house, that the ring wouldn't bring much money, but it had been his mother Hinda's engagement ring, and we should try to keep it in the family. "Someday," he said, "it will be yours."

❖ 15 ❖

O ne Friday my mother was on her hands and knees scrubbing the wooden floor to perfect whiteness. Since cooking and baking no longer occupied her time, she prepared for the Sabbath by giving an extra scrubbing to the center hall, which usually lay protected by two layers of rugs plus a top layer of newspaper when it rained.

My father burst into the house, looking wild.

"You crazy woman!" he said, kicking over the pail so that water sloshed halfway up the wall.

"What's gotten into you?" my mother shrieked.

A blast of smoke rushed at me through the open front door. I looked across the street and saw the reason for my father's anguish: the large synagogue was in flames! Jews were running in and out, trying desperately to save the burning Torah scrolls.

I dashed out of the house to the synagogue.

"They set this fire deliberately. Ten old men are being held hostage

The Skala Cemetery

under guard in the market square for trying to stop them," one Jew told me.

My two grandfathers may be among them, I thought, and raced to the marketplace. The ten elderly men — all highly respected but, thankfully, not my grandfathers — were being shoved and slapped, kicked and pulled by their beards and hair. I watched in horrified fascination how they maintained a dignified silence even as the Ukrainian militia intensified their assault.

Someone came up close behind me and whispered, "Go home." Jan's voice sounded more like a plea than an order. I left without turning around.

Later my father told me that the hostages had been released. They and other Jews put on their prayer-shawls, fasted and prayed, and then took the burnt Torah scrolls they had pulled out of the flames down the hill to the Jewish cemetery, where they buried them.

My father got a letter from his sister Esther in Nazi-occupied Paris. She wrote that the Germans were demanding that Jews with Polish citizenship register at the prefecture to be sent back to Poland.

In her letter, Aunt Esther asked, "Will it be better for us to come home rather than risk hiding in France? Will we be safe?"

My father sent Esther a postcard with one sentence: "If you come home, expect to see your mother." Grandmother Hinda had died during the Soviet regime. This was a coded warning, but we had no way to know whether they would ever receive it.

• • • • •

Erev Succos, September 25, 1942. Kelner, the SS commander of the region, came to Skala from Gestapo headquarters in Czortkow, demanding from the Judenrat "gifts" of leather and gold in return for letting the Jews remain in town.

Just before noon he, a few soldiers, and several members of the Judenrat burst through the door of our house. Without a glance at my mother, Arthur, and me — my father wasn't at home — Kelner ordered the soldiers to check each room, including the attic, for furniture and other valuables. Since everything of value had already been taken, there wasn't much for his deputy to record in his notebook.

Kelner conducted his own personal search under the bed, in the cupboards, and through the closets.

"You," he said to my mother, addressing her politely in the second-person plural, "you have lived in Germany?" My mother barely managed to shake her head no.

"Remarkable," he said to one of his soldiers, "but under her petticoat she's as filthy as all the other dirty sows."

Kelner left a message for my absent father: if he did not appear at headquarters by the end of the day, we would all be shot.

Later that afternoon, it looked like we might have a decent Succos after all. Kelner, evidently pleased with his loot, had announced, "The Jews of Skala have nothing to fear."

When my father came home from the hiding place where he had spent the night with Uncle Wolf, he was relieved that we hadn't been harmed. But he didn't believe Kelner and had a feeling that something was brewing.

"They'll come for us when we least expect it," he said. "We must all go immediately to the hiding place in the bathhouse and spend the night there."

Arthur and I begged him to excuse us from going straight to the hiding place in the bowels of the earth. We wanted to join the rest of the family for dinner at my Wasserman grandparents' house, as we always did on the eve of Jewish holidays.

"If there is an alarm," we argued, "we can all rush to that larger hiding place in the warehouse that you just finished building."

My father reluctantly agreed.

"But it's far from here to their house," he said, "so run as fast as you can."

I was ready to risk my life to go to my grandparents' for dinner. It was the eve of my eighteenth birthday, and we would celebrate with all the relatives gathered around the table for the holiday.

I had been tempted many times to barter away my curlers, and now I was glad I hadn't. The hairdo I would sport tomorrow would make me feel festive all day.

I took the curlers with me to my grandparents' house. I had no way to know that rolling my hair up in rows of metal coils and sleeping on them, despite the discomfort, or maybe because of it, would be my last vestige of a normal teenage life.

V

In Hiding After the Aktsia

Age 18: September 1942–August 1943

❖ 16 ❖

"Do you have any idea what you looked like when you stepped out of the hiding place with your hands full of curlers and your hair twisted into writhing black snakes?" Jan chuckled.

Jan and I had settled ourselves at the window of the attic hideout in his barn. Arthur was asleep. Jan and I were keeping watch for the approach of soldiers, for the inevitable attack sure to happen in five minutes — or next week.

We tried to appear calm for each other, but once in a while Jan revealed his anxiety when he raised himself to his knees and angled his body at the side of the window to get a view of anyone who might be skulking around the barn.

"I wasn't thinking of anything when we emerged from the hideout except how glad I was to be alive and how good it was to see you," I told him. "Tell me, what were you doing there anyway?"

"I was watching the warehouse the entire time you were hiding there under the floor, and keeping a lookout on your house as well."

The woman and child who had made us take them into our warehouse hideout were the aunt and cousin of a Jewish barber we barely knew. They had been staying with our neighbors, their cousins. The woman had apparently told the barber about our hideout before she joined us there.

"During the aktsia the barber left his bunker and came to find me. He tried to make a deal with me. His mother had been seized by the Germans and was being held at the Umschlagplatz. He said he would reveal your whereabouts in return for the release of his mother. He offered eighteen Jews for one, he said, and I would get the 'credit.'"

"He was going to tell the Germans where we were hiding, with his own aunt and cousin there?"

"Yes," replied Jan, "to save his mother. But I told him that I would kill him if he did. So I had to watch him, too, and make sure he didn't leave his own bunker again to go to the Germans."

Jan's face peaked with anger, his eyes wide and unblinking.

"Would you really have killed him?"

"Yes," he said simply. "Of course."

In a half-crouch to avoid the sloping beams, he moved over to put his arms around me. I was shivering in the chill that comes before dawn. Taking me on his lap, soothing me as if I were a child with a scraped knee, he kept assuring me that he would look after me, that I would be safe with him. The dark patch framed by the window turned light as we sat there, Jan holding me on his lap, his arms around me.

"You don't need curlers to make your hair beautiful," he said. "It's beautiful as it is."

The sunlight in Jan's attic was almost as brilliant as the moonlight had been by the time I settled into my crib in the hay next to Arthur. I lay with my eyes open, reluctant to surrender to the twilight of sleep.

• • • • •

Over the next two weeks, Jan came to see us every night about an hour after his house grew dark. We would hear him coming into the barn below our loft, and waited impatiently while he changed into the barn clothes he kept hidden behind the straw in order to keep his regular clothes free of hay and the odor of the barn. Then he would assemble the ladder he'd made himself to climb up to our attic hiding place and the top of the ladder would appear, followed by Jan himself.

When he left us, he would do the whole thing in reverse: he climbed down, pried apart, folded up and hid the long and rickety ladder and changed back into the good clothes he had left near the barn door with his rifle.

Jan had obviously thought this out very carefully, and his daily plan for taking care of us was a full-time job. Every time he came, Jan brought us food — a piece of sausage or some apples, a hunk of bread or a few raw eggs which we would eat with the bread if we had any. One time he brought a jar of delicious borscht, unlike any I had ever tasted; he disposed of the jar far from the house. Another time he came swinging a can of pork stew by the handle. It was already cold but it tasted delicious. Arthur and I scraped out the last of the sauce with our fingers.

Most of the food Jan brought us he stole from his mother, sometimes from her cooking pot and sometimes out of his own portion. He had to sneak the food out because his mother, as any peasant woman, knew exactly how much food she had on hand.

Jan's brother-in-law gave us a scare when he poked around in the barn one day, muttering as he searched for the hidden ladder. He cursed when he heard his wife call him, but gave up and left. Some days later, Jan's sister was crossing the yard on her way to the little garden shed; as I watched through the crack between two planks of the barn wall, she looked up speculatively at the window, standing and studying it for a long while, and then continued on.

The next time Jan came, I asked, "Would you please bring me the suitcase of clothes that my mother gave you for safekeeping? Perhaps I could give some of them to your sister. She would love the beautiful suits from Paris, the silk robes and dresses — and maybe she would agree to let us stay."

"It's gone," he told me. "My mother and sister must have found it.

95

And I doubt it would have helped anyway. My mother had chest pains not long ago, and she summoned me to her bedside. She said that it would kill her if she learned I was helping you. She says she already lost my father — do I want her to lose me too?"

What could I say? If I took Arthur by the hand and started walking, where would we go? I had to think of Arthur's life as well as my own. If we left and he was caught, he would be shipped off to Belzec; he was too young to join me in a fugitive existence. Yet if we stayed, and we were caught, Jan would pay with his life.

I begged Jan, "Take us somewhere else!" though this hidden corner of a barn attic was the only safe place I could imagine in the world.

"Arrangements are being made," he said. "Be good."

I got angry and started to raise my voice. "We're going before it gets light."

He slid down next to me on the straw and clamped his hand over my mouth. The firm pressure of his fingers on my lips silenced my frustration, but only temporarily.

"Until I find a place, you stay here," Jan said.

I decided to chance it a few more days. For Arthur, I told myself. We clung together and Jan rocked me back and forth in his arms. I held him tightly around the waist and abandoned myself to the movement of our bodies.

Arthur woke with a whimper and Jan gave him a piece of bread. Then he disappeared down the ladder. I didn't know how to comfort myself when he was gone.

❖ 17 ❖

I longed for word from my parents. Jan could tell me only that he had heard they were safe, but that it was a hard life in the Borszczów ghetto. One day he brought news.

"The Germans have set up their offices in your house. Thanks to your mother, it had a reputation for being the cleanest house in Skala."

This struck me as hilarious and I burst into hysterical laughter. Jan had to cover my mouth to mute the racket.

The days were rolled into a tight coil of waiting — waiting for Jan to bring more news of my parents or something to eat or just to come and sit with me while Arthur slept. Most of all I waited for the moment when they would discover us, when the Gestapo and Ukrainian militia would pounce and flush us out of hiding. Even though Jan had assured me he would rescue me from any truck or train, I knew the odds favored their killing us right there in the barn.

I longed to write letters, to try to influence those who could change history — Churchill or Stalin — to hurry up and end the war, but I didn't ask Jan to bring paper for letters or a diary. He had enough trouble scrounging for food without indulging my whim to record my thoughts. The dim light of the hayloft made writing or reading impossible, which was just as well since there was nothing to read anyway.

Time, plentiful time, added an indefinable peril to my rational fears. "True time," during which I sat and stared at a tuft of hay and allowed my thoughts to slip wherever they wished, clashed with "false time," chronological time, during which I gave my attention to Arthur or Jan. The challenge of waiting, for me, was to switch my mindset from one variety of time to the other without feeling violently disoriented.

Arthur seemed to be better at existing in limbo than I. He fell into long stretches of sleep, and I often hobbled over to him on my knees to check that he was still breathing. During sessions of "true time," when my body hovered over the straw-covered floor, my mind jumped about inventing ingenious schemes by which to distract attackers so that Arthur could flee.

Chronological time had become meaningless, since I had no clock or watch. On gray days, time played tricks — I would think it must be eight o'clock in the morning and it would turn out to be five. The neighbor's rooster could be counted on sometimes, but then one day his crowing stopped. Had he been sold or eaten? I named the rooster Phoenix and made up stories for Arthur about the fate of the rooster. The saga began to fascinate us.

"Tell me another Phoenix," Arthur begged several times a day.

I trained myself to use "false time" to advantage. Sometimes I persuaded Arthur to join me in braiding straw figures. I made a whole settlement of houses and people for him to play with. Other times I made up new stanzas for old songs, and Arthur joined in the refrain.

Arthur's favorite activity was to hear fantasy descriptions of what we would eat when the war was over, so I served up imaginary platters of meat and potatoes. His stomach had not shrunk. One day we had a piece of bread and I gave Arthur part of my share. I prayed he wouldn't eat it all, but he did.

How can I be so mean, I accused myself, *to wish the food from Arthur's mouth into mine?* My stomach rarely growled. Instead, a continual sensation of hollowness reminded me of an unfilled vase fated to sit on a table without flowers or water.

Losing track of the days led to whole chunks of them being outside of calendar time, but there was no way to ignore the November chill. "Bitter weather," the conventional term we had always used for extreme cold, took on new meaning. As a child, when I heard my mother say, "It's bitter outside," I saw wrinkled almonds hanging from frost-covered branches. Now "bitter" took the form of body-wracking shivers, of watching my exhaled breath solidifying as I sat wrapped in a coat of straw. Jan stuffed rags between the wall planks, but there wasn't much he could do about the window-hole other than to hang a double sack as a curtain.

Sitting on my legs kept them warm, but I had to remember to shake the stiffness out once in a while. I realized how fortunate we had been while still living in our own house — there I could stand without stooping and could go out to search for bread.

Day by day my legs began to atrophy, the deadening interrupted only when Jan came to allow Arthur and me a late-night trot around the barn floor once a week. Usually Arthur was too sleepy. Back up in the hayloft, I sat as inert as a pitchfork sticking out of a bale of hay. My unused legs cried to dance. Dancing with a partner — a smooth fox-trot with plenty of dips — became my favorite fantasy, but my partner's face was obscured.

Once, when Jan took me down the ladder to exercise my legs, he caught me in a bear hug and whirled me around, and I let myself go limp, enjoying the vertigo until he finally steadied me back onto my feet. I had to force myself to swallow my urge to laugh out loud, and that ruined the fun.

The smell of Jan's skin as my nose grazed his neck filled my mouth and became an agreeable taste, like a juicy pear or apple. When we sat or stood near each other I found the mixture of the odor of damp wool from his jacket with the scent of male skin, fresh from the outdoors, an intoxicant, a magnetic force. At times I felt heat flash across my forearms and chest and burn in my cheeks. Sometimes when Jan held my hand loosely while we sat together at the little window, he pressed it lightly, just a layer of gauze over palm and fingers, and I would find myself wishing he would press my hand longer and harder.

• • • • •

During the long nights in the attic, Jan and I told each other about our lives, what we had done and what we expected to do. We excluded present time, the war, its ferocity, its irrationality. The hours spent in the attic seemed unreal because they were not of our own choosing.

99

What an unlikely pair we made: a Ukrainian shoemaker and a Jewish high school girl! We had begun to think of ourselves as a couple, each one finding in the other a confidante, a person with whom to share any impermissible yearning or strange dream.

I told him naughty things I had done, in the belief that if I didn't get them off my chest now I might never have another chance. I told him about cheating on the oral exams with my Russian teachers. Jan admitted to poaching a goose at age eleven and told me some tales of early love-making which involved a lot of hay, moonlight, and lost undergarments. I told him about Izio.

"So you like older men," Jan said.

"Not only," I said. "I like Shimek. But boys my own age are so childish."

He told me what happened with his ex-fiancée. "She married someone on the rebound. Her father Dzsisiak has it in for me now. He calls me a 'Jewish uncle' right to my face."

"Aren't you worried?" I asked.

He waved it off. "I don't care — let people say what they like." His face darkened. "But Dzsisiak had better not talk like that to the Germans or it will cost him his life."

"Aren't you going to get married?" I asked.

"I have my eye on someone, but I'm not in a hurry." He grinned at me. "And you, you must become a doctor," he said, as if there were no doubt that I would still be alive by the war's end. "Why not study in Warsaw? I would like to see Warsaw. But Paris is out. I don't speak French."

"I'll teach you," I said.

He broke into a broader grin and poked me in the ribs. "I'll hold you to that."

I began on the spot with "Bonjour!" and he repeated with such a funny accent that I couldn't help laughing, and he began to laugh, too, trying to imitate my pronunciation. In a burst of frustrated energy, he put his arms around me and pressed his lips to my cheek. Somehow, in an instant between giggles, our laughter died and he kissed me on the lips. It was a light friendly kiss. I wanted to kiss him back but it was already too late; he was back at his post at the window.

When we were alone without immediate threat, when we talked or sat silently, we looked into each other's eyes in a way that was not embarrassing. It was like being undressed without feeling naked. Several times he was at the point of giving me more than a casual kiss, but the moment never seemed right.

One morning I arranged my handkerchief under the apple Jan had brought so that it made a ruffle, the white cambric setting off the tawny orange and yellow-green of the apple skin, which I had polished to a high gloss. When Arthur woke I would cut a third of it for our breakfast and save the sharp-edged core for a snack. The seeds were chewy and perhaps had some healthful properties.

Riveted by the sheen of the apple, I let my thoughts wander to Sluwa Kassierer, our homework tutor. I remembered how one day, when I was twelve, I had stayed behind to finish a composition after the other pupils left. Sluwa had picked up an apple, cupped it in her joined palms, and twirled it by its stem.

"I've never tasted the apple from the forbidden tree," she had said, and there was yearning in her voice and eyes.

I had wondered at the time what she meant. Now I knew she had been longing for a man's embrace. But tasting that "apple" was forbidden her as an unmarried woman.

I remembered how, when I had been a high school student a few years later, I read *Nana* and associated the prospect of sexual pleasure with a boudoir and its fragrance of sultry blooms, the room a pink shrine for a soft bed from which ecstatic sighs of love-making would rise. Now, with aching bones and itchy skin, picking bugs off my clothes and spitting one out of my mouth, I realized how little I resembled that foolish young girl. I lay on a pallet of straw. And whom did I imagine next to me for this embrace? The fleeting image of a tall figure, the head turned away.

Taste of the forbidden apple. The shiny cheeks of the apple nestled in its doily taunted me to take a bite.

Arthur slept and woke and ate his apple section and played a secret game in a straw fort he built with his jacket in the corner. The cold autumn day turned his hands blue before he stopped, lay down on his back, and, crossing his arms, tucked his rigid hands into his armpits.

Looking at him, I realized how dangerous it was to fall so deeply into reverie. I was so absorbed in my dream world that it was hard for me to reawaken my fear mechanism.

But I was responsible for Arthur. I vowed to train myself out of daydreaming.

•　•　•　•　•

After two weeks in Jan's attic hideout, my dreams began to shift from food — plates of schnitzel with eggs and anchovies; bowls of cherries with cream — to waterfalls, rivers, torrents of rain. It was not thirst but dirt — the feel of oily skin chafing under unwashed underclothes — that bothered me constantly.

Jan brought us enough water to drink and to rinse our hands, but warm water and soap were luxuries of the past. Lack of washing didn't trouble Arthur and, when I tried to comb my fingers through his hair to untangle it, he pulled away. I didn't know if the rank odor I smelled came from me or the barn, so I asked Arthur.

"It's you," Arthur said.

That night I told Jan, "Forget about bringing food tomorrow. Please, please figure out a way to let us take a bath!"

The next Sunday, when his family had left home to go to church and Arthur had been asleep for a long time, Jan appeared at the top of the ladder and led me down to the barn. He had brought a pail of hot water, a hunk of brown soap, and a piece of torn cloth, and apologized for not bringing a better towel. In my eagerness to catch the heat of the water before it cooled, I rolled down my stockings while Jan unbuttoned my sweater. I shyly turned my back as he gently soaped the nape of my neck. My undershirt became soaked, and I tore it and my bra and panties off, too.

It seemed natural to stand there on the straw-covered barn floor and have Jan scrub my back, legs and arms and then hand me the soap so I could do the rest. He told me to kneel and lean my head back; he poured water over my hair and worked some soap into it.

Finally he dumped the entire pail of water over me.

"But what about Arthur?" I asked in consternation.

"I'll bring more hot water another day, I promise," he said. Then he produced a boy's homespun shirt, with a clean sun-dried scent, and I wrapped it around myself like a sheepskin coat. We climbed back up to the attic and, seated by the window as usual, Jan signaled with his head for me to come. I sat in the niche of his legs between his knees, feeling light and new. He kissed my wet hair and I fell asleep.

It seems odd to me now that such a simple procedure as a makeshift bath could switch my mood from low to high, from a state of terror of imminent, violent death to a feeling of calm bordering on joy, even hope that this nightmare would end.

My gut instinct still told me that it would end, that I would survive. My father had said I would go to Paris and study medicine. I held on to that plan. It had become a mantra: Paris, Paris, Paris. The pictures that flashed across my mind were a succession of images: the Eiffel Tower, my father's books by Dumas, my Aunt Esther's face on an old photograph; the long, onion-covered baguette she had brought us on one of her visits to Skala.

One night, when Jan didn't come, I heard the barn-door hinges creak and voices whispering below. "I have to wake Arthur!" I thought. "We have to get ready to run!"

The sounds were soft — perhaps a nosy neighbor or Jan's brother-in-law. Maybe people in flight looking for shelter. I held my breath and pressed my ear to a crack between the floorboards.

I heard a familiar clearing of the throat. There could be no mistake. It was my father! And yes, of course, the other voice was my mother's.

Tossing the straw away, I stuck my head down through the attic opening.

"We're here," they whispered.

"There's a ladder hidden somewhere. Try to find it," I whispered back.

But Jan had hidden it so carefully, they couldn't find it.

It wasn't until the following night, when Jan came by, that they were able to climb up to the attic. Arthur and I threw our arms around their shoulders as soon as they appeared through the hole in the attic floor, even before they reached the top rung. The four of us and Jan were together again!

My father looked paler than ever, and I had forgotten how my mother had thinned out during the past year. She kept shaking her head from right to left in continual denial, as if she couldn't believe she was seeing her children again. Sitting on the loft floor, she looked up at Arthur standing before her.

"You look taller," she told him, but she shook her head from side to side as if to negate her words.

My father told us about the Borszczów ghetto, a few streets in what had once been the poorest neighborhood of the town, with run-down buildings and no sewers. There was almost no food or fuel for the communal stove in the room he and my mother shared with eleven other Jews. It didn't take a genius to figure out that the Germans had massed the Jews together because it would be easier to dispose of them that way.

"Living there we were as good as dead," he said, "so we had to leave."

My father knew one of the leaders of the Judenrat. Weeks of bribing and wheedling — begging for his life — had finally loosened a link in the Judenrat chain, allowing him and my mother to escape. They had run the 15 kilometers from Borszczów to Jan's barn and, miracle of miracles, here they were.

My father and Jan talked for a long time, examining all our alternatives. None of the hiding places my father had built were safe. Escaping to the forest, where the fascist partisans were killing Jews, was worse than staying in the ghetto. It was decided that we would stay here until Jan could work something out with people he knew in a distant village.

Jan took two apples and a penknife out of his pocket and cut each apple in half. After he disappeared down the ladder, I watched him hide the knife in a closet he had made behind a section of false barn-wall. The sharp slope of the roof — which even on its high end prevented any of us from standing up straight, except Arthur — made my parents hunch like cripples as they stumbled gratefully toward the hay bed. They fell asleep the instant they lay down.

In the moments before sleep, with the warmth of my father and mother on either side of me, I marveled at how swiftly the time had passed; a large block of "false time" had canceled the "true" kind for a change. I was happy.

❖ 18 ❖

We knew we couldn't all stay in Jan's barn hideout indefinitely and racked our brains for possible permanent hiding places. My father dispatched Jan to bring Marysia, a peasant woman from a nearby village, who had worked for us after Arthur was born. In our house she'd had a tiny alcove for a room and had worked night and day. The family had laughed at her habit of using a ruler to position rugs on the floor after cleaning, but no one could deny that she beat the rugs hanging on the line harder and longer than any other servant had ever done.

Marysia at first refused to come. Then one night, after midnight, when Jan had stopped in to bring us a can of milk and empty our waste pail, we heard little taps on the barn door. Jan sprang toward the ladder with greater agility than I would have imagined possible in a man with such a large body. I watched him — through a chink in the attic floor — leap to the barn door. Arthur must have been sleeping lightly, because he sat up in his hay bed and hugged his jacket, which doubled as a blanket.

When Marysia reached the top of the ladder, she barely acknowledged the rest of us, but headed straight for Arthur. He seemed glad to see her, too. She pinched his cheek and gave him a sweet roll wrapped in a cloth. When he finished eating, she blew her nose in the cloth and put it in her pocket.

"I'll tell you why I waited so many days to come. I'm being watched — and so are you, Jan," she said. "You should be more careful. It was foolish to come see me in daylight. It made the neighbors wonder why a poor woman with no money to buy loot would have a visitor, especially one connected to my former employers. Everyone knows that you are Benjamin Gottesfeld's 'Jewish uncle' and that the family has not been caught. It won't be long," Marysia warned us, "before they find you."

Marysia refused my father's offer of money to take Arthur and me.

My mother hoped to persuade Marysia and moved toward her. She had forgotten how Marysia had been afraid of her, so terrified of my mother's obsession with cleanliness that she had cleaned my father's razor and cut her hand. She had bled for weeks. My mother had thought nothing of it, or of the fact that Marysia hadn't shared our meals or even eaten the same food. She usually just got the bread left over after we had finished eating — that was just the way things were done.

My mother honestly believed that she and Marysia had been on cordial mistress-servant terms in the past, thanks to the occasional gift of a discarded pair of shoes or an unneeded plate. Marysia had always acted pleased with the gifts and, at Christmas and Easter, she had brought us samples of holiday goodies from home, which, of course, we could not eat because they weren't kosher. Although my mother had not permitted Marysia to nail her crucifix on the wall above her little bed in her alcove room, she had pretended not to hear when Marysia told Arthur stories from the New Testament.

Marysia recoiled from my mother's advance. "You have no right to ask me to take the children," she said defiantly as my mother fell to her knees and kissed her hand.

"Why did you come, then?" I asked.

"I came to see Arthur . . ." I knew she had stopped herself from saying, "for the last time" as she gently twisted a lock of his hair and traced the line of his cheeks to his chin.

"Be a brave boy," she said and turned to go down the ladder.

Arthur found his niche in the straw and began to suck his thumb, a habit he had broken years before.

"I should have given her better things in the past. Then she would have taken the children," my mother cried bitterly.

"It wouldn't have helped," my father assured her. "Taking the children would put her life in danger, and she has the right to refuse."

In one of the neighboring villages, the houses of people who had been hiding Jews had been burned — some with their owners still inside. Jan personally knew a Polish family whom the Germans had shot when Jews were found hiding in their chicken coop.

Marysia's visit had put us at serious risk. Even if she herself didn't report us to the authorities, she might carelessly allude to her visit during a neighborly chat. Someone might then denounce us to the Gestapo to get the promised reward. Before the aktsia, we had been reviled beings living in precarious times, but we had not been in immediate mortal danger. Now, ever since the aktsia, we were hunted creatures.

My parents decided to go back home. From there, my father would try to arrange a refuge for himself and for my mother, and possibly even for Arthur and me. They had no choice: Jan could find barely enough food to keep two people alive, never mind four. We all knew that each additional person, who might cough or sneeze at the wrong moment, multiplied the hazard.

One night Jan led them out while Arthur and I slept.

•　•　•　•　•

Several days later, Jan took us to the home of Lotka Sternberg's family, where my parents were now living. On the way he told us that her father Mottel, because he spoke fluent German, had managed to get himself certified as a *Wertvolle Jude*, a Jew who worked for the Gestapo. Lotka and her parents had hidden, in the crawl-space where Lotka and I had spent the nights after my aunt's rape, during the aktsia and in the ensuing three days before Mottel got a "hard" certificate — one that would stand up under scrutiny. What Mottel did, while working directly for a Gestapo chief, no one knew.

"Like wild animals," my mother said, as she pulled Arthur and me into the Sternberg's house. It was true; we looked like wild animals. We were dirty — straw and vermin in our clothes, our hair matted and snarled; and we smelled, I imagined, of rotted farm feed that had been out of the sun and air for too long.

Mother put an arm around each of us and then hugged Arthur and me separately. Then it was my father's turn. Tears trickled down from my mother's eyes.

"Animals don't cry," said Arthur.

We went to our room in the back of the house — Lotka's parents used the other room — and evidently Lotka was not there. I wondered briefly where she was.

Our high-ceiling room had a bed for my parents and a cot for me to share with Arthur, pushed flush against opposite walls, a chest, two chairs, and a table made of a plank resting on a pair of barrels. The kitchen was closed off and we did our cooking on the wood-burning stove in the back hall leading out to the garden.

"Even the pot and plate belong to Mottel and Szencia," my mother said mournfully. "But we have to stay here. It is not safe in our own house. Uncle Zygmunt is staying there, but he's in the Ordnungsdienst and that protects him."

That first night, Arthur and I attacked the large plate of cold potatoes my mother set on the table with the ravenous gusto of starved beasts. For once I didn't say to myself, *Please don't let Arthur eat so much.* Whom had I entreated? God? Either He was deaf or dead or I didn't know His language.

My parents just sat silently and watched us.

I asked, almost not wanting to hear the answer, "Where is Lotka?"

"Lotka is passing as a Christian in Lvov," my mother said.

"How is that possible?" I asked, thinking of the pampered girl I had known.

My father supplied the details. "The Polish priest who gave religious instruction to Catholic children in the Polish elementary school has sheltered several Jews. He taught Lotka Catholic prayers and liturgy every night for a month. He also got her "good" Aryan papers — those of somebody who had died — and made the arrangements for a middleman to take her to live with a Polish couple. She is living there as their niece, in return for money that Lotka's parents send."

Having saved the best for last, and almost beaming, my father then told us of our immense luck. "I myself can walk the streets freely now because I have a *W* insignia, a big round metal badge pinned to the lapel of my jacket. This insignia is based on a certificate testifying that I am a *Wirschaftswichtige Jude*, a Jew essential to the economy."

"What makes you essential?" Arthur asked.

"I am performing the essential service of gathering scrap metal and rags for conversion to ammunition for the war industry."

My father had bought the certificate and badge from a Ukrainian gangster — a thief, gambler, drunk, and womanizer who had grown up near Jews and spoke fluent Yiddish — with a portion of the silver he had buried in the yard. But the certificate was a "soft" one because the metal and rags he was supposed to collect were extremely scarce, and his "essential service" was therefore essentially obsolete. The W badge served mainly to intimidate Ukrainian militiamen so that they wouldn't drag him off to the Gestapo but, for the Germans, it had no meaning at all and, if they had caught him, he would have been killed. Trusting the certificate was like closing your eyes and believing you were safe because you no longer could see the danger.

Mottel and Scenzia came in to welcome us.

"In my opinion, we are in a more precarious situation than those Jews in hiding," my father said to Mottel.

"No, no, we are quite safe," Mottel insisted. "My Gestapo boss is a gentleman of the old school. He dresses impeccably, even if he does look like Hitler. He has vowed to look after the Sternberg family, and tell us when to go into hiding, and that promise now includes you, too."

The following night my father and Jan sat at the plank-and-barrel table. "What will happen if Mottel's Black-Shirt protector is transferred?" my father asked Jan.

"I hear he's a sick man," Jan said of the Gestapo chief. "He was injured in the First World War. He might be replaced at any time." That answer was typical of Jan. He never tried to give us false hope.

Arthur and I lay on the bed. We waited in a hungry stupor for the meal my mother was preparing from a beef bone, root vegetables Jan had brought, and some prunes my father had obtained in barter. It smelled like a feast.

To distract us as we waited, my mother began to tell of the Friday nights when she was a girl. "Friday was the only night the entire family sat down for a meal together. The kindling of the Sabbath lights in the silver candlesticks on the embroidered tablecloth beckoned everyone to the table. During the week the table was covered with an ordinary tablecloth, and we sat alone or ate standing up like birds balancing on one leg," she said. "But on Friday nights ..." My mother bit her lip and turned her head away.

Lying next to Arthur on the Sternbergs' cot, my mind drifted to other things that had nothing to do with the struggle to stay alive. They were the same thoughts I'd had in the very recent past when I was sitting with Jan at the little window in the barn.

Would that be possible here? I wondered.

• • • • •

The handful of Jews in Skala who possessed certificates lived the lives of ghosts. My father went out as seldom as possible. In a sudden random roundup, when men suspected of being Jews were ordered to drop their pants, not even his badge would save him. Arthur was never permitted to leave the house. My mother was too nervous to go out during the daytime, and at night she couldn't see well enough to find her way around.

That left me to take responsibility for organizing food and fuel. On dark nights I made forays into the fields to glean whatever sticks lay about so my mother could cook a little soup. Lately, I had found only twigs and we had no coal, either.

The nights seemed much longer than the days, probably because in the dark afternoons of winter we sat around without light. Even if we had a candle or a bit of kerosene for the lamp, we never kept a light on after seven in the evening, fearing to call the attention of murderers and blackmailers to our presence.

Unnerved by my father's floor-pacing, my mother often told him, "Stop wearing yourself out. You're wasting your energy and there's so little to eat as it is."

Jan's almost daily visits offered some relief from the tension. He and my father spent the time talking in the corner as Jan puffed on a cigarette and my father watched the smoke slowly fade away. Jan always had lots to relate: which farmer might be willing to sell me some potatoes, which Jews had been denounced or had given themselves up, and the war news that had filtered down to the Ukrainian militia.

I was hungry for news, but reports on the progress of the war were unreliable. One day Jan brought a map which we scanned under the candlelight to figure out the Russians' position.

"Do you hate the Germans as much as I do?" I asked him.

"I hate the misery they cause," he replied.

During those long months of the winter of 1942–43, Jan and my father became friends. My father liked him despite the fact that he was a Ukrainian goy — though, if he hadn't been one, chances are they would never have formed a connection.

"Jan, after the war, when we go to Paris, you must come with us," my father said one time.

"Yes, of course," Jan answered. "Do they need eight-fingered shoemakers there?"

He was still a mystery to me even though I saw him every day.

Most nights, Jan and I went up to the attic; he, the sentinel at the window, and I, the tower princess. We had a view of the marketplace from there and, as in Grandfather Jakob's house, we would be able to warn the others if the Gestapo was coming for us. I used my shawl as a pillow as I lay on the bare floor.

Our talk mostly concerned the amazing acts people were capable of in these times.

"One peasant's house was set on fire when Jews were found in the cellar," he told me. "The man ran into the burning building to try to save them and died in the flames."

Then, as if tilting a seesaw, he told me, "I know a tailor who went to Gestapo headquarters and denounced a pair of Jewish sisters, old customers of his, for the reward money." He told these stories matter-of-factly, as if reading to me from the newspaper.

Sometimes we sat in the dark, he smoking a cigarette, and I, if the sky was not cloudy, gazing up through the window at a patch of stars. Sometimes we sat on the floor with our backs to the wall, holding hands. Once in a while, usually right before he left, he put his arm around me and kissed me good-night. One time he made me laugh, and I reached over and kissed him on the cheek. He kissed me back in a way that I liked, but then I pushed him away.

❖ 19 ❖

I got a new job: laundress at German headquarters on Count Golochowski's former estate. The interview was arranged by Shimek's father, who had survived the aktsia along with his wife and son, and now worked directly under the protection of the new manager of the estate.

Mr. Bosek briefed me on this *Obergauleiter*, his German boss. "He is a veteran of the First World War with a glass eye and false teeth. He is a man who just wants to keep things status quo. He's harmless."

"Show me your hands," the manager said when I came to see him about the job. He wore a business suit and a tie. He was not much taller than I, and had a pinched face and a scar from mouth to ear. He gestured me to come closer. It was obvious that my soft hands and thin wrists wouldn't be much use at the washboard, but he agreed to let me try. That night my mother coached me on how to starch collars and remove stains.

The next day, as I scrubbed and rinsed clothes, water sloshed over me and I stood shivering in wet shoes on the stone floor. Ironing was a worse disaster; I scorched one of the detachable white shirt collars and burned my hand. The Obergauleiter seemed amused by my ineptitude, but the other laundresses, hard-working Polish girls, cursed me. They purposely left the door open as they went in and out so I would catch a draft.

The indoor temperature was only slightly less freezing than the air outdoors. The manager noticed my blue, goose-pimpled legs and called me into his office.

"Here," he said, holding up a pair of dark-brown cotton stockings. "Put these on."

I turned to go behind the screen.

"Put them on here," he said, gesturing to a chair facing his. I realized this was a condition of the gift. He reached for a glass, fished out a set of false teeth, and popped them into his mouth. His thin face bespoke his concentration as I put on the stockings.

"You have beautiful legs," he said. "Walk around a bit." He sat watching my brown legs as I walked up and down. Then he got up and brought a package with a brassiere, garter belt, and panties in it.

"Try them on. If they fit, they're yours."

I told him, "I have lots of underwear, but thanks anyway," as I edged toward the door. I was counting on Mr. Bosek's assurance that this Nazi was not one for whips or dogs. "Good night," I bade him quickly and scooted out the door.

The next day I took off the brown stockings when I arrived at the manager's house, fearing he would make me give them back.

"It's cold," he said. "Put the stockings on." Then he walked out of the room.

A short while later, the manager came back. He looked at my hands and said, "You're no washerwoman," and put me to work mending socks and sewing on buttons, which suited my talents better. I was vastly relieved.

My friend Zhenia lived in a tiny room on the estate and I went to see her. She still had her angelic blond curls. I sat on the soft mattress listening to her story.

During the aktsia, while our family was hiding in the egg warehouse, Zhenia had watched from behind a door as the Germans dragged away her mother, grandmother, and uncle. Hearing that they had been deported to Belzec, she bribed her way into an audience with the district commander.

"I asked to be sent to Belzec too," she said. "He jumped out of his chair and picked up his riding crop. When he saw that I neither cowered nor batted an eyelash, he put it down again. He told me that he would decide for himself where I would go and what I would do. He called me a Jewish whore and sent me to work as a maid in the German officers' quarters."

"So how did you get here?" I asked.

"In the officers' quarters I met an SS man who likes me. He's not scared of the non-fraternization rule. He set me up here in my own little room and provides me with food and clothes. I heard that my relatives are all dead, that they died before I ever could have gotten to Belzec, so I decided to use my position in the enemy camp to help other Jews." She smiled. "Remember how I played Queen Esther one Purim?" she asked me.

"Yes, I remember you as Esther. You wore a shimmering gown with wide sleeves, and when you extended your imperious arm to accuse Haman, the audience gasped!"

"Well, I'm still acting, but it's not a show anymore. Now I gather whatever information I can from the Germans, and pass it to a fellow who works here, a Jew passing as a gentile. He has contact with the underground," she told me.

"What underground?" I asked. It was the first I had heard of it.

"Didn't you know? There is quite an active underground," she assured me.

She went back to her story. "Once I realized that I was no longer living under God's protection, I felt great relief. I have nothing to be ashamed of," she said, and showed me cans of food she would pass on to starving Jews in Skala.

On the surface Zhenia looked as vibrant as ever. Yet, since I knew her so well, I detected a kind of wilting in her, like a declining plant that sheds random leaves and never blooms again.

I went to visit her a few more times in her room and each time urged her to search for a hiding place, to arrange an escape route for herself through her contact to the underground.

"No, it's not necessary," she assured me, "my Nazi lover adores me. And what sort of Queen Esther would I be if I ran away? On the contrary, why don't you come share my room? I'll set you up with a pal of my SS man."

I declined, though I knew she meant well.

One time I told her about Jan, how he looked after my family and me, and that I knew he wanted me but that I held back.

"Why? What are you waiting for?" she asked.

I would have felt foolish saying that it was because he was a goy, a shoemaker, ten years older than me, so I said, "He's never read a book."

Zhenia laughed. "Neither have I."

She told me that if I joined her I could help more people than just my family. "Your guy is small potatoes," she said, and shrugged when I still refused.

Most mornings Jan came to the house at seven to escort me to the job, and every evening he came around six to pick me up. He took my arm as we left. No one could doubt that I was his girl, his bearing telegraphing a lay-off policy to his fellow militiamen. To denounce me meant reckoning with Jan.

Once in a while, when the other girls were busy whispering gossip to each other, I sneaked away to Shimek's house on the estate. His mother always had a spare slice of bread for me, that she sometimes piled with sautéed onions and other times spread with honey.

Shimek, my source of world news, had a hideout behind the greenhouse, where he told me what his father heard on the BBC when the manager was away. He told me about the Russian offensive, and we were jubilant when the Red Army liberated Kiev and then Zhitomir. The following week the Germans retook Zhitomir, but we took heart that the constant rain would be sure to slow or even halt the German counterattack.

Shimek offered to steal a book for me from the estate library. I declined. He confessed that he was distracted, that he couldn't read a book to the end anymore. I told him that his father was foolish to depend completely on the estate manager, and that they should build a hiding place or find one with gentiles outside of town.

"My father doesn't trust Ukrainians and thinks that the Poles are almost as bad. But I don't feel safe here. I'm thinking of running away to the forest," he said. "Maybe we could join a fighting band."

"If you hear of one, let me know." I had heard about partisan groups, but none in our region. Some of them hated Jews more than Germans.

"Will you come?" he asked.

"Not to the forest." I didn't want to tell Shimek that I preferred a quick death by a bullet to starving in a cold dark hole in the ground. Besides, how could I abandon my parents and Arthur?

Shimek peeked around the corner of the greenhouse to where Jan was standing at the door waiting for me to come out. "It's because of him, isn't it? Do you love him?"

"Who said I love him?" There was annoyance in my voice. "Why do you listen to gossip?"

"All right." He sat down beside me again and kissed me lightly.

It hadn't occurred to me that Shimek might be jealous of Jan. He should have understood that Jan was protecting my family and me. It didn't matter how I felt about him.

I hissed in retaliation, "Does your mother have to sleep with the manager?" Shimek looked at me with a wounded expression. Only when I thought about it later did I realize that his comments were not the only reason for my discomfort with the subject of Jan.

Day by day the threatening atmosphere settled more heavily over the grounds of the estate, and I felt conspicuous as the only Jew on the domestic staff besides Shimek's father. The Polish and Ukrainian men passing through the house looked me over as if to say, "You stupid bitch, you'll get what's coming to you." I had overheard one of the Polish girls saying that it was a scandal for a Jewish girl to have the easiest job in the laundry. Once the other girls hid my sewing box and, when I found it, there was a dead mouse stuffed between the spools of thread. At lunchtime, when the manager and his staff went out to eat, I sat on a pail in a broom closet, hoping Jan would come for me early. Sometimes he did.

One evening, when Jan brought me home, I urged him to come in. He had removed my Jewish-star armband before we crossed town and put it in his pocket. Now he replaced it on the sleeve of my coat so that I wouldn't be caught without it the next morning.

"I'm too exposed there," I blurted out to my father and Jan, and explained why.

"Could you arrange a bribe, using two of the hides I gave you to store for us?" my father asked Jan. The next day Jan showed up at the estate late in the afternoon and announced that I had been fired. I was relieved not to have to go back there.

One night, later that winter, Lotka appeared at the back door. With her bleached blonde braids pinned around her head, her green eyes, and her self-confident carriage, she could easily pass for a gentile. Her thick eyebrows had been tweezed into arched crescents. She was wearing an embroidered peasant-style fur jacket that her father had sent to her via their middleman.

Only the Polish couple she was living with had known of her Jewish identity, and every safeguard had been taken to hide it, but Lotka herself must have slipped up in some way.

"A blackmailer threatened to turn me in. I barely managed to escape by giving him my last zloty."

Her parents bundled her away into their room, but not before I saw the shame in Lotka's eyes for letting her parents down.

This gave Jan an idea. "Why don't you come away with me to Cracow or some other large city? I'll get you papers from the priest of a neighboring town that say you are a Catholic. You'll just have to learn some basic practices and a few prayers." Jan knew as well as I did that I looked Jewish, particularly my "sad eyes," an unmistakable Jewish trait. And I had no *kennkarte* (working papers) to show I had a job. Still, I thought the plan might be the best available option.

"Maybe Lotka didn't succeed at impersonating an Aryan," I told my father, "but I'm willing to try."

"No, absolutely not," said my father.

I was angry. Was it because he couldn't bear to think of us as a couple? To have cared about that seems lunacy to me now.

I liked the idea. In a new city no one we knew would repeat gossip about me as Shimek had. No one would say, "Fanya Gottesfeld has a goy."

❖ 20 ❖

Alarms signaling flash roundups were becoming more frequent. The alarms would sound so suddenly that there was no time to get to any of our hiding places. My father would grab Arthur and we would each run anywhere we could, every man for himself. After one false alarm it took a particularly long time for my father to return with Arthur, crouched low on his shoulders, hands clasped under my father's chin. My mother lifted Arthur off and held him tightly for a long time.

Late one night, Jan hurried in, wearing a jacket over his nightshirt, with boots on but no hat. He quickly ushered us out the back door and gestured to my parents and Arthur to lie down on the floor of the horse-drawn wagon. Handing me a scarf to tie around my head, he pointed to the seat next to his.

In the predawn light, we pulled up to a house in the countryside where Jan had arranged for us to spend the day in the attic. At noon the householder came up with a bowl of cucumbers and sour cream. Another false alarm.

Late that night, Jan came to lead us home on foot under an extraordinarily clear sky, with stars that seemed close enough to touch. The wide-open road and the fields beyond suggested limitless space. I felt that if we kept walking like this — my father on one side of me, Jan on the other, and my mother and Arthur behind us — we would surely find an island of safety. And I vowed that I would eat cucumbers and sour cream every day after the war.

But Jan's coming for us with the horse and wagon did not escape the notice of his mother, sister and brother-in-law, and had revealed to them that he was still our "Jewish uncle."

Jan's fellow congregants at Father Derewienko's Orthodox church, where he had once taken his job as an altar boy very seriously, told him that his actions were sacrilegious and a defiance of the church. They made it clear that his absence would be welcomed.

"I don't need to go to church to pray," he said when he told me about this.

One Sunday morning, when an alarm had scattered us in all directions, I ran blindly for a while until I came to the door of a Ukrainian man who had attended gymnasium with Uncle Wolf. I pounded on the door. Hat on, ready for church, he motioned me in.

"Please let me stay for a few hours," I pleaded. I must have looked crazy, arriving barefoot in my nightgown. "Just while you're in church."

He looked at me for a while. An educated man, a high school graduate, a man with whom I'd had a few casual but intelligent conversations, a man who lived alone and would put only himself in jeopardy, he stood there clearing his throat nervously.

I dropped to beg on my knees. "If they find me, you can say you didn't know I was here."

He shook his head and held the door open. "You killed Jesus Christ," he said. "You people murdered him. It serves you right. I can't sit in church and pray with you here."

That night, while Jan and I kept vigil in the Sternbergs' attic, I quoted the man's words.

"That's what the priest told him," he said. "But not all priests would have sent you away."

That was true, I knew, remembering the one who had helped Lotka.

"Do you think Jews killed Jesus Christ?" I finally asked Jan this question that I had hesitated to ask him many times before.

He took my hand. Very lightly, he rested it on his palm so that what he was saying came through his skin as well as in his words.

"I don't know. I wasn't there. Christ was a Jew himself. I have no way of knowing. If they did, it was wrong."

"I don't believe it. Anyway, they can't blame us for it. We weren't there." I was close to tears.

He stroked my hand. "They do," he said.

When an alarm a few weeks later galvanized us to run in all directions, we had no time even to grab a blanket. My parents fled with Arthur riding on my father's shoulders.

Jan appeared at our house and led me through back alleys to the bathhouse in my Wasserman grandparents' yard. He hacked away the frozen cover of the hiding place behind the bathtub and we crawled in. Underground, with its low ceiling, the hole was a tight squeeze for a six-footer like Jan. Lying down was more comfortable than squatting, and Jan gave me his arm as a pillow.

Suddenly severe abdominal pains stabbed me so relentlessly that I writhed like a snake in its death agony. Violent spasms of diarrhea compounded by menstrual cramps racked my body with the ferocity of labor pains. In the vortex of pain, I lost my sense of time and place. My consciousness narrowed to the sensation of waves of agony advancing and receding. I rode the waves in Jan's arms, oblivious that night had turned to day and day to night.

I thought I was going to die, that my abdomen had exploded. I moaned like a coward. The blood and feces that involuntarily flowed from me soiled both of us. Jan held me in his arms until I was able to squat over a pail, and then he steadied me so that I would not faint and knock over the pail. I concentrated every fiber I could summon on one thing: not to moan or cry out. Tears could flow silently, but I knew that sounds would give us away.

Jan feared that dogs would pick up the powerful human scents. However, for once, the severity of the winter came to our aid. Everything, even odor, froze within a short time, and only the closeness of our bodies prevented us from freezing.

During the second night, Jan released his hold. I begged him not to go but he left, promising to be back soon. I rolled myself into a ball, sure I would be dead when they found me.

I didn't know how long it was before he lowered himself down next to me again and said, "I made it just in time. It's almost dawn. The *razzia* (raid) is still on. Here, drink this." He lifted a little can with a handle and took off the cover. Milk. It was still lukewarm. I cupped the warm can in my hands as I drank it. He had gone home and heated milk for me and carried it back in the dark.

We must have dozed through that day because it was deep night when we finally ventured out and back to my parents. Frantic with worry since they had returned from their own hiding place, they had not found us in the cellar or garden shelters.

Arthur woke up. "You stink," he said when I kissed him.

From that time on, a new intimacy developed between Jan and me. Jan had seen me at my worst — but neither moral weakness nor stench nor filth nor danger of discovery had turned him against me. I knew I could trust him completely.

Some weeks later, my father toured our hiding places and reported back that the one in the bathing shed was no longer safe; someone had used it and left a pail of frozen human soil encrusted with blood. Jan, who happened to be in the room at the time, managed to keep a straight face.

• • • • •

By spring, my father felt that our stay with the Sternbergs was becoming too dangerous. He warned Mottel not to trust his Gestapo boss and not to wait until the last minute to prepare an escape plan. Mottel insisted that he and his family were safe and that he would decide for himself if and when it was time to leave town and go into hiding.

My father and Jan, trying to come up with someone who would hide us, spent weeks reviewing the names of gentiles my father knew from his lumber business and from his stint on the Soviets' bridge-repair project.

"Try Sidor Sokolowski," my father told Jan. Sidor, whom my father had protected from punishment when he worked on the bridge, had moved to Trujca, a village not far away, when he had married a

Ukrainian woman with a bit of land.

"I'll bring him, but it will take a while. Sidor may be poor, but he has fields to prepare for planting."

"At least Fancia," my father told Jan. If Sidor couldn't take the four of us, at least he might be persuaded to take me alone.

In the meantime, Jan told us he was enlarging the hiding place in the attic of his barn, and he and my father collaborated over the plans. "Watch out for the saw," my father teased Jan. "You can't afford to lose any more fingers."

Jan smiled. "The day you make me a pair of boots I can take five steps in, I'll give you a horse."

They both laughed at the thought. What use would my father have for a horse?

"I'll settle for a horseshoe," he said and went back to his design.

Time dragged on until high summer. Sometimes, as I lay awake during the night, I would think fiercely: "I want to live." Not, "I don't want to die," but "I want to live." I wanted to accomplish something before I died, some work in which my life would be of use; I wanted to fall in love. I wanted to kiss and to be kissed back.

At the kitchen table, my father and I were speculating one evening on where the Russians, who had launched a new offensive, might be. We were arranging knives and forks to mark their positions near the Dniester River when we heard Jan's special knock on the door.

We welcomed him warmly. Jan looked mischievous as he put his rifle in the corner. Tonight, instead of the usual bit of cheese, matches, or few pages from a newspaper, he plunked a bottle of homebrewed vodka down on the table. He had never brought vodka before.

My mother put cups on the table for us and a large jar for Jan.

"What do you think I am? A Russian?" Jan said in mock umbrage. He got up and found himself a small cup on the shelf.

We laughed. We knew that the Ukrainians drank as much as the Russians, maybe more, but the Ukrainians hated the Russians.

"Drink up," my father said, "while we're still . . . healthy." He almost said "alive."

I got up. "Come on, let's have a little fun. Let's sing a song. How about the one that Russian officer used to sing when he drank too much?"

"How he loved my gefilte fish!" My mother said. "Jan, after the war you'll taste my fish. And you'll drink tea in a glass with a silver holder."

"Yes," Jan said as he refilled our glasses, "after the war ..." He looked as if he could see it somewhere down the road, and gave us the confidence to see it too. He started to sing a song I had learned from Ukrainian schoolmates, and I joined him.

What none of us allowed ourselves to think at the time was that we were sitting around a table drinking like goyim with a goy. Not even a Pole but a Ukrainian, one who was poorly educated; a man who said, "Holy Mother of God" when he cursed. Jan would never have been sitting with us in such intimacy before the German occupation. We wouldn't have wanted him, and he would have declined our invitation anyway. All the old social rules had been broken.

Every Jew I knew had always believed that the goyim hated us, but it was not clear why this was so.

My mother had said, "They hate us because we have nicer things than they do."

My father believed, "It's because we're smart and not lazy."

I had always countered, "There are gentiles who have nicer things than we do, and they hate us anyway. And I know Jews who are dumb and lazy."

Late one night I quizzed Jan: "Do you hate me?"

"Would I be sitting here if I did?"

"Why is there . . . ?" I didn't even know how to finish.

"You ask questions," said Jan. "I don't have answers. Must you understand?"

"Yes."

126

"I don't know. One day in the square I saw some Jews pushed into a corner, and one — maybe you know her, the one who wears a red wig — "

"You mean Chaya? Chaya the Wig?"

"Yes. Suddenly she was on the ground screaming. 'The baby,' someone shouted, and I saw that she was pregnant and her labor pains had begun. The baby was born in the street. And Stanislaus, a guy I went to school with, took the baby and tore it apart." He was silent for a moment. "I try not to tell you things like this, but you ask me why. Should I say Stanislaus is crazy or that he holds a grudge because a Jew once cheated him? No. He did it because he wanted to. He has a good head on his shoulders, he doesn't beat his wife, he goes to church. He wanted to do it, and there's no law against it. He's the law. The law is behind us. Kill. I'm supposed to kill you. And Stanislaus? He'll do it again, given half a chance."

Jan had not spoken like this before. I felt cut and slashed by his words and by his tone because it was so dry, as dry as parched earth. I didn't dare go near him.

In the morning Jan was still sitting at the window. He hadn't gone home, as usual. I sat down next to him.

"Can't you talk to Stanislaus? Tell him what he does is ..."

"No. I do what I can. That's all I can do."

He looked at me. For the first time I saw a look of pity, not because I was a Jew or stupid, but because I talked like a child, an overgrown child who didn't understand limits.

He hoisted himself to his feet wearily. The early sun was bright but not warm. I stretched on tiptoe to kiss him on the cheek, to say, "Jan, what you do is enough. It is enough."

VI

Under Sidor's Wing

Age 18–19: August 1943–March 1944

❖ 21 ❖

With a thick shawl over my head and paper lining my jacket to keep out the chill of the midnight air, I set out with Jan for Sidor's house in the next village, Trujca. I had decided not to wait another day until he might come to us.

We walked along the river at a swift pace, alert for the German patrol whose men were stationed in various spots. When we saw a German we ducked and waited until the soldier looked away for a moment before going on. The patrol was watching for Jews; the Ukrainians had given the Germans a list of the Jews who were still alive, and they knew that the Gottesfelds were still at large.

Despite the danger, I felt an animal exuberance at the freedom of being outdoors. Jan and I almost ran the eight kilometers. I heard the river flowing to my right and, closer by, the hoot of an owl. The novelty of striding in step with Jan's long legs opened the throttle for my young, vigorous limbs to carry me where I wanted to go. At one point I tripped on a rut in the road and Jan helped me up with his left hand. I covered the three fingers of his left hand with mine. He urged me to take his right hand instead, but I told him that the missing fingers didn't bother me.

"How did you lose your fingers?" I asked.

"Water under the bridge," he replied evasively.

My father had instructed me, "Stay at Sidor's for a few days and gauge the situation. What kind of person is Sidor's wife? Can she be trusted? Is their little girl, who is Arthur's age, the type who would blab to neighbors that Jews are hiding in the house? Is there enough space for the four of us? If it looks promising, try to persuade Sidor to let us come."

Jan planned to stay with me, rather than chance being seen going back and forth. He would do some work around the house, so that the neighbors would find his presence normal and natural in the future.

"How do you know they will let me stay?" I asked him.

"Because I know Sidor," he said. Jan had once repaired a harness for Sidor, back in the days when the peasant had owned several cows and a horse. More recently, Jan had spent several days convincing Sidor to shelter us. Jan's description of Sidor's one thin cow — "you can see right through her" — muffled the sounds of approaching feet.

It was a German patrol. Jan threw me to the ground, dove on top of me, and started to grind his hips into mine.

The patrol leader kicked Jan in the ribs. I felt the blows in my body.

"What are you doing?" the patrol leader demanded.

"What does it look like?" Jan replied. A few of the men laughed coarsely. We heard their joking as they wandered down the road.

After they left, adrenalin made my head spin. What if they had seen me, seen my Jewish face? We had to be more careful. Hands clasped, we set off again.

When we finally arrived at the house, Sidor directed us to a little alcove separated from the main room by a thin curtain over its small opening. We collapsed onto the bench with its pillows.

After a few hours of dead sleep, Sidor woke us at dawn and beckoned us to sit at the table. I looked around the kitchen. It had a stove, a bed where Sidor, his wife Marynka, and their young daughter all slept together, a small wardrobe, and a few stools. Everything — cooking, eating, sleeping — was done in this one room.

Marynka sat on the bed, pulling on her thick stockings. She resembled the fiancée Jan had brought to our house: full figure, high Slavic cheekbones, and pug nose. Her blond braids framed her face to advantage. I could see what had attracted Sidor: she held herself in the self-possessed way that a pretty woman does. Only her glistening gold-rimmed front tooth, a Ukrainian fashion which signaled prosperity, marred her good looks.

Sidor, a stocky man with black eyes and close-cropped hair, had a serene expression on his face. But when Marynka, who was taller than he, came over to the table to slice some bread, I could see that she wasn't happy to have us there. Still, she cut each slice equally and gave us our breakfast. Then she wrapped some bread in a piece of cloth for the three of them to eat at the market in another town, where they were going that morning.

Their little girl, Hania, woke up. She was blond like her mother and dark-eyed like her father. She rubbed her eyes and peeked out from behind Sidor while she looked me over.

I was wearing the last ring we had, a gold band set with one large and one small garnet. My father had instructed me to give it to Marynka. It was hard to part from this ring, a birthday gift from my father, but I took it off my finger and put it in her hand. Marynka tried to fit it on one finger after another by greasing the inner side with lard, but it would not slide on, not even on her pinkie. She knotted it into the corner of her handkerchief and tucked it into her blouse.

Before leaving for the market, Sidor gave us careful instructions. "There's not supposed to be anyone at home. Don't go near the window or open the door. Don't cook — the neighbors will see the smoke. Use the slop pail instead of the outside privy." He told Jan, "Make yourselves a bed in the attic. We'll be back at nightfall." Sidor took Hania's hand

and led her out. Marynka turned as she left, and her half-smile made me uneasy.

"She's Ukrainian," Jan explained to me after they left, "and Sidor is a Pole. It's an unusual combination."

"Is he really as good-tempered as he appears to be?" I asked.

"In the morning," Jan said, "he gets out of bed on the right side and Marynka on the wrong side. What a couple!"

Jan shook a mound of straw onto the attic floor and I helped him spread it. The straw had the musky smell of sunshine. For once, instead of positioning himself at the window, Jan lay down next to me.

• • • • •

That morning, in the snug burrow of that straw bed, Jan and I made love for the first time. We took a long time. Gentle Jan. I prayed it would always be for us as it was that day — losing track of time as we caressed each other, our bodies pressing and rocking high above the rest of the world.

A warm ray of sunshine shone through the small square window of the attic and warmed the small of my back. "I'm glad it's daylight," said Jan. "You're beautiful." Lying there with him, I felt that I was.

Resting in Jan's arms, I found myself spilling happy tears. Lovemaking surprised me: it felt so right, the only sane thing in a time of madness. All awkwardness had left me. Jan, this most unlikely partner, felt right to me. Somehow I had imagined that he would feel heavy, but I had no sense of my body being crushed under his, only of lightness and light.

"Why are you so surprised?" Jan asked.

"I just am," I said.

Through my new eyes, the world sparkled. The ordinary view from the window of the late-fall meadow was enchanting; my fingers stroked fabric, wood, metal as if learning touch for the first time; and at times my breasts and my inner places announced themselves as if brushed by a satin glove.

I tried to persuade myself, over the next few days, that it was the wrong thing to do. No use. Even as I swept the floor and washed the dishes, sudden elation would overcome me. I missed the familiar dark mood that had enveloped me since the coming of the Germans. I had to summon dread consciously from where it had taken a back seat. "My pleasure," I was thinking, "could lead to our destruction; in this high mood I could be lying in Jan's arms instead of listening for the sounds of German motors and dogs."

I made a mental list of the reasons I should despise myself: I had been intimate with a goy — a Ukrainian! Not a doctor or a member of the intelligentsia — but a shoemaker! A man ten years older than I, a rifle-carrying member of the militia. Although Jan's affection for me was clear, he had exerted no pressure on me to become his lover. I had no one to blame but myself.

I remembered my father's injunction, "Be nice to him." But now I feared his anger. Had he intended me to go this far? My mother, I knew, wouldn't say a word but would pity me. A few years before, when I had confided in her that I liked a certain boy in my class, she had told me to remain friends, nothing more; to wait until I got married. Then she recounted the horrible nights of her honeymoon. It hadn't been that way for me. It had been sweet, and I hated myself for wanting more. Despite my anxiety, my heart had expanded and opened a forbidden room to envelop Jan.

During the next few days, when Jan was repairing Sidor's window frames, I tried to gather my wits. I was in the country but could not step out the door. Jan and I drank fresh milk while my family starved in Skala. Sidor was sheltering me today but might denounce me tomorrow.

It occurred to me that Sidor had said "Make a bed," not "beds," and that Marynka's half-smile as she left insinuated that she knew how we would spend the day. Perhaps Jan had made an arrangement with Sidor. Anything was possible. These were murderous times. But I knew that Jan's first priority was to see that I was safe.

• • • • •

On the third morning of our stay, Marynka was adamant:

"The girl can come live with us and help me with the housework. If Jan brings wool, she can earn her keep by knitting sweaters for me to sell. But I refuse to take in the rest of them. It's too dangerous."

In the neighboring village, a man who had sheltered Jews had seen his wife and children shot in front of his eyes. Then he was tied up within sight of their corpses, which the neighbors were forbidden to remove and bury.

Sidor tried to persuade Marynka. "Her father has done me good turns, and I am grateful to him. He will give us whatever they have." I could see that they were very poor — a few cooking utensils and tattered quilts, a small trunk, summed up their household goods. God knows they could use any contribution we might make.

Looking out the window, I watched a few scrawny chickens run between the legs of a cow so undernourished she barely gave milk. Not a single pig lived in the pen. Their one limping old horse was all skin and bones. The tiny field did not grow enough food to support them, let along feed four additional mouths. Anything we might give them could be used toward seed for sowing a field of early spring wheat or for more chickens.

"She can stay," Marynka said to Sidor, gesturing toward me with her head, "but you keep your hands off her." Sidor looked at Jan, whose face remained impassive. Suddenly it was clear that I belonged to him. Perhaps Jan had made love to me to protect me from Sidor. Maybe he didn't love me, just wanted to see that no harm came to me, for my father's sake.

I decided to trade on Sidor's respect for my father to persuade them to accept my parents and Arthur. "My father is a man of his word. After the war he will reward you splendidly — we have rich relatives in Paris."

Marynka scoffed at my assurances. "Promises," she said to Sidor. "In the meantime we don't have enough to eat. Do you want to take the food out of your child's mouth?" Hania looked up at her father, expecting an answer, but he turned away.

Late in the evening, we sat around the table drinking the vodka Jan had saved for our last talk.

I told them that the mania to rout out the last Jews had reached fever pitch, with neighbors searching every possible hole for hidden Jews.

Jan added that Uzbek deserters from the Red Army had joined the hunt. "When the Ukrainian militia searches for Jews, no stone remains unturned," he said.

Sidor and Marynka looked bewildered. It meant searchers would come here, too.

Then Jan told them about what had happened to Dr. Steuerman, who had once relieved Sidor's agony during a gallbladder attack.

"The doctor was hiding in a bunker under the Strusover Synagogue in Skala with his wife, daughter, and a young woman who ran away from the Borszczów ghetto and had become his lover. The Germans drove the four of them out of the hiding place and gunned them down on the sidewalk. Then the Ukrainians stripped off their clothes. They put Dr. Steuerman's naked body on top of his lover's and left the two of them on the street for days. Ukrainians and Poles came from far and wide to see this spectacle, laughing at the sight and spitting on the corpses."

"I liked him," said Marynka. "May God have mercy on his soul."

"If you don't let me bring them tomorrow," Jan said quietly, "it will be too late."

Sidor agreed. I took his hand as if to kiss it, but he shook my hand instead.

Marynka went over and knelt by the bed in front of the tacked-up picture of Jesus on the cross, and she began to pray.

❖ 22 ❖

That night, past 4:00 am, Jan left me at the Sternbergs' door. As I groped my way toward my cot, I heard the striking of a match and I saw my father's face lit by candlelight. He had been sitting in the dark waiting up for me.

I'll never forget the hurt look on his face. The corners of his mouth were drawn in so that he looked as if he might burst into tears. I was sure he knew I had been intimate with Jan. But how did he know? Perhaps I looked different, my face glowed, or maybe I moved with more confidence. The uncertainty about what was going to happen between Jan and me was now gone. And I had become a woman. The sixth sense of a loving father must be telling him this.

"Where have you been so long?" he asked sorrowfully.

I eased my shoes off and let them drop to the floor. "There's a full moon. We had to go around the long way by the woods."

After Jan calculated that the patrol had passed, we had taken a shortcut that led through the fields from behind Sidor's house. In the bracing air, my tightly wound nerves had room to explode and I had burst into a run. We ran together, this time not from the patrol but toward a small clump of trees which would shelter us for one more embrace before I went home. I looked for traces of pine needles on my sleeves but there were none. I felt devalued under my father's gaze, undeserving of his vigil.

My mother lay on the bed next to Arthur's, her headache compress across her forehead, her red eyes staring into the void. Tears ran down her expressionless cheeks.

"What happened?" I asked. She remained immobile, silent.

The next night, Jan came to take my parents to Sidor's. He promised to come for Arthur and me the following night.

Before she departed, my mother gave me her favorite sweater, a beige cardigan with brown stripes and wooden buttons. Through the window, I watched my father and mother walk down the street, carrying a few small parcels of clothes — the only possessions they had left.

As I looked out, I saw the darkness envelop them and prayed they would evade the German patrol. Once I would have prayed that the soldiers would fall off the riverbank and drown, according to the elementary premise of war that if there are fewer of your enemies, you have a greater chance to live. Now, accustomed to the idea that my life would come to an early end, I decided that the drowning of a handful of Germans wouldn't save me, that blood-thirst assuages nothing — it didn't even diminish my fear.

I started my new knitting career the next day as I waited for Jan to come pick us up by unraveling an outgrown sweater of Arthur's so I could use the wool to knit a new one for Marynka. Perhaps Jan could get me a skein of wool to add to what I had.

The next night, Jan came to get us. I wore layers of the little clothing I still owned — dresses, a shirt, and a blouse — and carried my mother's sweater on my arm. Jan carried Arthur piggy-back, and the rocking motion soon put him to sleep.

"My parents know," I said. "They were waiting up for me when I got home."

"What did they say?"

"Nothing. My mother was crying. And my father, well, I could tell how upset he was by his face."

"That's not the reason they were upset. I have something to tell you." He stood still and held my arm to keep me from going on. "While we were at Sidor's, someone came to tell your parents that your grandfather Jakob and grandmother Miriam were murdered in the final liquidation of the Borszczów ghetto."

Jan sat me down in a ditch by the side of the road and I cried in his arms. "Why didn't they tell me?" I repeated over and over.

It was too cold and too dangerous to stay there. We got up and, as we walked, Jan told me the rest of the story.

Jakob and Miriam had lived with nine other people in one room in the ghetto. The constant fear of a raid, the starvation rations, the continuous harassment for contributions by the Judenrat, and the spreading contagion of typhus and typhoid must have brought them to despair. They had no money for bribes with which to buy their freedom, no chance of escaping to the forest, no Jan to look after them. And they were in their sixties.

When the alarm reached them, they rushed to their hiding place in the cellar. Grandmother Miriam and some other people managed to get in, but by a fluke Jakob was caught outside. As the Ukrainians dragged him off, he broke away. Running to a German officer, he fell to his knees and offered to tell where Jews were hiding in exchange for his life. A red scarf was tied around his neck and he led the Germans to the hiding place, calling, "Miriam, it's safe. You can come out."

As the trapdoor opened from inside and people crawled out, the Germans kicked and beat them, with Jakob looking on.

They were taken out of town with the rest of the Jews, forced to dig a pit, ordered to undress, lined up, and row after row they were shot and their bodies tumbled into the pit. In a short time the pit was overflowing with corpses and blood, and a deeper one had to be dug.

As she went to her death, Miriam knew that her husband had betrayed the bunker to the Germans. She saw him standing there by the pit among the Germans and the Ukrainian militia, who forced him to watch the shootings.

What she didn't live to see was that, after the other shootings, the German officer came up to him, gun in hand, saying, "This is how we repay traitors," and shot him in the mouth.

Jan knew all the details. I didn't ask him how he knew — undoubtedly from the Ukrainians who had been there to loot, rob, and see the big event first-hand.

This, I now understood, was why my father had decided we had to leave immediately for Sidor's instead of postponing our departure until the last possible moment. That moment had now come: more mass murders were about to take place.

As we walked on, I suddenly realized that I had lost my mother's sweater and I began to cry as if someone I loved had died. Nothing Jan said brought me any comfort. He became upset that I was so distraught. Strange: here I was, running for my life; I had learned that my grandparents were dead, and the sweater was the only thing I could think of. Later, Jan went back across the fields and searched for it, but it was gone.

❖ 23 ❖

Sidor was kneeling by the bed in front of the crucifix saying his Paternoster. Illiterate, he garbled words he had learned by hearing them over and over. "Our Father, who art in heaven . . ." It was the first day the four of us were together in his house.

He then took Hania on his knee and told her that my parents were her uncle and aunt, and Arthur and I her cousins, only it was a big secret and she mustn't tell anyone that we were living in the house. Marynka came over, hairbrush in hand, and undid the child's braids. The girl, stolid as a wardrobe, never flinched or complained as her mother yanked her hair into strands and raked her head with a fine-tooth comb, on an unending crusade against lice.

As Marynka worked, she warned Hania not to mention us at school or to the priest. And Hania never did; in fact the only time I heard her speak of us was to Rex, the family's alert German shepherd, when, during a rainstorm, he was allowed in the house to dry off in front of the stove.

"Don't tell," Hania warned the dog, "or I'll slice you up and cook you in the soup."

That evening, I began to teach Sidor the words of the Paternoster. At morning prayers in Polish elementary school, when we Jewish students sat silently on the sidelines, the words had etched themselves into my memory.

Marynka said to Sidor, "You should be ashamed to take lessons from a Jew. God knows what you mean no matter how you say it."

But Sidor took my efforts as a sign that I deserved protection. My parents concealed their pain when they heard me say the prayer, and my mother said to me later, "I suppose I shouldn't worry, God will wash the words off your tongue since there is no faith behind them."

We settled into the attic, which we reached via a ladder from an unused room filled with straw across from the entrance hall. The attic was small — we couldn't stand, and we could barely crouch.

When the time came for the evening meal, Sidor closed the shutters, as he would do many times over the next weeks, and called us down from the attic. Plain though it was, Sidor invited us to share their bounty. Marynka set on the table a steaming bowl of potato stew made of whatever vegetables and grain she had thrown into the pot on the back of the stove that day. On market days, she added a few scraps of meat or a bone but, after our first weeks there, such luxury was seldom repeated.

Besides the nourishment of the food, Sidor's good-natured presence had a cheering effect on me. We took turns dipping our spoons into the communal earthenware bowl.

But during the first few meals, my mother sat at the table with her lips pressed together when her turn came. By the end of the first meal, Sidor's glare had fixed on her.

My father and I thought that agitated nerves were preventing her from eating. We tried to persuade her to eat.

"It isn't kosher, but so what?" my father remonstrated. "God will forgive us."

On the third day, my mother consented to taste a spoonful and immediately ran to the slop pail to vomit.

Marynka interpreted this as a comment on her cooking, and she was not pleased. Luckily she hadn't noticed that my mother had spent an hour scrubbing the tin cup attached with string to the water pail. The cup, bent and battered, had kissed so many mouths and ladled out so many brews that no amount of elbow grease could alter its blackened complexion. Giving up, my mother cupped her hands from then on to hold water when she drank from the pail.

Later, when I went up to the small space under the attic eaves where my parents lay on a straw bed, my mother admitted that it was disgust that had twisted her stomach into knots.

140

"I watched Marynka wash bed linen, floor rags, and clothes in the bowl we all eat our soup from. Nobody in the house uses toilet paper. Peasants," my mother explained, "don't wear undergarments, so when Marynka menstruates, not all of the flow is caught by the tail of the shirt she ties between her legs — did you notice the trail of blood she left on the floor? The bloody shirt also had its turn in the bowl."

My father, who used to claim that he had to "walk on his hands" in order not to muddy the immaculate carpet at home, shook his head.

"Stupid, stubborn woman, if this food keeps you alive, nothing else matters," he screamed at her. "And if you're going to die it won't matter either." He despaired of trying to reason with her. After five days of refusing food, she gave in.

Early in the fall, on the day she reckoned was Yom Kippur, my mother fasted from sundown to sundown. Said my father, "God understands this is no time to fast." Neither hunger nor his words budged her. Sidor allotted her an extra piece of bread when she broke her fast, since he respected religious observance.

❖ 24 ❖

It didn't take me long to get used to my surroundings; after all, it had been a long time since we had owned a bar of soap or a cache of food. Even the country cottage smell that continued to make my mother nauseous had, for me, the scent of safety. It was a mix of coal, when there was any, unwashed bodies — neither Sidor nor we ever bathed — and stewing beans or cabbage.

Once Hania brought home a bunch of daisies she had picked and arranged them in a jar. Sitting near them, my mind transported me back to a Saturday afternoon, strolling through a meadow near the ruins of the Turkish Tower. *In another life,* the refrain drummed in my head, *that was in another life.*

Time became telescoped into alarms separated by anxiety. Every act, every move from chair to bed — taking care not to pass too close to the window — every gesture of courtesy or greed, was magnified: life or death. It wore us out.

Our lives depended on Marynka's whims. We did as much as we could to help with chores but, since we couldn't leave the house, she had to carry out our waste in a bucket, which, understandably, did not thrill her.

She had assigned me to knit sweaters and stockings from home-spun wool, which she then bartered for food. During the day, sitting in the half-light near the small window of the attic, I could count the rows, but once it got dark I would lose count and sometimes drop stitches. Marynka bought a pair of needles for herself so that I could teach her fancy patterns and she could then show off her skill to the neighbors. My father couldn't persuade her that this sudden proficiency would arouse suspicion.

Sidor and Marynka had a next-door neighbor, a Ukrainian bachelor she had her eye on. When Sidor was out drinking at an inn, she would invite the neighbor to come drink with her in the kitchen. And, when she was drunk, she sat on his lap. Crouching and vulnerable in the attic, trying not to make a sound, we heard their laughter and movements.

Marynka traded one of the sweaters I had knitted for a new white blouse, embroidered in the peasant style. She wore her new blouse to church one Sunday. Sure enough, this bachelor neighbor came by the house that evening, on the excuse of wanting to borrow a bit of flour, and we barely had time to scamper up to the attic before Marynka opened the door.

From then on, we remained in the attic except for an hour or so late at night when we came down to exercise, walking back and forth on the earth floor that was hard-packed except for muddy spills around the water and slop pails. During the day, while Marynka and Sidor were away in the fields, we ate the pieces of bread doled out to us in the morning. Some days, when neither Sidor nor Marynka had filled the drinking pail at the well, I was tempted to dip my finger in the soup for a drop of moisture. I knew Marynka would notice, so I redirected my thoughts to rainstorms and flooding riverbanks. Sometimes this made me even thirstier, but it was better than risking Marynka's curses. We gave Arthur a morsel of our rations, but a spoonful of kasha is hard to divide into portions.

The discomforts of hunger — gnawing emptiness, headache, dizziness, disorientation — all familiar sensations since the Germans had come — would have been easier to disregard if we had been occupied, but I had nothing to do but clack my knitting needles together when I had any wool.

Having almost nothing to eat for days at a time, we again became obsessed with food, an engrossing subject that gave us a break from the constant anxiety about falling into the hands of the Gestapo. My father recalled meals he had eaten in student cafés in Czernowitz, and my mother dropped all vestiges of a delicate pious nature when she had the chance to fish a bit of pork bone out of the soup with her fingers or eat some of a chicken that Marynka had found lying dead on the road, delicious road-kill.

My mother could sit for hours without moving, but my father's natural restlessness plagued him. He was a veteran floor-pacer, but in the attic there was no room to stand up straight or walk up and down. He had to content himself with shifting his weight back and forth on his buttocks or jiggling his leg.

His university education at Czernowitz passed across his memory as if pages were being displayed consecutively on a lectern, and he would sit reading them off to us. He spared us algebraic formulas but reeled off long portions of history, novels, and poems in Yiddish, Polish and German, his voice low and rich with vibrato when he recited romantic and philosophical passages. Though no longer the pious believer he had been as a young man, he chanted portions of the Torah that he had read aloud when called to the podium in the synagogue.

The Torah portions did not necessarily come to his mind on Saturday mornings. Calendar time had become superfluous. If Marynka went to church we knew it was Sunday but, when the weather was fine, she and Sidor went out to work in the fields on Sundays and only took a few hours off in the afternoon. With a nail or stick I began to scratch the mark of each day on the wood of the eaves and, on the seventh, I would slant a line across the previous six with a satisfying finality that I knew to be meaningless. The seventh day, like a paper calendar page, neither ended nor began anything.

As we neared the end of good weather and sensed the early traces of winter, I would catch a look on my father's face that said, "You, if only you make it through ..." He would mention aunts and uncles in Paris, and I knew that he was trying to impress on me that I must get there and tell them what had happened.

I adopted my father's approach to coping with our circumstances — to take what comes and go on from there, to avoid wasting time and energy bemoaning our fate or cursing God for turning away from us and, above all, to do our best to stay alive.

• • • • •

In the early morning darkness one day, even before he arose to light the lamp and she to add wood to the embers in the stove, we heard Sidor and Marynka begin to bicker.

Marynka cursed Sidor in Ukrainian for the danger hanging over them since "his" Jews had arrived, and he bombarded her with Polish insults learned during his years in the army.

"You're a dumb, ignorant slob. You can barely write your own name," she taunted him back.

"I'm sorry I ever signed my name to our marriage papers!" he retorted.

This roused her fury. "How dare you! You have less loyalty to your own family than to those Jews of yours. I swear, I'll report them if you don't manage to squeeze something out of them. Where are their clothes, their furniture, their gold?"

We had come to Sidor's with about $250 in glued-together and ironed American bills. Each of us had had some of them sewn into our clothing since the first days of the German occupation, in case we got lost or separated. Mine were in my bra and once, when we were still at home, they had gotten wet when I washed. Arthur's were in his undershorts and little jacket.

My father collected the bills from us when we got to Sidor's and doled them out to him one at a time, cautioning Sidor to be careful when he exchanged a note to buy food, kerosene, and candles. A bed sheet bartered for a small bag of flour would go unnoticed, but a five-dollar bill was a red flag. In the anonymity of a city or large town it might have been possible to convert money inconspicuously but, in the nearby villages, everyone knew that Sidor and Marynka had next to nothing. And why would an evidently self-sufficient peasant have to buy food — in addition to the small amounts of kerosene and salt that all farmers bought — and where had he gotten the bills?

When there had been nothing in the soup pot but water and old turnip peels for several days, my father gave Sidor our last five dollar bill. At the market, Sidor reported, he was teased about his sudden riches. My father feared that someone would come nosing around to see whether Sidor was sheltering Jews.

That night, we took our blankets and slept in the barn. Sidor felt contrite for not managing to change the bill without being noticed. I could hear it in the way he told us he would bring us food twice a day and change our pails.

The next evening, the bachelor neighbor came to call on the pretext of having heard there was a cow for sale.

When Marynka came to bring us back into the house the next day, she said, "That was a close call. Sidor told him that the cow is old and gives no milk, and isn't worth her fodder, and distracted the fellow with vodka so he wouldn't come out to the barn. You're lucky he's so good to you."

Jan, slipping in and out at odd hours, brought our only relief. He almost always arrived with some oddment of food — cornmeal, a sausage, maybe some cheese. None of us would touch the food until Sidor, Marynka, and Hania came home to share it with us.

One night, Jan was searched by a German patrol on the lookout for smugglers. He explained the slab of butter he was carrying as being a gift to his married mistress whose name he couldn't divulge; the German newspaper, which he couldn't read, he said he used for cigarette paper.

The next time he was caught, he got a beating and a warning that he would be taken to headquarters if he was caught again. Even the Germans knew by now that he was a "Jewish uncle" who was hiding Jews somewhere.

On some visits, Jan would bring only bad news. Ferreting Jews out of hiding places had lost no momentum. One time, when Sidor and Marynka were out of the room, he told us of a peasant who had killed his Jews when their money ran out, and left their bodies lying in a field.

We could no longer pay Sidor and Marynka for our upkeep, since our money had run out.

My father asked Jan, "Why make such a secret of the neighbor's action? Surely everyone knows."

"Probably," said Jan. "It doesn't matter if Sidor knows, but Marynka, well . . . why put the knife in her hand?"

None of us trusted Marynka, Jan least of all. He would sit with her at the table for hours when he came to see us, eating the eggs she had put aside for him and parrying her flirtatious remarks. He played her game at the beginning because he wanted her to be good to us and knew that this was part of the price she demanded for letting us stay.

Marynka would ask when Jan was coming and prepare for his visits. She would wash with nice soap and put on her beautiful embroidered peasant blouse, bleached white in the sun, and a long full skirt. Only boots were missing to complete her costume, and she longed for them as for a loved one.

As consolation, she would clasp around her neck my mother's gold chain with the heart pendant that bore tooth-marks from when Arthur and I had teethed on it as children. She kept the pendant, which my father had given her when he and my mother had first come to live at the house, tucked inside her blouse. Sidor forbade her to sell my gold ring with the garnets no matter how little food remained in the cupboard.

• • • • •

One night, when Sidor had taken Hania and Marynka to visit her family in another village, I was dawdling in the dark by the stove. My parents and Arthur had already gone up to the attic.

Suddenly Sidor slipped in the door. He told me that Marynka and Hania had decided to stay overnight. Without lighting a candle, he fetched the all-purpose tumbler and a bottle of vodka that he offered to share with me. When I declined to drink, he muttered, "She thinks she's too good to drink with a peasant like me." I denied it and accepted a sip.

After a while, when I sensed that he had dozed off, I stood and started to tiptoe to the ladder. In one lunge, Sidor sprung up and pressed himself against me. "A Jewish beauty," he said. I pushed him away, but he kept grabbing at me. Locked in the vise of his arms, I considered biting him, but he let go before I had to.

"Don't tell Jan," he said, sitting down hard. He looked terrified that Jan would kill him if he knew that Sidor had touched me. He tried to say more, but a sob stuck in his throat. I had the impulse to comfort him but turned and climbed up to my bed. "Don't tell Jan" was a change from the old days, when he would have been afraid I would tell my father.

My parents had never let on when they first realized that Jan and I were lovers. They treated us at Sidor's as they had before: the "young people." Young people just stay up late. We always waited a decent interval to give them time to fall asleep in the attic before we lay down on the bench in the little alcove downstairs. Each morning, after Jan left at dawn, I expected my father to be sitting there waiting when I parted the alcove curtain, to stab me with a look. It never happened.

A word, even a reproving word, from my mother would have been welcome. I wanted to tell her that Jan was very gentle, careful not to rush me, passion so well anointed with affection that during those first three days of our intimacy I could not have said precisely when I had stopped being a virgin.

"Lost my virginity." That's how my parents would have put it, but I didn't feel loss; no, I felt that I had become a woman, gaining the full intelligence of my body, its capacity to respond, to invent, and to send to Jan's body waves of devotion that partnered with sensations of pleasure. The hours Jan and I managed to spend together may have been furtive, but they were intense and filled with tenderness.

Even these moments of peace bore a price tag of fear. A faceless baby floated in my imagination. Each week after Jan's visit, I would see the floating baby in my dreams. Conceiving a child, a great blessing under other circumstances, would now have brought great misfortune. The floating baby would be my death warrant. Even if I had the strength to carry it, I would have to go off by myself to give birth and then get rid of it. A crying baby! I often thought of Wolf and Malcia's child whimpering during the aktsia. The child could have given us away or been suffocated in an attempt to keep her quiet. For me to become pregnant would mean the end of all of us because I would no longer be able to help save my family.

I wished I could talk to my mother about ways to avoid getting pregnant, though Jan had said that this was his responsibility. In a dark corner of my mind I knew this wasn't true but, short of refusing to sleep with him, I didn't know what to do. I wondered how my mother had managed to have only two children. By putting on her headache compress? Here in hiding, of course, her periods had stopped — starvation had taken care of that.

I thought once or twice about asking Marynka. People who live in the country know about such natural things as a matter of course, though their information is often twisted by superstition. But I was convinced she would laugh at me. I had to rely on my own instincts, handle each question as it came up.

Jan said I could trust him. And I did. He didn't want me to die. I knew it by the way he held me in his arms. And now that I knew how it felt to be loved, I didn't permit myself any stray, let-come-what-may thoughts. No. I wanted to live more than ever. I had bitten into the apple and found it sweet.

Yet, in the eyes of God and my parents, we were sinners. I glanced at my father at casual moments, during a scanty meal or a game of chess that he played solo, on a chess set assembled from rocks and straw, and I saw a suffering look, the pain I was causing him. The rebuke on my father's face troubled me; it haunted my dreams. His look, as if he were seeing an injured bird, belied his soothing voice saying, "In Paris no one will know. You'll be clean again, I promise you."

I didn't feel dirty or wounded during those hours when Jan's arms were around me in the alcove, but I couldn't say that to my father.

I couldn't explain to him that there was something between Jan and me that transcended the physical: we had been allied, entwined, intimately involved with each other for over a year before we made love. Nor could I explain to him — or to myself — why in a hidden corner of my heart I felt maidenly and inviolate.

My periods had become irregular, then stopped, and when some spotting began again I couldn't wait to whisper the good news to my mother. "Look," I intended the news to say, "I'm healthy, I'm not starving." But I hadn't realized that she thought I would become pregnant each time I had been with Jan.

"A gift," she said to me, her wayward daughter. "The dear Lord has sent you a miscarriage. Say a prayer of thanks to God."

• • • • •

Our friends and relatives knew that they could contact us through Jan, and he sometimes brought us letters from them. Jan surprised us one Sunday with a request from Rose Bradler, the married daughter of the family I had roomed with as a high school student in Borszczów. She had given birth and was now hiding with her baby not far from us. To give birth to a baby in these times, foolish as it might be, was simple compared to finding someone to hide a mother and new baby. But now Rose's milk had dried up and she needed sugar for the infant.

I watched my mother untie a few lumps of sugar from the corner of a ragged handkerchief. With our last coin, Sidor had procured a bit of sugar to go with the tea leaves Jan had brought.

"If we give it to her, we won't have any," my father said. "No, the answer is no." My father, known by all for his charitable heart, told Jan, "Tell Rose that we have no sugar; that we too are starving. Tell her we'll send sugar when we have some." Jan nodded without looking up. "And see if you can find a little milk for her."

Jan's eyebrows went up as if to say, "Easier said than done," but he said nothing.

My mother poured hot water over the tea leaves in the pot for Sidor, Marynka, and Hania, who were expected back from church soon, retied the few broken sugar lumps in the handkerchief, and put it back in her pocket.

Another time Jan brought a letter from Aunt Sophia asking if she, Uncle Zygmunt, and Dolek could stay with us at Sidor's. They were being sheltered by a peasant named Wasil in a village a few kilometers from us. Sophia and Dolek had gone to Wasil's right after the aktsia and for a while, as long as Zygmunt was still in the Ordnungsdienst, he had brought them food every weekend. But, when it had become too dangerous for him to live openly in our house, he had joined them. Now, the letter said, they expected to be turned out imminently because their funds were almost gone.

My father sent back word with Jan: "You'll have to search for another place. In any case, we may all meet at the river before long," meaning that we might all commit suicide together rather than submit to certain capture and mutilation.

Jan brought yet another letter from Aunt Lolla's sons. It said that Lolla herself could not write because she had been stabbed through the skull by the same Ukrainian peasants who had killed her husband in the fields where they were hiding after the aktsia. The part of her brain which had controlled writing was damaged. Lolla, an intellectual like my father, could no longer read or write.

Lolla's sons also asked my father if the three of them could come stay with us. My father asked Sidor, who said that if they did we would all have to leave. My father chose to save his own children and sent back word to Lolla and her sons: it was impossible for them to join us at Sidor's.

The forest, in my father's opinion, was not an option for us. According to Sidor and Jan, people hiding in forest bunkers scrounged for food on night forays to distant cottages and were frequently dragged away to the Gestapo.

When I mentioned to my father the possibility of joining a partisan group, I set off an explosion. "In the forest," he said, "the partisans themselves are the greatest menace to the Jews. When they are frustrated by lack of supplies and their own limited military success, they massacre fleeing Jews."

When I asked Jan about the fighters in the forest he said my father was right. "How can they fight if they have no arms and nothing to eat?" he asked. Seeing my disappointment he added, "Maybe there are more sympathetic groups to the west, but not around here." For an instant I doubted them both, yet not enough to take off and find out for myself.

I thought of Shimek. "Maybe Jewish partisans?"

"Dreams," my father said. "In Palestine maybe. Not here."

At the end of Jan's next visit, while we sat waiting for the last rays of light to disappear, he handed me a letter. It was from Shimek. He had given it to Ulanowski, my father's Polish friend whom Shimek had met at our home before the war. He knew that Ulanowski kept in touch with us via Jan or Sidor.

"I've been carrying this around for weeks but I couldn't bring myself to give it to you," he admitted. "I was jealous of your feelings for Shimek."

"How do you know what I felt for Shimek?" I asked in amazement.

"The way you looked at him in your garden." Ancient history. Those days when Shimek and I sat on a bench talking about a book we had read seemed to belong to an earlier incarnation.

I told Jan, "I only admired Shimek for his intellect and taste in books." As soon as I said this, I realized by Jan's face that it was the wrong thing to say.

"He's dead," Jan said flatly.

For a moment my mind closed, threw out all images, left me lost in fog. I was chilled to the bone, and the only thought that swam into my head was the need to put on a sweater, my mother's lost sweater.

Shimek's father had trusted the promise of sanctuary that his German boss swore would be honored. Jan said that the German protector had been arrested for helping Jews and taken to Gestapo headquarters in Czortkow. When the Gestapo came to take Mr. Bosek to Czortkow as well, Shimek and his mother had slipped out of the room.

"They only made it as far as the greenhouse. Their brains were splattered all over the glass," Jan told me.

In his letter, Shimek had written about a point that had recently occurred to him concerning the tale of the Grand Inquisitor in *The Brothers Karamazov*. He also wrote that he intended to join a partisan band if he could only make it to the forest.

❖ 25 ❖

While visiting her parents' house, Marynka had obtained a warm jacket that her brother had stripped off a Jewish woman before taking her away to be killed. Marynka taunted Sidor with the jacket — "I have to look out for myself since I get no benefit from your cheap Jews" — driving him into a frenzy, until he smacked her across the face.

"Find out where they buried their gold," she snarled, "or I'll earn myself a pair of new boots." It was common knowledge that the Germans used boots to reward informers who turned in Jews. She glared at us as if to say, "See what I get for feeding you and carrying out your slops?"

Over the weeks and months, Marynka's resentments increased, particularly against my mother. My mother could barely conceal her contempt for Marynka, and Marynka was no fool.

"Anyone like that dirty hussy who threatens to denounce human beings for a pair of boots deserves to be called 'murderer,'" my mother insisted.

My father was treated with more courtesy by Marynka — in fact, when Jan wasn't around, she flirted with him — and my father's suave responses concealed his distaste. Marynka, vain about her small feet, would tickle his leg with her toes, and he would promise her a pair of red boots from Paris as soon as the war was over. Talk of fancy boots when there was not enough food to eat didn't seem ludicrous at the time; to us it made perfect sense.

When Sidor and Marynka fought, Marynka would throw the nearest shoe or broom against the wall. Then Hania would come up to the attic to sit with us. Arthur slid over so she could sit next to him. None of us said a word.

Often I could hear Sidor banging his fist on the table, and variations of the same argument.

"He's a good man," he said of my father. "I saw how he treated the men who worked for him on the bridge. I can't send him to his grave."

"Yes. Instead, you're digging your own and mine and Hania's. They'll shoot us in our own yard!"

"I'm the boss here. I know what I'm doing."

"You're a miserable dirty Polack," Marynka shouted as something heavy, probably the kettle, hit the wall; the wall vibrated against my back and I felt her fury all through my body.

Every time Marynka and Sidor had one of their periodic fights, she would threaten to denounce him for hiding Jews and say that we had to leave, and Sidor would refuse. My father would go down on his knees, kiss her hands and feet, and say, "If you insist, my wife and I will go; we'll go, but keep my children."

After each fight, the atmosphere would throb with fits and spurts of alternating animosity and amiability. Then, a few days later, the drama would repeat itself. The fights terrified us — we knew it was inevitable that, eventually, something had to break.

It was not Sidor and Marynka's screaming and yelling but an altercation between my parents that traveled out the attic window and brought the inquisitive bachelor neighbor for another surprise visit. My father was again trying to dissuade my mother from a scheme such as bartering her gold filling or my hair — which Marynka coveted — for a bath or for food.

"If we are meant to die of dirt and hunger, one bath or one ham won't prevent it," he insisted more loudly than he should have.

How Sidor and Marynka got rid of the neighbor they did not say. But we were banished to the barn, to sleep on the hay between the wheezing horse and the dried-up cow. To protect us from the intense night cold, Jan unloaded a box from his horse-drawn wagon. It contained the down quilt and blankets my mother had given him for safekeeping. It was wonderful to have them to wrap ourselves in.

My mother gave one of the blankets to Sidor in return for permission to cook in the house so, that night, Sidor came to the barn to get her. When he brought her back to the barn before dawn, she was carrying a pot of corn soup.

"You thoughtless woman," my father muttered as he ate the soup. A few times after that, she sneaked into the house when Sidor, Marynka, and Hania were working in the fields and returned with a few pancakes or a little gruel. My father always warned, "The neighbors will see the smoke."

"We have to eat," she said.

The barn had no window. Through chinks in the vertical planks I surveyed the courtyard where a few chickens pecked half-heartedly, dispirited by the absence of a rooster. Peeking into the yard when it rained, I could see the ruts in the ground fill up with muddy puddles that splashed Sidor and Marynka's legs when either of them ventured out with a dish of scraps or to empty our slop pails. At least in the barn I was spared Marynka's raucous voice raised in argument or coarse jest. I missed Sidor's face and the benign look of his eyes.

Arthur grew listless now that Hania no longer came to sit near him. At first Arthur and Hania had ignored each other, but soon they had started to make up an occasional game. They would play ball with one of Hania's rolled-up stockings, rolling it back and forth to each other across the floor without speaking a word, their faces blank. Later they had taken to playing furious games in which the rules changed constantly. Now all that was over, and Arthur became depressed.

The incarcerated feeling of my first few days at Sidor's, when I had felt the urge to run across the meadows, was gone; now I wanted to remain here, ensconced alongside the horse and cow. The manure smell, strong as it was, didn't bother me after the first few hours. The barn at least had pacing room for my father. We constructed a sleeping nook for ourselves with bales of hay and blankets but, during the day, we dispersed to different corners of the barn. Arthur liked to sit near the horse, and I favored the cow.

Sidor's report that the Allies had landed in Sicily and were fighting in Salerno was cause for celebration. *Dare I let myself feel good?* I wondered. The Germans might push them back into the sea. Still, the news gave me a twinge of hope.

My father and Jan built a hiding place in the barn intended for an emergency, to hide us for a few hours, at most a day. The hideout was in the miniature chicken coop that was attached, like a malignant growth, to the exterior wall of the barn. The cow's feeding trough, filled with hay and straw, stood against the barn's interior wall at the spot where the coop leaned against the exterior of the barn. Crawling between the legs supporting the trough, my father made a hole through the barn wall into the coop. He concealed the hole with a brick. Then he made a flimsy false wall of logs within the coop to separate us from the chickens, which were on shelves at the other end.

The space we stole from the chickens was the size of a closet. Wide enough for two people, it was a tight squeeze for four. The roof was too low for an adult to stand upright, and there was not enough room even to lie down. The angle of the slanted roof took getting used to. At first only Arthur managed to stand without bumping his head. We crouched on the ground against one of the walls.

In our drills, when my father made us practice disappearing into the coop, we squirmed snakelike on our bellies through the hole in the barn wall in a fixed order: first Arthur, then my mother, then me, then my father, who pulled the brick closed behind him.

"We've got to do it faster," my father told us sternly as we sat in the barn, worn out after several trial runs. "It takes the four of us much too long to hide. Let's try it again."

•   •   •   •   •

Early one morning, not fully awake in the barn's gloom, I heard Rex barking, which he always did when strangers were approaching. I peered through a chink in the barn wall: Gestapo men were swarming out of cars and motorcycles. Ukrainian militiamen were gesturing with their rifles.

Rex's barking saved us, giving us the few precious seconds we needed to disappear into the hiding place. My father had barely pulled in his legs after mine before I, lying on the floor, saw boots passing back and forth in front of the hole in the barn wall. There was no camouflage over it; my father hadn't had time to pull the brick to the wall.

We heard the clank and bang of heavy implements, the grind of rusty hinges, the swish and clomp of the cow and horse being prodded out of the barn.

"Cursed dirty Jews," rang out when the slop pails spilled over their polished boots.

"Where are those damned Jews? Damn that Benjamin Gottesfeld with his sow of a wife and two lousy children!" a voice bellowed in German a few inches beyond the wall. He shouted orders to the Ukrainians to search every corner of the barn.

Our blanket and down quilt, which they had found in the barn, evidenced that we had been there. I strained to hear Marynka and Sidor's voices. They would be tortured to betray our hiding place.

My mother put her hand over Arthur's mouth. It wasn't necessary. We were too stunned to move or cry out. My mother's teeth chattered for a few seconds until she managed to clamp her jaws together. My father dug some old throat lozenges out of his pocket and popped one in each of our mouths. The tearing of the paper wrapper sounded as loud as a rock-slide.

The Germans ordered the Ukrainians to dig holes in every part of the barn in the belief that we had a hiding place under the ground or had dug a tunnel that led under the river to the forest.

As they dug with their pitchforks, straw and dirt piled up in front of the hole in the barn wall. They were sealing us in and covering our hideout without realizing it. We had barely enough air to breathe, but at least our entry point was now invisible.

The Germans, increasingly maddened by each hole that did not expose our hiding place or supposed escape tunnel, threatened the

Ukrainians with severe consequences if we were not found.

"Come out, Jews," a militiaman called out in Ukrainian, "we'll wrap you in white linen." He was referring to burial shrouds.

I heard our bachelor neighbor's familiar laugh and knew that he was the one who had betrayed us. I heard other people laughing and cheering the diggers on. There seemed to be a large crowd in the barn, making a holiday of waiting for us to be pulled out of hiding and shot.

"It's only a matter of minutes," I said to myself, "it will be any second now. It will be quick, right in the courtyard, up against the wall." A quick bullet to the brain would be merciful, I knew. So often had I imagined my last moments that now, when the guns were only a foot away, I felt a queer numbness.

Then I thought of Dr. Steuerman's lover and what the Ukrainians had done to her body. They would shame me as a Jewish whore. Just as being Jan's girlfriend had protected me up until now, it would cause my body to be defiled after my death. Jan would not be able to prevent my shame.

Tears and saliva flowed from me. All my sphincters opened and left nothing inside. We soiled ourselves and each other over and over again.

The sound of spades digging first in one corner of the barn floor then in another continued for hours. We lost track of the time until we heard the chickens squawking. No one had come to feed them. The Germans and the militia were there digging all night. Off and on I would hear a spade hit a rock — and then curses.

It was quiet the next morning but we stayed where we were.

Late in the afternoon, we heard Sidor's quavering voice. "Are you there?" he called over and over again. We didn't answer; we weren't going to fall into a trap. Obviously the Germans had come back and were forcing him to act as though there was nothing wrong. Then Sidor said, "I swear I'm alone. They're gone. Come out. You can come out now."

But we couldn't come out, even if we had believed him. Finally, he realized that he had to clear the straw and muck away from the hole in the wall.

We crawled out of the coop, filthy and stinking. Sidor hugged each of us in turn, and we all cried, sometimes falling against each other. Sidor kept crossing himself, saying over and over, "It's a miracle. I expected to find you dead."

For a moment I caught sight of Arthur standing alone, almost upright, yet sagging a little to one side. He stood on the spot like a stalk of corn in a field after the harvest, alive at the base only, deserted despite our being near him, neither awake nor asleep, blinking in the light, whimpering like the rest of us.

My mother, Arthur, and I sank down on a pile of hay while my father hobbled about in an effort to get his legs working. Sidor, picking his way around the holes in the ground, went out and came back with water for us. The horse and cow were gone.

Sidor told us that he and Marynka and Hania had been in the fields when the Germans had come looking for us. On their way home from the fields, someone had warned them that the Gestapo was waiting in the barn for them to return. They had hidden in a neighboring village until the coast was clear, but they had been warned that the Germans had announced to the peasants that they planned to come back.

Sidor returned to the house and I expected to hear Marynka ranting.

There was only silence.

• • • • •

A few hours after dark, Sidor returned to the barn and held out a whole loaf of bread. None of us reached for it. Finally he put it in my mother's hands.

"You have to go," he said to us. "They're coming back within twenty-four hours. They left a message."

Every second brought the Gestapo closer and yet we didn't move. To my mind there was only one place to go: back into the hidden area of the coop.

My father sank to his knees. "Have pity on my children," he begged. "Don't make them go. After the war there will be no end to the rewards for you and your family. Clothes. Money. A new house. You will be members of our family as long as you live."

Sidor's face, a mask of stone, was new to me. He went into the house again. He came back with the blanket we had given him and cut it into four parts.

"It's cold in the forest," he said. "I'll take you there."

A few rags from the blanket the raiders had torn during the razzia lay about in the barn debris. I picked them up and stuffed them into my blouse while my mother foraged under the straw for anything that might have remained in one piece. She found the handle of a knife, turned it several times, then gave it to Arthur. We retied the rags around our feet. Our shoes had long since fallen apart, and their remains had disintegrated into the muck of the barn floor.

At the courtyard gate, while Sidor scouted the road, I turned around and saw a figure at the window. Marynka. She had her wish now. For a moment I wondered if she had earned that pair of boots for herself. "May her legs break off if she did," I thought, but I was actually sure she hadn't denounced us. She must be furious with Sidor for taking us to the forest. He would be killed if he was found with us.

That march to the forest, through back roads out of the village, through fields and ditches and quagmires along the river, my feet following the path trodden by my mother ahead of me, seemed longer than any three hours I had ever lived through. My father and Sidor took turns carrying Arthur. Once in a while we stopped, so that whoever was carrying him could pass Arthur to the other one's shoulders.

It was still pitch-dark when we arrived at the first line of trees. Sidor lowered Arthur to the ground. "I'm going," he said, but he stood rooted to the spot. He started to say "May God...." A crackle in the underbrush drove him away.

161

My father lifted Arthur onto his shoulders and took my mother's hand.

"Wait," she said and broke off a piece of bread for each of us. We ate as we walked straight into the forest. It seemed to swallow us up. From having read about walking into the ocean, I imagined it must cause the same terror I was feeling. We were walking away from the killers at our rear and toward their victims ahead. "Let's stop right here," I wanted to say to my father, but it was too much of an effort to speak.

Picking our way between pine trees, we came to a sudden clearing. Before we could duck out of the moonlight, a figure approached. A scout for hidden Jews, he had been tracking us, but fearing we might be decoys, had waited until the moon revealed my father's face and he could be sure we were not being followed.

He led us to an enclave of earthen dugouts — some protruding into contoured rises, some level with the forest floor — all camouflaged with branches and leaves. About 150 Jews from Skala and shtetls in the area had fled to the forest, one or two at a time, after the aktsia and after the liquidation of the Borszczów ghetto. These bunkers were their last hope of shelter.

"He's here, Benjamin Gottesfeld is here," passed along their grapevine.

I knew my father had been held in high esteem in our town, but these reverent whispers elevated him to the status of a wizard, someone with a sixth sense who knew how to escape the enemy beyond the trees.

One of my father's old friends came to find us. "You're here. Now the war will end," I heard him say. The man took us to a bunker where a group of men eagerly interrogated my father for news about the Russian advance.

After my father told them what he knew of the progress of the war, they told us about the lives of the Jews in the forest. They spent their daytime hours in the underground bunkers. After dark, some of the men and boys would venture out, one by one, to beg or steal a little food from the peasants. This was dangerous, but it was a matter of life and death to scrounge for food. Many of these volunteers never returned. The Jews were all starving; many had already died of hunger and exposure.

The Ukrainian peasants knew where the Jews were hiding. Individual peasants and German units had periodically invaded the forest to ferret them out, and some Jews had died in these attacks. My father's friends told him they had received warnings that a full-scale assault on the forest was planned and they were expecting it at any moment.

My father motioned us to sit under a tree and told us quietly that we were leaving as soon as it got dark. "If we stay in the forest," he said, "it will be our death."

"Can't we stay only one more day?" my mother begged. "I just found my brother Wolf and his family. They escaped to the forest just before the Borszczów ghetto was liquidated. They feel alone here. He told me that they are pariahs because everyone thinks my father betrayed that bunker full of people to the Germans. He complains bitterly that people don't trust him. They say, 'If your father could do such a thing, so could you.' But I don't believe it. It's a lie, and I won't believe it until my dying day. It's only slander from those Ukrainians because no Jew lived to contradict their story."

My mother picked nervously at the pine needles on the ground. "Wolf begged me for bread for his children, but I said I didn't have any. What should I do?" she beseeched my father. "Should I give him some?"

"Am I Solomon?" my father asked, walking off toward someone who had waved to him.

I also wanted to stay there a little longer because I had found Lotka.

• • • • •

Lotka had crept up with soundless forest expertise, and bear-hugged me from behind. I turned around and embraced her skeletally thin body.

Traces of the forest stuck to her hair and her ragged clothes and lodged under the nails of her swollen blue fingers. One foot was wrapped in a makeshift bandage anchored to the remnants of a shoe.

"Refused to make way for a burning log," she said, pointing to her foot. "Damn thing won't heal. You don't have any ointment, do you?" I had nothing to give her and took care not to burden her with sympathy. She shrugged.

It was already light when she led me to the bunker she shared with Rubcio — our old classmate Rubcio, whom I had once had a crush on. He had always preferred Lotka, and now here they were together.

"It took months to learn the forest and how to build underground bunkers covered with earth," Lotka said. "But we've gotten good at it. We transplant saplings and scatter dry branches and needles to camouflage the roofs of the bunkers. You've probably just walked over the heads of dozens of people without even noticing."

"The bunkers are different sizes, depending on how many people — two, three, six — live in them," she continued. "Every few weeks, when we feel that the Ukrainian peasants are becoming too aware of us, we move to another part of the forest."

"But what do you eat? How do you cook? Where do you get water?" I asked.

"Whenever Rubcio can scratch a bit of cornmeal from an abandoned sack we pick wild mushrooms, make a fire deep in the forest, and cook a little soup. We have no water except what we can save from rain and dew."

"But what about the smoke?" I asked. "Surely people living near the forest must see it!"

"We only risk building a fire very late at night," she said. "True, people might see the fire itself if they are nearby, but it's too dark to see the smoke rise above the trees. Rising smoke is visible from a much greater distance so it's far more dangerous."

Lotka rewound the bandage on her leg and I saw the festering wound.

"We work every moment," she said, then she blushed; perhaps she was thinking of stolen moments with Rubcio. I wanted to ask if her parents, who in the old Skala days had forbidden an alliance with him, knew about her and Rubcio, then realized it didn't matter.

"There are no secrets here and all the old rules are gone," she told me. "In the next bunker a high-born girl, you would remember her, lives with a former water-carrier. That woman over there, who was from such a fine family, lives now with Skala's only Jewish thief since she lost her husband and child."

"My father will be devastated when he learns that girls from the best families are living with old men who have lost everybody and everything," I said, thinking that the rules had changed for our family as well.

"Why not?" shrugged Lotka. "We'll soon be gone anyway."

Lotka told me that her parents no longer lived in the house we had once shared with them; they slept where Mottel worked — in Gestapo headquarters. Holdouts to the last in Skala, the Sternbergs still counted on their Gestapo angel for protection.

"It's crazy," I said.

"I know." She thrust her hand under her ragged jacket and drew something out between her fingernails. She laughed as she squashed a louse and dug in for another one. "I prefer to associate with these vermin rather than with the ones they rely on."

We sat there for hours catching up. I told her about Jan and me, and the asylum my family and I had found at Sidor's, and about the razzia there a few days before. After we sat in silence for a moment, choked by private agonies and common terror, Lotka began to talk of the forest itself, how it kept her going: birdsong in the trees, the ingenuity of nature evident in a mushroom that appeared overnight after a rain, the forest's silence and how it soothed and cleansed the spirit.

"Rubcio and I tried to join a Russian partisan group, but they wouldn't take us," Lotka told me. "Only one Jew from here has succeeded in joining any of the four partisan units that passed through this part of the forest."

"We're starting a Jewish group," Rubcio said. "Will you join us?"

Lotka added, "Anyone can shoot a gun."

"Yes, but first we have to have one to shoot," I said. So far they had nothing: no arms, no leader, no military know-how. "I'll think about it," I said, in order not to discourage them. I admired their ambition to go down fighting, and it was tempting to join in their dream, but it was difficult to accept deserting my family. Anyway, my father and Jan would never let me.

I walked a zigzag path back to my parents, passing people sitting at the entrances of their bunkers. Some, too weak to manage more of a greeting than an almost imperceptible nod of the head, sat immobile, taking full advantage of the fresh air in their lungs before another suffocating night underground. Some picked over bits of clothing looking for lice. Others lay limp or tossed on the ground in an agony of high fever. Typhus. "Water," a small girl moaned as I passed, "a little water."

A woman I knew who used to live on the next street had a baby at her breast. "I have nothing for him," she said, "but I let him suck."

This was not the only baby born in the forest. One woman whose children were already grown, and whose period had stopped before she escaped to the forest, told me that she had given birth to a girl. Her husband had bitten off the umbilical cord. Then he took the baby and left her on the steps of a nunnery. Later, they learned that by the time the nuns found the baby and took her inside, she was dead. I shuddered when I heard the story, thinking what would happen to my baby if I got pregnant.

My mother gestured for me to follow her behind a clump of bushes and gave me my share of bread. Arthur sat next to my father, chewing his mouthful slowly, which enraged my mother. "Hurry," she said. "Someone will see."

My father returned the rest of his portion to her. "For Wolf's children," he said.

He had seen Lolla — we had all seen her and her two sons. They were living in a crude dugout. The once beautiful Lolla had a deep scar on her bald head from the knife the peasants had plunged through her skull into her brain. She and her two boys were starving.

Lolla wanted my father to build a shelter large enough for all of us. My mother pleaded with him to do so. "If we go, we're leaving them to die," she said.

My father refused. "Staying here is our death," he repeated. "I learned it in the ghetto: Jews who band together invite their own destruction."

But where to go?

My mother did not give my father's portion of bread to Wolf's children but kept it for us. Retying the rags around Arthur's feet, she told him to hurry up and finish his bread.

"We have to get a message to Jan," my father said.

"I'll go as soon as it gets dark," I offered.

"Not yet," Father said, "we'll wait a day for him to find us and, if he doesn't, then you can go."

I thought about my options and decided to join Lotka and Rubcio's band after I had made sure that Jan would lead my parents and Arthur out of the forest.

I spent the rest of the day with Lotka and Rubcio. He spoke of plans to acquire guns and ammunition, and promised to teach me how to shoot. His hand rested on Lotka's knee as she sat cross-legged beside him. It made me sad to think that Jan and I had never held hands when anyone else was present. Each stolen encounter was accompanied in my head by a refrain: "This is the last time." The last time together, the last time to make love — that thought must have been with Lotka and Rubcio, too — but Lotka's hand, as she squeezed Rubcio's thigh, signaled an acceptance of the situation that Jan and I had never known.

Rubcio walked me back to the tree that was sheltering my family for one last night.

"For me, not having a gun is harder to bear than hunger, freezing nights, and lice. One night the Germans and Ukrainians came through with bayonets fixed on their rifles, and the only weapon I had was a paring knife. But they passed over my bunker."

"Talk to Jan," he said. "Convince him to be a courier for us."

I promised I would enlist Jan as a gunrunner.

• • • • •

As we went to sleep on the bed of pine needles carpeting the ground under the tree, my parents and I agreed that we would leave the forest at first light.

Shots and screams woke me. Lying on the ground, I felt the pounding of feet even before my eyes could make out figures running in all directions in the predawn darkness.

Gunfire and explosions erupted around us, and bullets whizzed past our heads.

"Keep down," I screamed as my father and mother sheltered Arthur between them.

Smelling smoke from bunkers hit by grenades, hearing the screams of people trapped inside, I got to my knees before my father yanked on my ankle and I fell flat again.

The Ukrainians dropped armfuls of smoking, burning straw into the remaining bunkers to roast and asphyxiate anyone who did not crawl out.

Voices yelling orders in German and Ukrainian mingled with the screams of the wounded and burning people. Human sounds alternated with shots and explosions, became louder, then ebbed and became louder once again.

End of the line. Nowhere to run. No hole in the ground to crawl into. At least I would be spared the degradation of my dead body that I had dreaded during the razzia at Sidor's.

"Let it be quick," kept repeating itself in my head.

We lay there, motionless, as if we were already dead. Paralysis set in. I was sure I wouldn't be able to stand when the moment came. They would have to shoot me lying down. I started to feel limbless, a useless thing; when I would finally die, there wouldn't be much left to kill. Numbness replaced fear, which barely kept ticking in a low throb all that day.

By evening, when it was quiet at last, most of the Jews in the forest were dead.

Morning.

The shadow of a pair of boots fell across my face. I opened my eyes.

Jan.

It seemed natural for him to be there. Without conscious thought, I had been waiting for him.

Once he had seen me blink, he checked my father and mother and Arthur. They weren't hurt. I was sure I had been shot in the back, as I had been sure during the aktsia in Skala. Jan examined every inch of my body but could find no bullet or bleeding. Somehow, miraculously, all four of us had survived the bullets, the grenades, the fire, the smoke. None of us could believe we were alive.

Jan told us that when a militiaman, after the razzia at Sidor's, had claimed that "the Gottesfelds escaped to Russia," he went to check with Sidor. Sidor told him we were in the forest.

"I had to wait till it was over." He gave me a sip of water from a tin canister, then held my face in his hands as if my cheeks were the petals of a rare flower he had never seen before.

He told my father he would sneak me into the attic of his barn, come back for Arthur, and make a third trip to fetch my parents. "It may not be until tomorrow," he cautioned.

Walking close behind Jan, I heard a branch behind us snap, and then the sound of footsteps. "Run!" shouted Jan.

Turning around, I saw a big fellow, a Jewish boy whom I recognized from my class in Polish elementary school. He was two years older than me and had been left back in school, but in the forest he had become a leader.

He was chasing Jan and me. Perhaps he was afraid Jan was going to betray the few Jews left alive after the massacre. We didn't know what he wanted — to kill Jan or stop us from leaving — but we didn't stop to find out.

I ran my fastest and managed to keep Jan in sight as he sprinted back and forth, doubled back and jumped over fallen trees and gullies. Every time I looked back, our pursuer, brandishing a stick, was still dogging us. Finally, at the edge of the forest, we lost him.

• • • • •

In his barn that evening, I followed Jan up the ladder into the hideout I had left what seemed like several lifetimes ago. Jan held me in his arms for a while, but I could not release the dam of tears that were ready to burst. "Go get Arthur," I said.

He sat down near the window opening and I went over to sit by him as I had done so many times before. "Please," I said. He had just risked his life by going to the forest, and now I was sending him back into the jaws of death.

He bent down to kiss me and I received it but could not return one of my own. I saw my father and mother and Arthur lying side by side on the pine needles. The raiders might come back. They usually did. "Go — please. Now." He got up and disappeared down the ladder without a word.

When Jan handed Arthur to me from the top of the ladder, his limp little body and expressionless face alarmed me. Had Arthur been wounded after all? Even the empty blob he had learned to impersonate when a cough or a sneeze could give us away, even the inanimate, thin little figure curled in my mother's lap or clinging to my father's shoulder or Jan's back, had now lost any apparent vestige of life-force. He just lay

170

in apathy on the straw. I kissed him, rubbed his hands and feet, held him and rocked him, and finally, as if after a deep sleep, he opened his eyes.

"He won't come back, you know," he said.

"Who? Papa?"

"No, Jan. I heard your friend say he almost caught Jan when he ran out of the forest with you, and that he would trap him the next time."

I gave Arthur a drink of water from Jan's canister. "Well, he didn't succeed. Jan brought you, didn't he?"

"Yeah, but that was because they were distracted by some shooting we heard and we ducked past them. They're going to kill him. I heard them say it. They said he's a murderer like the others. They're going to do it."

"Stop it," I said. Maybe a somnolent Arthur was better than this doomsayer. I glared at him.

"You'll see." He turned to the wall with an emphatic twist and went to sleep.

The following night, after Jan and my parents had returned safely from Jan's third trip to the forest and Jan and I had settled down together, I asked him if he knew what had happened to Lotka and Rubcio.

"The Germans captured them. Rubcio, with his mother and sister and other Jews, was taken to another place in the forest and shot."

There was no longer any need to ask Jan to become a gunrunner for Rubcio and his fighting band.

"Lotka's father, through his Gestapo boss, managed to save her from being shot. Somehow he got them to bring her to where he and his wife are living — Gestapo headquarters."

From our hiding place in the barn's attic, we all heard Jan's neighbors come into the yard and greet each other.

A voice screeched, "The forest has been cleaned out. No more pigs."

Jan's mother shouted, "Finally got their due," and his sister added,

"About time."

A list of dead Jews was recited and amended: "So-and-so's family but not the son," and then, "No, they got the son too."

"Benjamin Gottesfeld, did they get that swine yet?" someone asked. Jan's mother answered with authority, since we were known as her son's Jews: "They ran away to Russia. Don't worry; we'll get them when they come back."

"They got the wife's brother, you know, Wolf Wasserman, the one with the egg warehouse."

Jan's sister chimed in, "Yeah, the whole family." Wolf, his wife and children had been killed by a grenade thrown into their bunker. Lolla and her sons had perished the same way.

My mother rapped her fist slowly like a dirge on her heart. "He asked me for a little bread for the children." Barely forcing the words out, she kept saying over and over, "for the children, for the children. It was a sin not to give it to him."

"What good would it have done?" my father whispered. Nothing we said could distract her from obsessing over her sin. Her grief solidified into despair at the creature she had become, an animal like the wolf, the diametric opposite of her good-natured brother.

She wrapped her arms around her head. "A wolf can at least howl," she said.

Down in the yard, the neighbors laughed and jeered about how uppity the Jews used to be, how they had believed they knew more than the peasants.

"What they knew was how to finagle what they wanted out of us."

The group must have pulled into a small knot because they spoke in hushed tones interrupted by bursts of hilarity. We heard them gossiping with scandalized delight about the immorality in the forest, how couples had paired in random combinations. "They all screwed in the open, like animals."

"And she was pregnant," I heard someone say. "Her father thought he was a big shot, that his boss would save her."

A sick feeling hit me. They were talking about Lotka. A man reported that, after Lotka was reunited with her parents, the Germans had lured away Mottel's Gestapo boss, then shot the three of them in their beds.

"That was too good for them," Jan's mother said. "I would have known what to do with the sinners."

I couldn't bear to think of Lotka lying in a pool of blood.

"How often did I tell Mottel not to wait any longer?" my father said sadly.

"Stupid," my mother said, "to let herself get pregnant."

That night Jan brought me a note from Lotka. The ending was:

> *I have a feeling I will join Rubcio soon. I did want to live long enough to have the baby. Now I think, what for?*
> *It was wonderful to see you in the forest.*
> *Remember me as your good friend and cousin,*
> *Lotka*

I asked Jan why he had kept Lotka's death a secret from me.

"I was waiting for the right moment," he said.

I turned on him.

"What right moment?" My throat seemed to be lined with sandpaper.

"You're always mad at me when there's bad news." His voice was no smoother than mine. "What do you expect from me? I can't save the whole world."

❖ 26 ❖

For the next two weeks, Jan traveled from town to village, from house to house, trying to find someone to hide us. Anyone he approached could have denounced him on the spot. A Polish saddler spat at him, saying, "You're as bad as a Jew," hurling "Jew" at him like a curse word. Among Ukrainians, only one agreed to have us for a few hours, at most overnight, as a personal favor to Jan.

My father said to Jan, "Forget about trying to find a place for all four of us together; just find a place for Arthur and Fancia."

When my mother heard this, her face contorted as if to scream, but no sound came out. After a minute she gasped a few times and said, "No. Arthur stays with me."

Every morning I thought, "This is the day we'll go to the Gestapo."

The host of time-bomb guests, Jan had every right to put us out and slam the door behind us. But he didn't. "Something will turn up," he would say when all he could find to bring us were a few potatoes or a jug of water. I understood that he had protected us for so long that our lives no longer belonged to us; they belonged to him, too. If he put us out now, he would hear the door slam for the rest of his life.

One morning, during the special quiet that meant it was a Sunday, I heard Jan enter the barn. After his usual clothes-change, he appeared in the attic in his knockabout clothes, holding a small red zinnia. He plopped down on a hay pillow with a sigh of relief and rubbed his neck.

Skipping church didn't save him from wearing a stiff collar; it was part of his courting outfit. His mother had begun accusing him of hiding me somewhere since he showed no interest in finding a wife. So the charade of finding a girlfriend had begun again. Every time he took off to search out a hiding place for us, his family thought he was chasing girls.

"They're all the same," he said. "Blond, blue-eyed, and round-bottomed." No one could accuse me of those things, especially not of having a round bottom. My skirt, once tailored to fit snugly, hung straight down like a curtain with nothing much behind it.

Jan took me down to the barn to exercise my legs. He sat in a far corner, patiently watching me tramp from trough to horse stall, up and down; and the more hungrily he looked at me, the more determinedly I marched about. Finally I gave in and went to him, to the half-circle of his seated body waiting ready to receive me. His desire sparked mine and, even though it was foolhardy, we made love. "Last time, last time," I thought. And that thought gave way to: "They haven't got me yet, not yet."

We climbed up the ladder again and my father and mother awoke from their nap. Arthur, hovering near the window, said, "A man's coming."

Jan sprinted downstairs before the visitor could knock. It was Sidor. I heard him ask, "Are they here?" Jan brought him upstairs.

"I've come to take you back," he said, sitting down on the straw. "Italy has capitulated, and I think you were right when you said that the fall of Italy would be the sign that Germany would lose the war."

My father nodded. "The Germans are too smart to commit suicide, Napoleon-style, in Russia. The war will end before winter."

With just a trace of his old beaming smile, Sidor assured us, "It will be safe to come back. Even Marynka agrees that now no one would dream you were hiding there." He paused. "Even I was afraid you were killed in the forest."

We returned to Sidor's that night. It was bitter cold both outside and indoors, and we were freezing and exhausted when we arrived. All seven of us slept in the kitchen on their one bed, stretched horizontally with our feet resting on the bench that Sidor brought from the alcove.

The next morning, Sidor shoved a ripped and almost featherless quilt in after us before he closed the entry hole of the hiding place in the chicken coop. No more spending time spread out in the barn, and no more leaving the brick cover for my father to pull shut from the inside. Sidor sealed us in.

When I crawled inside, I couldn't imagine how I would make it through the next day. Braided like a horse's tail, the most we had ever spent in there at a stretch was two full days. Now, even crawling out for a five-minute break would be a special treat.

When bright daylight forced itself through the cracks in the coop, I cherished the strips of illumination that transformed each bit of wall or cloth from black or gray into tones of color.

Sidor had spread fresh straw in the coop, but it was still the same tight fit. We sat squeezed against the wall, unable to lie down, and, when one of us turned, the other three had to turn as well. Sometimes Arthur had to sit on my father's lap. We twisted and bent to avoid the rats scurrying through the coop; they often bit us.

Even in September the temperature fell below freezing at night. No matter how much I wiggled my fingers and toes, my hands and feet felt numb, but my body sweated from being pressed against three others. The two people on each end always pulled Sidor's old quilt around them to cover the side exposed to the icy air, but the two in the middle wanted it off.

Sometimes Marynka or Sidor came by to bring stewed potato peels or other scraps, but some days neither one came and our chamber pot got very full. Often it spilled as we changed places to use it.

Ravenous lice, reminding me of Lotka's lice-killing expertise in the forest, crawled through our clothes and hair and fed on us with gusto.

All day and night we picked off the lice and killed them, but it was a losing battle. Since it was too dark to see them even during the day, we had to rely on touch. More came to replace every one we killed. My mother was the champion louse remover; it became her full-time occupation.

There were so many lice on my head that my hair was moving.

• • • • •

One day Marynka came by with a small pot of beans and said that Sidor was very sick but she was afraid to call a doctor. Sidor, in his delirium, might say our names.

"Maybe I should call the priest."

"Same risk as with a doctor," my father said.

"Not for his soul," she retorted.

Sidor had typhus, apparently having contracted it from infected lice we had brought back from the forest. Typhus kept him in bed for three weeks.

Not long after he recovered, my father and I fell into the daze of illness. Of those weeks I only remember waking at moments to an agonizing thirst and then sinking again into a stupor. Both of us at different times, my mother said afterwards, appeared to sink without rallying, and all she could do was pray. I pulled out of the coma before my father, then I lay despondent, convinced he would die. It was four weeks, according to my mother, who pressed her lips to our foreheads as a thermometer, before my father and I were fever-free.

My recuperation brought a consuming interest in what Sidor or Marynka would bring us to eat. I had previously thought of hunger as a gnawing mouse in the stomach; now it became a rat that took up residence in my body and chewed on my mind. All I wanted to talk about was food: wiener-schnitzel with eggs and anchovies and fried potatoes. Though my mother gave me part of her and my father's portions, each morsel whetted my appetite for even more.

Often, in that hole, inhaling each other's breath as our only sustenance for twelve or thirty-six hours at a time, we fabricated dream menus: my mother reciting ingredients for recipes — "Take a nice fat carp"; my father reminiscing about dishes he had sampled in Czernowitz cafés; Arthur recalling his favorite jam or the orange he had once been given for Chanukah.

As my mother fell silent, too exhausted to formulate complaints and criticism, conserving every iota of energy to keep her inner pilot light burning, so my father became more expansive, drawing on his intellectual reserves, reciting Goethe or Schiller or Shakespeare's soliloquies. At times his mood called for prose, and Arthur and I would listen to partly paraphrased but nonetheless extensive portions of novels by Polish and Yiddish writers. My father made me and Arthur promise him that we too would teach our children Hebrew and Shakespeare, and we swore to it.

When my father was not in a literary frame of mind, he would try to boost our spirits by speaking of what would happen after the war. We would all go to Paris, of course, have plenty to eat and pretty clothes; for me, medical school, and for Arthur, what? Stuck on what Paris had to offer Arthur, he would find a panorama to view: Paris from the top of the Eiffel Tower or from the steps of the Sacré-Coeur. Arthur reminded him that heights made him dizzy.

My father began to reminisce about long ago. He would offer bits of family lore to cheer us up. He spoke of his father, Grandfather Azriel — whose portrait as a young man with a flower in his tunic I had often seen in the family album — as a military man with a distinguished record and a medal to prove it. My father's voice trembled proudly with habitual admiration, evidently choosing not to acknowledge that the Austro-Hungarian Empire had been a swirl of whipped cream that had soured long ago. The Grandfather Azriel who had been lost in Belzec did not exist; in his place my father gave us the debonair soldier executing a smart salute for his emperor.

❖ 27 ❖

Christmas Eve, 1943. After midnight, Sidor invited us into the house. He carried Arthur from the barn since his legs refused to support him. In the shuttered house, the room's single candle seared my eyes. A bottle of vodka stood in a place of honor on the table. Sidor took a swig as he carried a large pail to the fire on the stove, and Marynka contributed a kettleful of hot water.

I cried as I washed my face, hands, and chest for the first time in many months. My mother unbuttoned Arthur's shirt and scrubbed him with a heel of brown soap, then stripped to the waist and washed her face, neck, arms, and chest. When she finished toweling Arthur and herself with a bedsheet, I asked Hania to hold it up as a screen, which she did conscientiously. Since she wasn't very tall, Sidor and Marynka were still afforded a full view of my body, but I didn't care.

Hania whispered to me around the edge of the sheet, "I wish you would come live in the house again. Then I wouldn't be so afraid."

"Afraid of what?" I asked, assuming she meant her mother. I had often seen Marynka smack the girl without warning across the face and head.

"The Germans are coming to shoot me and burn down the house," she said. "And they're going to kill Rex, too."

"How do you know that?"

"My mother says it will happen when they come for you."

I stifled my impulse to deny what her mother had told her. She stood there, a child with solemn eyes, clearly not asking me to deny her fears, but wanting to ask something else.

She had difficulty finding the words. "I have seen cows and pigs and chickens slaughtered, but a bullet makes such a small hole. Does it hurt while the blood is coming out?"

I put my arms around her. "No, no, it all goes very fast. Besides, they don't want you. You don't even have to think about such things today, on Christmas. Next Christmas I'll have a lovely present for you."

Marynka washed my hair with kerosene to kill the lice. "I wish I had your hair," she said, as she had often said in the past.

"You're welcome to it," I told her. What would she do with a switch of black hair? Even if someone could be found to make it into a wig for her, it would have to be dyed blond, the only color considered beautiful.

After a few more rounds of vodka, she started in on my breasts.

"How round and firm they are. Mine," she complained, "are no more than pimples, even when I'm pregnant."

Here I was, all skin and bones, and Marynka was jealous of my figure. What could I say? Instead of raising her spirits, drinking had made her querulous. At any moment she might order us out of the house.

We sipped vodka from the communal cup and took turns making toasts. When it was my turn, I thanked them for the bath, which they had guessed was my dearest wish. On my father's turn he toasted friendship; but when my mother stood up, she stood frozen. Even in the best of times she had never been much of a public speaker.

"Oh God," I thought, "she's going to look at Marynka and say something like 'Cleanliness is next to godliness'".

Raising the cup she said, "Let's drink to Sidor and his family. May they have a healthy Christmas, and let's hope the Russians get here soon, and" — she hesitated, looking at my father and me, and then said — "and that the ring of dirt we left on the pail isn't so heavy that it can't be scrubbed off." We applauded, and for a moment I looked around in astonishment. This was the first time any of us had smiled in Sidor and Marynka's house, and it was my mother who had cracked the joke.

The little alcove in the far wall, with its lumpy pillows, seemed to taunt me. I couldn't help thinking how it had constricted every shift in position when Jan used to join me there, yet I had thought of it as a bower of comfort. That had been before the razzia here and the aktsia in

180

the forest, when we still had daily food and water and the glow of heat from the stove, when Jan visited at least once a week.

At least my father still promised to take us all to Paris after the war. But then it occurred to me: Paris might be as demolished by now as the Jewish enclave in the forest.

Hania took a stool and went to sit by Arthur. He ignored her. She offered him a worn-looking top — a toy Sidor must have made for Christmas years before — and a few walnuts her mother had hidden away since the harvest. Arthur took the walnuts. She demonstrated how the top worked, but he refused to look at its mesmerizing revolutions. He twirled each walnut in turn, but none of them would spin.

Then Marynka mixed a basin of dough, put out some sugar Jan had brought, and fried so many pancakes that the last batch was left on the table when Sidor, with Arthur in his arms, led us out just before dawn. Even Rex couldn't eat any more. We all had stomachaches that day. I cherished every spasm.

● ● ● ● ●

About twice a week, Marynka uncovered the opening of the hideout, gestured to my father to come out, and then sealed us in again. Usually it was in the afternoon when she came home early from the fields or when Sidor went to a peasants' fair. At first I assumed that she wanted my father to do a chore in the house; but then she began to appear in the middle of the night.

I didn't ask my mother what Marynka wanted him for because I had already guessed the answer. I tried to downplay my own suspicions. "Now that Jan isn't around much to flirt with Marynka, she needs someone to listen to her fanciful speeches," I theorized to myself, "or maybe she likes to hear my father speak of city life. All they do is talk," I lectured myself silently. "If there's anything else going on, my father is a more resilient man than he looks." We never spoke of these incidents; we just pretended they didn't happen.

Then Sidor came to get my mother. She looked at my father and he nodded.

"Has Sidor discovered Marynka's pranks and vowed to get even?" I wondered. "And how can he possibly allow her to know about his own transgressions without risking severe consequences?"

The first time my mother was gone, my father launched into one of his recitations. This time he recalled his favorite biography, of Napoleon. Arthur and I, guided by my father, observed Napoleon's triumphant visits to conquered cities. Enchantment with the Napoleon mystique had long gripped my father, and in the hiding place the conquering emperor thrilled him more than ever, but each accolade to Napoleon diverted me less and less as I grew anxious over my mother's long absence. Eventually she crawled back in with a large hunk of bread in her hands, but my father remained imperturbable as he went on with the story.

Occasionally Sidor came for my mother again, but not as often as Marynka came for my father. Once Arthur, addressing no one in particular, said, "No one ever asks me to come out."

This frenzy puzzled me: either they did very little or they had huge appetites. Jan had not come for a while, but in the past when we had managed to find a few moments together, we spent most of our time talking and just held each other. Did Sidor and Marynka take aphrodisiacs? It didn't make sense to me that they would choose this late stage to exercise their mastery, like feudal barons, over dependent Jews.

As the weeks elapsed and the hardest months of winter alternated between the sounds of storms and the silence of snowfall, our chances of remaining alive until the war was over seemed to leak away.

I felt my life force ebbing slowly and it was tempting to let it go. *Uberleben*, the Yiddish word for "survival," made me wonder, "Survive another day — and then what?" I envisioned only a ruined world populated by creatures out of a painting by Bosch who would torture me with hells I had not yet experienced. To live — if that word could be used for the existence in our coop — to live *uber*, over and beyond our current existence: what did it mean? "Over," in the sense of floating disembodied above everything as in a dream? Or was it a challenge to prevail beyond physical endurance?

Each day I thought, "To live one more day will be a miracle. But I have to, I have to try my utmost to live another day. My mother, my father, and Arthur's lives depend on me."

• • • • •

Jan hadn't seen me since my illness, but when he finally came I could tell by the way he looked at me that he was frightened by more than my physical emaciation. I tottered on his arm as he led me around the barn. My joints had ossified, in fact I felt that I had no joints at all, and I begged to sit.

We brought each other up to date. His face was bruised and the side of his mouth was encrusted with dried blood. A German patrol along the river had taken him for a smuggler, and when they found on him only a sausage and some bread, they beat him and vowed to waylay him on his return.

"The hardest trial for me is not knowing how much longer I have to hold out," I confided. "I must know when the Russians will come."

"Ask me for medicine and I can go to the pharmacy. Maybe there's none to be had, but at least I know where to look for it. Where do you want me to go for predictions about the war? Should I ask a bird to fly over the lines?" He grew increasingly agitated. "There are plenty of rumors. You want rumors?"

Sidor couldn't buy a newspaper because everyone knew he couldn't read German. Besides, the news was doctored by the Germans to make it look like they were winning the war, when actually they were losing.

Even when Sidor could repeat the rumors about troop movements he had heard from other peasants or in the marketplace, and even when he got the geography right, the original reports had been distorted by German lies and Ukrainian fears of Soviet conquest well before they filtered down to him. By this time the Ukrainians no longer trusted the Germans or believed they were going to give them an independent state, as they had once hoped and expected, but they hated the Russians even more than the Germans, and they hated the Jews more than both put together.

Sidor and Marynka's food deliveries to us fluctuated, not only with how much they had but also with the rumors about the progress of the war. We could guess that the Russians had won a victory when they brought us a little bowl of soup or stew. When Sidor heard that the Germans had withdrawn from the west bank of the Dnieper River, he came to celebrate with a small pot of kasha. We ate every grain as if it were a delicacy and begged him for more bulletins.

But, when they would hear in the marketplace that the Germans were advancing, they wouldn't bring us anything to eat. Sometimes Sidor cursed the day he had taken us back. Sidor was a sweet, decent man, but he was also sick and tired of the risks of sheltering us, of the work it involved, of the fear, the suspicion, of the war itself. His family's life hung in the balance of which side would win the war.

Once Sidor called my father out into the barn to say he had lost belief in the prophecy that the war would end in the spring. He said he didn't believe in spring anymore; there was nothing to eat in the house, his child was starving, and he would have no seeds to plant even if he had the strength to plow the ground. Sidor admitted that the battles with Marynka had begun again and that she still had her eyes on a pair of red boots if he himself didn't drive us out.

Through the opening I saw my father fall to his knees in front of Sidor.

"Please, for my children's sake, don't drive them to their death." I could see Sidor's shoes pacing up and down past my father. "The war is ending," my father pleaded. "We'll be like one big family."

"Talk," Sidor said, "just talk," and he motioned my father back into the hideout.

On one of his visits, Jan brought a letter from Aunt Sophia. She and Uncle Zygmunt and Dolek, still hiding in Wasil's attic, were close to despair. For seven days they'd had no bread. There were rumors of a razzia.

The Gestapo had come to search the house and found Wasil singing while working on his gate.

"Why are you singing?"

"Why shouldn't I sing?" Wasil replied. "I have nothing to worry about. I am a poor man. I live alone. Go to the peasants who don't sing. They're rich from the Jews they hide in their houses. They worry. I sing." My aunt wrote that the Gestapo had left without entering the yard but with a promise to return.

She was keeping a diary, Aunt Sophia wrote, in which she inscribed many such stories. She prayed daily for Dolek to be saved. She closed her letter, "Death is no longer frightening."

My father instructed Jan, "Tell her I say that they should hold on, that the war will end soon." His message, I realized, was meant to instill resolve in her, but the offhand way in which he spoke the words betrayed that at that moment he didn't believe them himself. Though certain the Germans would be defeated soon, my father admitted that "soon," if it meant more than a week or two, would be too late. One "soon" miraculously followed another. No more "soon" was all I wanted.

I told Jan to find someone who listened to the news reports from the BBC. Hardly anyone had an illegal shortwave radio, and among the few who did, he said, "Who do you think will admit to a militiaman that he listens to forbidden broadcasts?"

He held me close, and his eight calloused fingers felt like salve on a wound as he stroked my cheeks. We were too exhausted to talk or move. "I'll be back," he said before he left.

❖ 28 ❖

When Sidor came to bring us some bread and muttered something about February coming to an end and "bringing an end to everything," I realized that Jan had not come by since sometime in January. Then one evening he arrived by horse and wagon with his friend Stasiek.

This was the same Stasiek who had sat behind me in class and had rolled up and pinned my hair so the commissar teacher wouldn't pick on me. Stasiek was one of Jan's sources of food for us — he would take the food from his mother. Now he had consented to come in the wagon, since Jan had trouble getting past the patrols alone. He waited in the house with Sidor and Marynka.

Jan and I sat opposite each other in the barn on bales of hay, and he reached for my hand. I knew I stank to high heaven, but so what.

"The news is bad," he said. "The Russian offensive to liberate the Ukraine has stopped." He spoke in a monotone, as if he were talking about shoe leather: that's what had been delivered, take it or leave it; it was all the same to him. Shoes were on my mind since the rags around my feet were giving out. When the Russians came, I would have to try to get some shoes.

"Fancia, you're not listening." It was true. I didn't want to hear what he was saying. He was telling me about Zhenia.

"Her SS man's superior officer threatened him with a court-martial for fraternizing with a subhuman Jew. The SS man vindicated himself by driving her to the town square, where he threw her out of the truck like a sack of potatoes, shouting, 'Run, dirty whore!' She tried to but did not get far. He shot her in the back."

"You saw this?"

"Yes. The whole town was there, laughing and jeering." Jan's face, unshaven, gray — the eyes sunk deeper in their sockets than I had remembered — set into a blank expression.

"They tore her clothes off and ..." His voice gave out.

He held both my hands in his, and as I looked down at the dirt encrusted on my skin and under my fingernails, I thought of Zhenia's hands the day of her sixteenth birthday. Her parents had given her a gold ring with a tiny ruby.

From his pocket Jan pulled a salmon-colored scarf with a geometric print.

"It's Zhenia's," he said. "Stasiek put it aside for you when her things were given away to the Ukrainian militiamen and peasants." It was not a scarf I recognized — German-made, good quality raw silk. I held it to my nose to inhale the faint scent of floral perfume which clung to it — the last evidence I would ever have of Zhenia's life.

Jan, who had always dragged me up from the depths of despair, sat there looking so forlorn that I felt I had to do something.

"Let's lie down," I said.

He stood up.

"I'm going out with a girl, the daughter of my father's friend." He spoke as if repeating a lesson he had learned, though not very well.

"What do you want me to say? Congratulations?"

"Look, you know I don't want to. You're the one I love. I'm still known as a 'Jewish uncle.' At my cousin's funeral, the priest said right out that I wasn't needed there. Nobody has enough to eat. This girl's family is well-off." He spelled it out for me as I sat there, the tears running down my cheeks. I didn't want to use Zhenia's scrap of silk to wipe them, so I let them drip off my chin.

"You're not coming anymore?"

He kissed me. He belonged to someone else now.

At the barn door, even after he opened it a crack, he came back and took me in his arms. He kissed me again. So, he had really lost all hope.

"What's the news?" my father asked as I crawled back into our coop.

"Not much." I told him that the Russian advance had halted. It hardly seemed to matter.

My father wanted to know how soon Jan would come again and I shook my head, but of course it was too dark to see.

"What day?" He prodded me, his finger jabbing my shoulder like a stick. "What day?"

I made him understand that it was over.

Now that Jan would not be coming anymore and whatever he might send would amount to next to nothing, even asking for war bulletins came to seem absurd. No more pleading with Sidor to prevent Marynka from getting her pair of boots; no more saving a bit of bread for later. From then on, we existed from moment to moment.

The chickens, our only clock, informed us of the full turn of the earth, but sometimes I heard them and believed it was only a dream. I was in a stupor. Most of the time I didn't know where I was and could not keep hold of the days. I stopped thinking and existed on a battery that required the most minimal charge.

I knew my name and that my parents and Arthur were within arm's-reach. They seemed less palpable than my vivid imaginings of that earlier time when I had lived at home and went to school. I would see myself, perpetually thirteen, wandering around the garden and cleverly evading my mother's commands to come and help her in the house. It seemed vitally important that I remain alone and not reveal my hiding place in the lumber pile. I would fear my book was lost, but then it always turned up and I would be floating in the world of a story that never reached its end.

I tried desperately to keep my eyes open in the murky dark of the hiding place, since keeping them closed, an easier choice, led to restless sleep. Waking from either a short doze or a longer slumber left me feeling shattered. I frequently woke from a repeated dream: a bare tree standing alone in the tundra after a cataclysmic storm, one twisted branch on the icy ground still tossing in the wind.

Each time I floated up into full consciousness after sleep or lolled out from limbo, I registered faint surprise that my body was not yet a corpse, that my life wasn't yet over. Once in a while, my mother still offered me a "wash rag" on which she had dribbled a few drops of water so I could wipe my face, but I refused it.

Since my rational mind had quit, and only the vestigial after-twitch of what had governed me remained, I have no recollection of that time. I can only compare it to the apathy that takes over when a person who knows for a fact that she is about to die, and is confident that nothing can be done to reverse it, lies back on the pillow and sails on.

VII

Liberation

Age 19–20: March 1944–July 1945

❖ 29 ❖

One day Sidor brought us a bowl of water in which beets had been
boiled.

"It's all I have to give you." I heard in his choked voice how much
this pained him. "Such a comfortable house you had," he said, "and
now you're squirming in that rat-hole."

Then his own chord of despair seemed to frighten him.

"Don't do anything rash." Suicide was apparently on his mind.
Some Jews had bought cyanide pills with their last zloty, and he didn't
know if we had any, supplied by Ulanowski through Jan.

I had brought up the cyanide alternative before my parents left for
the ghetto, but my father had been adamantly against it. Back then, I
had still believed it was noble to die by an act of your own will. This
seemed naive to me now. Though it would have saved us a year of tor-
ment, by continuing to live and suffer, at least we had not wounded
Jan and Sidor. For all of us, religion forbade it. Now the act had lost any
glamorous note of defiance or courage. Suicide was no longer necessary.
We would achieve the same result by eating only beet-water; it would
just take a little longer.

Sidor told us, "A neighbor asked me for advice. He said, 'When some Jews asked me to hide them, I consulted a Gypsy fortune-teller, who encouraged me to do it. Now the fortune-teller has been killed. Should I drive the Jews out?'"

"How did you respond?" asked my father.

"I advised him to keep them." Sidor chuckled. "I told him, with the fortune-teller dead, you no longer have to worry that she will denounce you and them. My neighbor went home happy."

One day, early in March, Marynka came at noon. The light pouring in through the opening, though filtered through the windowless barn, hurt my eyes. She asked us to come out and eat a bowl of potato soup which was still steaming on the trough. My mother told us not to go, but my father pushed Arthur and me out, and she followed us.

"Burial," said Marynka, "costs money — the wagon, the horse, the coffins. If you turn yourselves in, I'll see that you have a decent funeral."

I stared at her. I didn't know whether to laugh or cry. My father said nothing. Finally my mother put down her spoon.

"You know we have nothing. Why are you torturing us?"

Marynka said, "You have things stashed away, probably with Jan or Ulanowski. I bet you have jewels buried in the cellar."

My mother assured her, "You have already gotten the last of our jewelry."

Thinking of all the times I had imagined that in a few minutes I would be shot, my body defiled and then thrown into a mass grave, I found the idea of a funeral more like a ludicrous joke than an attempt at extortion.

"Marynka," my father said, handing her the empty soup bowl, "we're going back in now, and I promise not to mention this to Sidor." He knew she was afraid of Sidor; he had beaten her many times, once almost to her death.

"We'll see who has the last laugh," she muttered as she sealed us back in.

That night the temperature fell, and the quiet from the yard told us it was snowing.

Three days passed before Sidor brought another bowl of soup. It had been over two months now since the Russians had taken the city of Sarni and fought their way to the Dniester River.

"In a few days, perhaps even a few hours," Sidor said, "the Russians will arrive."

Marynka came by with a bowl of sour milk. I ate it and fell asleep immediately.

A heavy rumble and shouting voices woke me.

"Tanks," my father said. We didn't know whether they were German ones in retreat or Russian ones on the offensive. It seemed like a long time until Sidor came and removed the cover of the coop, but he didn't motion us to come out.

"Yes, it is the Red Army, but there are groups of Germans on the run who'd be happy to use their last bullets on you."

A loud pounding on the barn door stopped Sidor in mid-word. He closed the coop opening, and I could hear him tossing a few bales of hay against it. We heard the barn door open. German voices came nearer and mingled with Sidor's. Obviously they had shoved past him. Cut off from their unit, they asked to stay in the barn until nightfall. Sidor told them it was impossible, the Russians had already requisitioned it.

"See, we have no guns," one said. Sidor stood his ground.

"At least give us some bread," another said.

We heard the barn door close as Sidor led them to the house. Germans begging for bread perked up our spirits more than the vision of a thousand tanks passing by our door.

• • • • •

I burned to leave the hiding place. Something in me shouted for Sidor to let me out. It was an eternity until he came by. I crawled out, a worm, a spineless thing, and lay on the straw while Sidor hopped up and down with delight.

"You should have seen them," he said of the retreating German soldiers, "dogs with their tails between their legs. Dirty, one wounded, bleary-eyed. I directed them to the forest. The *Banderowtzi*" — the roaming partisan gangs that had arrived in the region from the forest — "will take care of them." He laughed so hard that I would have joined him if I'd had the strength.

Sidor went to Ulanowski to find out whether the war was really over. He brought home some butter Jan had given Ulanowski for us. Sitting at the kitchen table, eating the gruel in which Marynka had melted Jan's butter, I looked at the room and the familiar faces and felt neither glad nor sad. The phrase "it's over" was as empty as the prayer of gratitude to God my mother instructed us to say. Marynka and Sidor knelt down in front of the picture of Jesus to give thanks.

"I don't believe it," I said. "Maybe they'll come back." My only response to the news that the war was over was skepticism, which everyone jeered at except my father. Still, he decided that we could sleep in the attic instead of the hiding place. Foul hole though it was, Sidor thought to seal it up in case more fugitives would come poking around and find it.

"Why bother," I thought. "No animal except a rat would enter that hellhole voluntarily."

"The only way to clean it is with fire," I told Sidor.

"Burn it," Arthur said. They were the first words he had spoken in ages.

"It saved our lives," my father said.

I looked at Sidor, Marynka, and Hania. They and Jan and Stasiek and Ulanowski. All of them had saved us. What about them? Did only God and the hiding place get the credit for saving us?

Just before dawn, Aunt Sophia, Uncle Zygmunt, and Dolek arrived from the neighboring village. Their hiding place had been less than three kilometers away, but it had taken their weak legs several hours to reach us. We looked at each other, pitying the emaciated creatures we saw before us. The skin around their eyes looked bruised. "Do I have those eyes?" I wondered. What difference did it make? Looking at anything or anyone was an effort, so I fixed my gaze on the ground.

Uncle Zygmunt, Aunt Sophia, and Dolek slept on the dirt floor near the stove. Marynka stumbled over them in the morning dimness — on purpose, Aunt Sophia said — which I doubted, since they were lying in Marynka's path when she got out of bed.

"She delights in our misery," Aunt Sophia whispered, and recounted the "spiteful" way Wasil had treated them.

"Once a month he brought a pail of water so I could wash our clothes." Once a month! Ours hadn't been washed in six months! Aunt Sophia's contempt for "peasants" kept her mind off the lack of food, beds, and blankets.

Marynka's flour substitute, made of roots, resembled the powder used for concrete. She absently dragged her fingers back and forth through it and then tipped the canister for us to see the white worms that stuck to the bottom of the sieve. Turning it upside down, she gave it a few whacks to shake the last of the flour out and made a batter, which she boiled because there was no fat to fry it in. Each of us got a dumpling. There was nothing to scavenge for in the thawing fields, not even rotten potatoes. All the chickens had been bartered or eaten.

A few days later, while sitting in the kitchen and sewing yet another patch onto my father's jacket, I tuned in and out of the men's discussion. Uncle Zygmunt said they had to risk going to Skala to find food and a place to stay. Sidor cautioned against it, but my father, reluctant at first, agreed to go when it got dark.

"I'll go," I said. I knew all the shortcuts off the main roads. Adept at procuring food before we had gone into hiding, I also had the advantage of being able to speak Russian, German, Ukrainian, or Polish in case I was stopped. True, I didn't have any ID papers, but I could say the partisans had taken them. I went over to my father and, taking his hand, promised, "I'll be back tomorrow night."

"Out of the question," he said.

"That would be asking for it," Sidor added, meaning rape by the Russians. No woman was ever safe during the first wave of oncoming troops.

"I'll wear Sidor's pants and Father's jacket. Cut my hair," I ordered Marynka. She looked at my father for a cue, but he shook his head.

"She stays here," he said to Sidor. "Swear you'll guard them with your life. They are to remain in the attic, and Hania should stay with them there."

I was sure I would be just as vulnerable in the house as on the road. Banderowtzi swooped down on village or town and took what they wanted. No sport short of obliterating a German division would give them more pleasure than to roister through this place and kill a few Jews.

Suddenly I no longer wanted to be the tractable daughter. I decided to slip out at dawn when everyone was still asleep.

•　•　•　•　•

I groped my way down the stairs from the attic after only a few hours of sleep, but I was already too late.

"Zygmunt and your father left an hour ago," Aunt Sophia informed me.

In late morning I suddenly heard the heavens crack apart. Arthur and I ran out to Sidor in the courtyard. Above our heads, an aerial battle lit the sky with swathes of fire and smoke as planes zigzagged toward and away from each other. Neither Sidor nor I knew the German planes from the Russian ones until Arthur pointed out which ones had a swastika, which a hammer-and-sickle; he had spotted the insignia when the planes swooped in low.

My mother dragged Arthur back into the house, but Sidor and I stood there in the deafening roar, watching as some planes caught fire and nose-dived. It looked like there were more Russian planes, and they eventually chased the struggling Luftwaffe away.

I worried that the Germans were still not defeated. Perhaps they had come back to Skala.

"Your father has a good nose for trouble, but this time he's jumped the gun," Sidor said.

Annoyed with Sidor for voicing my own fears, I defended my father. "Look, he had to go. There's no food in the house. He'll come back or send Jan." Sidor picked up a stiff old harness and began to polish the badly corroded buckles with his sleeve.

"Jan won't come around for awhile," he said.

"Why not?"

"I didn't tell you. He ran into a German patrol the last time he left here, and they beat him to a pulp. He's not going to come again until he's sure the Germans are gone."

"But even if the Germans go, the Russians consider the Ukrainian militiamen collaborators," added Sidor, "which is why some have disappeared along with the Germans. And Jan's militia buddies are itching to beat him up for all the times he was nowhere to be found when they went out hunting Jews. And the Banderowtzi would love to get their hands on a 'Jewish uncle.'"

I understood that Jan was in considerable danger from every side, no matter who won the war.

Sidor put a brotherly arm around me.

"Don't worry about Jan, though. His mother and girlfriend watch him day and night." He threw the harness against the wall.

I started to ask "How can he help my father if he's . . . " but I couldn't find one word to cover everything.

"He will help in any way he can," Sidor said.

There was only one thing to do.

"I'm going to Skala," I said.

"Not if I can help it." The determination in Sidor's eyes left no doubt that he meant it. I had no choice but to wait.

That night I told Aunt Sophia and Dolek to take my father's and my place in the attic. I wanted to be awake when my father and uncle returned. I sat at the kitchen table and got up to shake myself awake whenever I began to doze off. At dawn Sidor came to sit beside me.

"It's too soon for them to return," he said. "Why don't you get some rest?"

But I couldn't rest until they were back in one piece.

Marynka gave me a sweater of Hania's to unravel, and I sat there, ripping and winding, watching the small wool torso on the table shrink bottom upwards as the ball of wool grew in my hands. There wasn't enough to make Hania another sweater, but I decided to start one anyway to occupy my restless fingers. Hania came to sit with me and I taught her to knit.

The day dragged on. We were distracted by our hunger pangs, waiting for my father and Uncle Zygmunt to return with food and news. Marynka put onions and salt on the table.

"Eat some of this," she said, "and drink lots of water." It worked. My stomach stopped badgering me and I resumed my knitting.

Arthur and Dolek found a rusty old bicycle wheel in the yard which they brought in and took turns spinning in creaky gyrations. Hania sat down beside them, hoping for a turn.

Those three days without word from my father and Uncle Zygmunt were like the period following the typhus crisis when my inert body seemed weightless, free to fly back and forth just below the ceiling of some unknown room. I seemed to be in that room again, but I kept crashing against the wall and falling to the muddy floor. My mind raced continuously with scenarios involving my father while my body, thin as it was, felt heavy. It was a burden to keep it functioning. By virtue of my gender I was a target of the Russians and thus constrained to be inert as a slug.

❖ 30 ❖

Late in the afternoon of the third day I could stand it no longer. I snuck out and set off for Skala. If I wanted to use the back routes I had learned from Jan, I had to go while some light remained by which to see the landmarks. Once I was out of sight of Sidor's house, some untapped strength helped me to jump over a stile and a high, jagged fence. I stopped in a ditch to retie the rags on my feet.

I saw a peasant carrying a sack on his shoulders walking towards me along a parallel path a few yards away. I knew he wouldn't see me if I flattened myself in the ditch. But the next moment I jumped up again and ran toward him. The country jacket and sack had almost fooled me, but his loping gait identified the man as Uncle Zygmunt.

I pulled him into the ditch.

"Where's Papa?"

His fingers, as he patted my hand as if to say, "Wait, wait, wait," had a clammy touch.

"Fancia, take me to Sidor's," he said in such a feeble voice that my blood ran cold.

Before I hoisted the sack on my shoulders, I peeked in. It was filled with straw. I left it lying there.

We sat at Sidor's kitchen table as my uncle told his story.

"Benjamin and I reached Skala three days ago and went to the marketplace. Jan ran up to your father, happy to see him again. In the marketplace square we found other Jews who had emerged from hiding, and we all shared information on who survived and who was killed. The worst news we heard was that Benjamin's brother Leo, and Leo's daughter Micia, were murdered very recently, just a few weeks ago, by Germans or Ukrainians, no one knew who actually did it. It was quite a shock to Benjamin."

Uncle Zygmunt continued, "We went over to a group of Russian soldiers who were washing at the fountain. Your father rushed up to them, fell on his knees, kissed their boots, and began embracing them and thanking them for liberating us. 'We're Jews,' he said. They didn't seem to care, but they gave us two loaves of bread." Uncle Zygmunt pulled a partial loaf from his pocket and set it on the table.

"Then, in front of the Russians and everyone else, Benjamin vowed revenge — not only for Leo and Micia but for all the Jews who had been murdered," said Uncle Zygmunt.

I had never heard my father speak vengefully, but perhaps hearing about Leo and Micia's murder, so frustratingly close to liberation, had been the straw that broke the camel's back. It was not like him to act so irrationally, and I hoped that, in his frustration, he had not done anything reckless.

"I could see women watching all this from behind their curtains, and men stopping and pointing at Benjamin and me. '*Zhids*,' they said. One called out, 'As cheeky as ever.' Another yelled, 'I thought we had gotten them all.'"

Uncle Zygmunt continued, "Benjamin hung around the Russians, listening to their talk about the Red Army's activities. I tried to tear him away but I couldn't budge him. I told him I would meet him at the fountain around midnight, and I left. That was the last I saw of him, three nights ago — at the fountain talking to a group of Russian soldiers."

"Did you return to the fountain at midnight, as arranged?"

"There were no bells, so I had to guess the time, but it must have been about midnight when I got there. I waited for hours, two or three at least, and finally went to Jan. What a beating that man's been given! Jan took me to his barn and told me that Benjamin had been there earlier but had already left."

"Where had he gone?" I asked.

"To Ulanowski. I stayed in the barn all that day. Jan said it was foolish to walk around in daylight because the Germans, encircled only by the Russian partisans who had arrived in Skala, had broken through the lines, killing Jews in town right and left. Ulanowski had told Jan that two Jews he knew named Finio Finkel and Chaim Gottesfeld — you know who I mean, he's not our relative, he's one of the other Gottesfelds who lived on the road to the brewery — had been killed over the past few days, after coming out of hiding. Their bodies were found in the road."

"So where is Benjamin? At Ulanowski's?" my mother asked.

"I don't know where he is."

Sidor shook his head. "Did you go to Ulanowski?"

My uncle nodded. "Yes. Ulanowski is still sheltering Dora there, the one whom he took in when her parents and sister were deported during the aktsia. He said Benjamin never came to his house."

"So where is he?" my mother demanded.

We stared at Uncle Zygmunt as he shrugged his shoulders. Then he shrugged again.

"I went back and stayed in Jan's barn the second day, too. That night, as I wandered about, I met a neighbor of Jan's who said that he had seen Benjamin leave Jan's place that night, but that's all he knew. I went back to Ulanowski. Ulanowski said maybe he went to Father Derewienko. I don't know. I didn't go to him. I decided to come straight back here. And then Fancia found me on the way." He patted my hand with his cold one. If there was blood coursing in his veins, it must have been like slush in an icy stream.

• • • • •

Sidor returned from the market in Skala the next day with a small sack of cornmeal he had bought on credit, to be paid for with hay in the summer. We needed food, yes, but I had sent him to Skala to find out where my father was.

The moment I saw the grim look on his face, I had the terrible feeling that my father was dead.

Sidor reported that he had gone to see Jan and Ulanowski, who had corroborated Uncle Zygmunt's story: My father had been to see Jan, left to go to Ulanowski, never arrived there, and no trace of him remained.

"What does Ulanowski say?" I asked Sidor.

"Ulanowski is very upset, not only about your father, but also about Dora." I knew Dora, a smart, sweet and affectionate girl in Shimek's class.

"What happened to her?"

"She ignored Ulanowski's advice that it still wasn't safe to go out. Some women threw stones at her as soon as she stepped out on the street, and one of them hit her in the eye. Ulanowski blames himself for not stopping her from leaving the house."

Sidor added, "Another young girl slipped out of hiding yesterday." He hesitated before continuing, "Well, she's dead."

How naive of me to have thought that the move from the coop to the kitchen meant that anything had changed. Almost all the Ukrainians and Poles wanted the Jews dead, whether the Germans were gone or not.

"Ulanowski calls it a 'false liberation,'" Sidor continued. "The Russians are only an advance force, the partisan irregulars. The Germans are back in Skala; they returned the day after Benjamin and Zygmunt got there. There's fighting going on right now north of town," he added. "The Jews were in a panic and ran to hide wherever they could. Some joined the Russians as they retreated from town."

A spasm of hope gripped me: perhaps my father had gone with the Russians. Maybe he had been forced to work for them, once again, as an engineer. Perhaps he was caught somewhere in a battle. Maybe wounded. Wounded is better than dead. Finkel's and Gottesfeld's bodies had been found on the street, but not my father's. Maybe he was still alive!

Sidor took my hand.

"It's not over yet," he said. "Jan says he will come by tomorrow and perhaps he'll bring some news."

When Uncle Zygmunt heard this he, Aunt Sophia, and Dolek went into the old hiding place in the chicken coop and asked Sidor not to tell Jan they were hiding there.

201

Jan arrived the next morning. He had a bandage over his ear. When he spoke I saw that one of his teeth had been knocked out. The small bouquet of early purple and white flowers he held out to me were wilted, but they perked up in a beaker of water.

"The battle is over," he reported. "The Russians are now firmly entrenched in Skala."

"Where's my father?" I spoke with such challenge that he answered me sharply.

"I don't know. I made inquiries and no one knows. When he'd arrived at my house he was crying," Jan said. "He had just heard about Leo and Micia. He told me he was going to get the guy who killed them. Maybe other people heard him make the same threat and repeated it. Maybe the guy who killed Leo got him first."

"Speculations!" I said. I looked Jan in the eye: "You shouldn't have let him leave your place."

Jan sprang up.

"Let him leave? I couldn't stop him! He said he had to find food. I told him I would get some in the morning, but he said no, that he was going to Father Derewienko while it was still dark."

That made no sense. First of all, it contradicted what Uncle Zygmunt had said Jan told him originally: that my father had gone to Ulanowski. And, anyway, why would my father go to see the priest, an arch-collaborationist, when the Germans were back in town and fighting was still raging? It didn't sound like something my father — whose strong instinct for survival had saved us on many occasions — would do. But after hearing about his making public vows of revenge against murderers, I wondered whether my father was being his usual careful self. Maybe he had put himself in danger in some way.

Uncle Zygmunt wasn't there to confront Jan; he and his family were hiding in the chicken coop.

Jan tried to comfort me, but I pulled away from him.

"I'm going straight to Father Derewienko," I announced. "I have to

202

find my father."

I waited alone in the priest's parlor — Jan would not enter the church that had kicked him out — until he finished his duties. Father Derewienko looked genial and healthy. His cheeks were red, and the war's privation had not diminished his big belly. He sat with folded hands.

"Please," I beseeched him, "you must tell me what happened to my father, no matter how bad the news is."

"My child," said Father Derewienko, "your father never arrived here. I have no idea where he is. But there was a battle north of town around that time. I suggest that you go look at the bodies that still lay unburied in the fields."

I thanked him. I did not mention the ring my father had given him for safekeeping three years before, and neither did he.

Jan offered to go with me to the battlefield to look for my father's body. As we approached the spot, the stench of rotting bodies penetrated my nose and throat long before the hundreds of dead came into view. Jan tore his handkerchief in half, and we tied masks over our mouths and noses.

In one corner of the field a crude, partially filled, mass grave surrounded by German battle debris indicated that the Germans had hurried away in the middle of burying their dead and left their soldiers' bodies to rot. Many were very young, Hitler's last fighters. There were also bodies of Russian soldiers and of civilians. The boots had been removed from the feet of some, and the ring finger cut off of numerous hands. Randomly scattered, the bodies were hard to sidestep. At first we looked at each face together as we turned the corpses over but after a few dozen we split up.

Some incalculable strength held me up, pushed me on, and kept me going even at the moment when I saw a button I was sure I had sewn onto my father's jacket. The button was on the ground near a corpse that lay face down.

I screamed and Jan rushed over. There was no shirt under the jacket. The torso had swelled, making the buttons pop off. Perhaps he was a German deserter who had thrown his uniform away and stolen the jacket from my father. Jan thought he was one of the Banderowtzi who had come from the forest to loot in town.

I bent down to pick up the button. "This thread is brown," I said. "I sewed my father's button on with black thread."

Jan took the button out of my hand and threw it away. "It's a common kind of button. Come. We'll keep on looking."

None of the other corpses or body parts offered any hint of my father. We had to give up the search.

Now all I wanted to do was to get washed. If it had been warmer, I would have gone to the river.

"Come to my barn after dark to bathe," Jan suggested.

"No. Your mother and sister have not changed," I told him. "I'll go back to Sidor's. You needn't come with me."

"I insist. A woman isn't safe walking alone with so many Russians around."

"Why weren't you so firm with my father?" I asked. I was furious with him. "You killed him! You let him walk out of your barn door."

"Is that what you think?"

We walked to Sidor's along back routes. Neither of us said a word. The dead bodies on the battlefield kept juxtaposing themselves in my mind with wishful thoughts of Jan wrestling with my father to keep him in the barn. After all he had done for us, why couldn't he have done this one last thing?

At Sidor's door he turned to go back. He did not say goodbye.

❖ 31 ❖

Two days later, the six of us left Sidor's and split up to investigate which Gottesfeld and Wasserman houses had not been occupied by Ukrainians. We were looking for one with a roof, floors, and a door.

My mother and I found some Ukrainians living in our home. In my Wasserman grandparents' house, the windows were gone.

Aunt Sophia had gone directly to her childhood home. Although the windows of Grandfather Azriel's house had no glass, boards had been nailed over them. We joined her there and settled in. Two sisters we had known casually before the war had appropriated one room. My uncle, aunt, and Dolek took another that miraculously still had a double bed in it. My mother, Arthur, and I improvised sleeping arrangements in the only other habitable room, the kitchen. My mother put together the remains of some old beds for her and Arthur. I slept on blankets on the floor.

"So, where is he now, when we need him — your bridegroom?" my aunt asked. It was said as a joke, but her tone revealed her scorn.

I had no intention of discussing Jan with her. "What do we need him for?"

"To help construct a new hiding place," my uncle said. "Even if the Germans have not come back, there are Ukrainians and Poles ready to finish Hitler's job."

"I'll tell you why he's not here," my aunt said, addressing my mother. "He killed Benjamin and he can't face us."

"No," said my mother. "Benjamin is in Russia. He's alive. I heard at the market that some Jews went off with the advance party of Russians when they retreated." She addressed Arthur. "Papa will write us. Or he'll send a message."

My mother put on the table the small cache of beans she had managed to wheedle from a farmer. I was carefully picking through them for stones when the two sisters, their bellies swollen just like ours, came in — they too had a small bag of beans. Who would use the single cooking pot first?

"Cook them all together," I suggested.

The women looked at me as if I had spoken curse words. Our family had six stomachs to feed, and the sisters had only two. We let them use the pot first.

The older one, in a gesture of conciliation, told me that the Russians were looking for a girl to work in the office of the Soviet military command located in the building of the former Polish garrison. I eventually got the job because I knew Russian and other Slavic languages and also because I was not a Pole or a Ukrainian. My co-workers were all Ukrainian girls who were eventually phased out.

Our job was to make lists of the local men of military age whom the Russians could draft into the Red Army — the war was still going on — and to write letters. There were no typewriters, so my clear handwriting was useful.

I also had to write autobiographies for the officers. The army constantly required them to update their autobiographies, but many — even the top commanders — were illiterate. Some had risen through the ranks as a result of their service during the civil war. Others had distinguished themselves as war heroes in recent battles with the Germans.

I met my Communist cousin while I worked in the army office. He had returned to Skala with the Russians and learned that his family had been murdered. He advised me to study medicine in Russia.

During my first morning on the job, a message came in: Jan was in jail. All the Ukrainian militiamen had been arrested as collaborators.

• • • • •

It upset me to see Jan lying on an undersized pallet of straw in a filthy cell the size of a small cubicle. I had never seen him hurt anyone, and even Uncle Zygmunt, who had disapproved of my father's trust in Jan, admitted that no one had ever seen Jan harming a Jew. Looting, maybe.

Through the grates of the cell I passed Jan some white bread I had obtained at lunch in trade for the coarse black bread we got at the bakery. My fingers were sticky with the honey I had spread on it.

I went to visit Jan in jail every day. I didn't tell anyone at home that I had been to see him. My mother asked me where he was, but I said I didn't know. On one visit it looked as if he had been beaten.

In a way I was glad he was in jail. Reprisals against Poles and Ukrainians who had aided Jews were being reported through the grapevine. Jan told me about a Polish friend of my father's who had given sanctuary to Jews in Czortkow. His car had been waylaid on the outskirts of town. The car was set on fire with kerosene while he was inside, and he died of his burns.

Once when I arrived to see Jan I found his sister already there. Before I could leave I heard her say to him, making sure I would overhear, "She isn't worth it, your little Jewess."

I had met his sister once before, at her house, when I asked her to return the suitcase of silk dresses and suits my mother had left with Jan. Of course she had denied that she knew anything about it. I also knew that she and Jan's mother had made numerous visits to the headquarters of the Ukrainian militia, during the war, urging them to find our family. His mother wanted me dead.

On the way home from one of my prison visits with Jan, some former classmates from Polish elementary school stopped me on the street.

"What, you're back?" they exclaimed, as if dirt that had been swept into the sewer had miraculously reappeared on the sidewalk. So far, fifty out of the fifteen hundred Jews who had lived in Skala before the German invasion had come back. For most of the townspeople, this was fifty too many.

We started to pick up the pieces of our lives.

Marysia came to see us in Grandfather Azriel's house. She kissed

Arthur, just as she had when she came to the attic of Jan's barn after the aktsia.

"Get the hell out of here," I told her. "You didn't want to have anything to do with us before, you didn't even bring us one rotten potato. We don't need you." I threw her out of the house.

We learned that Suza and Munio had been murdered only a few weeks before the Liberation. They had been hiding in a little village. Munio was working there as a dentist, making teeth for the Gestapo and for the Ukrainians.

The SS men took a liking to Munio so, when they got wind of orders to kill him and Suza, they warned him, "You'd better go, we'll be coming back in an hour." When the Germans returned, they found the couple still at home. They had not found anyone to hide them; with the war drawing to an end, perhaps they did not believe that the Gestapo would bother to kill two more Jews. But they did.

My mother and I went to the village and asked the Ukrainians what had happened to Suza and Munio, and were told they had been shot and thrown into a ditch, though they refused to tell us which ditch it was. We went from ditch to ditch, looking for traces of their bodies, but never found them.

After a week in jail, Jan was released and began to accompany me home from the Soviet headquarters as he had done when I worked for the manager of the count's estate. Once in a while the Ukrainian girls in the office whispered just loud enough for me to hear as we passed, "What does he see in her?" "He risked his life for her?"

Jan ignored the remarks. He would take my arm or my hand to show how he felt about me. I knew he was getting lots of flak at home. He told me that his mother and sister had suggested he move to another town because no one in Skala would want him to repair their shoes.

I'll never forget the eyes of the Ukrainian girls seated at desks at the Russian headquarters the time I submitted a deposition for Jan to keep him out of the army. As I entered the commander's anteroom, half a dozen girls stared at me so hard that I froze in my tracks.

"You came back," one said as if spitting at me.

"Look at her," another one said, "she has the nerve to show her face."

I walked right past them into the commander's office. He was not impressed that Jan had saved the lives of four Jews, but permitted me to fill out a form.

"Why are you so interested in this man?" He had a sophisticated, almost debonair manner.

"I'm his girlfriend."

"He's too good to fight for Russia?" he asked, elevating an eyebrow.

"Jan risked his life for years to keep us out of the clutches of the Germans and he deserves some respite," I told him. I knew that the gift of a watch would make my argument much more convincing, and I wished I had one to offer. But I knew that mercury — a cure for VD — was even more prized than a watch. "And I can guarantee you a vial of mercury the next time a pharmacist friend of mine receives a shipment."

Happy to see me alive, Moizesevich had beckoned me into his pharmacy the first week we came out of hiding. During the war he had supplied my father with medicine through Jan, and Aunt Sophia through Wasil. He was troubled that my father had disappeared.

Moizesevich had not had an easy time during the war. An Armenian who by name and looks could well have been a Jew, he had repeatedly been forced to prove otherwise by lowering his pants.

I knew to offer mercury because Moizesevich had told me that day, "All the Russians have gonorrhea and syphilis. Don't let any of them touch you."

I could not tell from his response whether the commander would have excused Jan anyway, but my allusion to a cure for VD seemed to have offended his dignity. Abruptly, he signed the sheet of paper releasing Jan from army service, indicating that I was to take it, and turned his back to open a file. As I walked out through the silent anteroom, followed by the eyes of the Ukrainian girls, I felt cloaked in a cape of triumph.

Avoiding conscription was the topic of conversation one day when Sidor dropped in, as he did once in a while, always with some item, usually food. This time he came to say that he had obtained an exemption because he had a job in the vodka distillery, which the Russians had geared up for full production.

Sidor declined my offer to make a deposition in his favor.

"They like me, the Russians," he said. We understood that he had already managed to purloin a stock of vodka to sell privately.

"You're not smart enough to cheat the Russians," I told him. "Be careful."

He laughed. "Marynka says the same thing."

❖ 32 ❖

When the Jews who had "run away with the Russians" during the "false Liberation" returned and told my mother that my father had not been with them, she concocted a new theory: Yes, her husband was dead, and only one man could have killed him — Dzsisiak, Jan's ex-fiancée's father. Early in the German occupation, when Jan had broken his engagement, Dzsisiak had let it be known that he would avenge the insult. My mother decided that he had.

"Everyone knows he's a drunk," she said.

The next Sunday afternoon, as we walked to Dzsisiak's house — which was not far from Jan's and, like his, near the old Jewish cemetery — my mother cued me: "You must make him see that we only want to hear the truth and that we won't report him." She had designated me spokesperson but, once we were sitting on the stiff horsehair sofa in his second-best parlor, she took over.

Even though Dzsisiak was a wealthy landowner and she an impoverished widow, she addressed him in the familiar second-person singular: "My husband was seen coming into your house and never heard from since."

Dzsisiak, a burly man with a pipe clenched in his mouth, said, "It's a lie. Benjamin Gottesfeld did not cross my threshold."

"I won't prosecute," my mother told him, "I just want you to admit your crime and I will forgive you."

"You Jews are worse than ever," he said.

My eyes wandered across shelves crowded with porcelain figurines and vases and rested on a gray earthen vessel inscribed with a large blue six-pointed star.

"My daughter didn't need Jan," he said. "She's well-fixed and has a bouncing baby boy." He looked me over, appraising my thin body for motherhood, and stood up. "Too many of you have come back," he pronounced.

We made a second outing to Father Derewienko's beautiful house next door to the church.

Without much formality, my mother demanded that he return the diamond ring my father had deposited with him.

"My dear lady," he said, a grin on his shiny red face, "the ring is not here. Your husband came and picked it up himself." He threw the doors of his large cabinet open as if inviting her to search through it.

"When?"

"The first week in March," he said.

"That is impossible," my mother told him, "because we were still hiding at Sidor's at the time and he couldn't have gone to Skala. And you told my daughter he had not been here."

The priest's expression made it clear that he took offense at being called a liar.

"Wait here," he said. He came back with a five-pound bag of white flour. "This is to show you that I forgive you for your unfounded accusation."

When we got home, Uncle Zygmunt fumed at my mother. "What are you trying to achieve, running off half-cocked to confront Dzsisiak and Derewienko? You are just asking for trouble."

A conflict had already been brewing among the four of us. Each of us — Zygmunt, Sophia, my mother, and I — considered ourselves in charge of the family's welfare, now that my father was gone. The day we had walked from Sidor's to Skala, my uncle had put his arm around my mother and said, "Now I have two wives and three children."

But my mother did not think my uncle had done all he could for our family, and suspected he still had some hides in safekeeping.

"He could roll up a nice skin and go to Russian headquarters and get them to find out what happened to your father. The Russians have methods of extracting information from people."

"From which people should they try to extract this information?"

I asked.

"Jan," she said.

"Jan! How can you even suggest that Jan be subjected to torture after he has saved our lives thousands of times?"

"Papa was last seen alive in his house," she insisted.

❖ 33 ❖

Except in the dead of night, our kitchen was a hubbub of movement and chatter. I could hardly believe the contrast when I remembered how we had sat pressed together in the coop at Sidor's, a four-limbed hydra-monster quiescent for six months, how we could barely be roused even when Rex barked his alarm.

Now the storm was over and yet the wind blew as hard as before. Survival required a new kind of daily struggle. Sleeping on the kitchen floor, hungry, in rags, lice-ridden, a turtle with its shell torn from its back, I felt exposed, half-blinded, ignored by the world.

My father's disappearance and probable death galvanized my mother, who had let my father take the lead throughout the war, into improvising ways to keep us clothed and fed. She directed me to pry wood moldings from the doors and windows and to barter them for food in the market. There was never enough wood to keep the house or even the kitchen warm.

The clamor in the market jarred my frazzled nerves; the pushing and screaming reminded me of the time I went for cucumbers and was nearly trampled by the starving mob — the day Jan had first appeared in my life.

One day Aunt Sophia heard of a shipment of coal and we rushed to buy some with dismantled window frames. When she heaved the sack onto my back, my knees buckled and it slid off. I assured her that I could carry it, but after the fourth try I had to admit I was too weak. We divided up the load and I used my skirt as an extra sack. A trickle of black perspiration ran down my chest, evidence of my feeble body's shame.

I knew I looked awful: I was badly underweight, and my skin had the pimply dullness it had acquired in the chicken coop. I still had lice, and Aunt Sophia continued to wash my hair with kerosene. And we needed something to wear to replace the rags we had lived in for years.

Aunt Sophia had found in the house two items of clothing: a long, black, shiny coat that had belonged to Grandfather Azriel and a black shawl of Grandmother Hinda's. We kept the coat intact, but I unraveled the shawl and used the wool to knit sweaters for my mother, my aunt, and myself. Then Aunt Sophia got back two kimonos she had left in safekeeping with a non-Jew, one blue and one made of black rayon. She gave me the black one. I promised a seamstress a hand-knit sweater if she would make it into a dress for me.

The day I picked up my new dress, Jan showed up with a pair of black grosgrain sandals with white-accented stripes and platform soles. I felt like an elegant lady in my new outfit. Jan said the sandals showed off my pretty legs. I loved the shoes and wore them everywhere except to bed. I refused to take them off even when I went with my aunt to sift through garbage heaps for leavings to put in the soup.

One day, a woman ran after us in a back alley and pinched me to a halt.

"Your shoes," she said. I was about to tell her that I hadn't stolen them when she continued, "I'd know those shoes anywhere. They were custom-made for my mother." Her mother had been killed.

I had no idea how Jan had gotten the sandals — maybe he had looted their home, maybe they had been given to him or to a friend to hide, maybe he had bought them from a looter. I had never asked.

Aunt Sophia hurried me away from the alley.

❖ 34 ❖

September, 1944. The new semester was about to begin in Czortkow, the nearest town with a functioning high school. It was important to me to finish my one remaining year of school and get my diploma. I decided to study in Czortkow and, around the same time, my aunt and uncle decided to move to Lvov.

Combing Czortkow to find a room for rent, my mother and I ran into her best friend from her business school days, Mrs. Axelrod. She was now a widow and lived with her bachelor brother. Since the brother, a doctor, had resumed his practice, and it gave them enough to live on, it was agreed that, with the supplement of a handful of kasha now and then, I would live with them.

Although the Axelrods welcomed me, I wasn't comfortable about living with them. The kasha my mother brought them from time to time hardly repaid them for my room and board, and I felt like a burden on their household. My mother had told Mrs. Axelrod that I was seventeen, not nineteen, and since the widow considered it her duty to act as a surrogate mother, she treated me like a child. She would shampoo me vigorously with kerosene to try to get rid of the lice I still had months after the Liberation.

Still, Czortkow suited me. The mental stimulation of schoolwork in the morning exhilarated me after three years of not having a book to read nor pen and paper for writing. The system was basically the same as it had been in the Russian high school in Borszczów — Marx, Lenin, military training, and encouragement to spy on fellow students, who included a few Jews with the rest being Poles and Ukrainians.

My afternoon duties for the Russians in their military headquarters, to which my school assigned me, were similar to those I had performed in the Skala commander's office: writing letters and dictated autobiographies for the constantly updated dossiers on the generally illiterate

Russian officers. From time to time an attractive officer would try to tempt me to visit a café with him, but I always declined.

Jan rented a room with a Ukrainian family in Czortkow soon after I arrived there. He told me the Russians were still arresting militiamen, and that the harassment for his being a "Jewish uncle" had not abated. He had found it difficult and unpleasant to remain in Skala.

I felt very conflicted about Jan — grateful to him for saving my life but tormented by the unresolved accusation that he had killed my father. Even so, Jan always waited at the gate like a faithful dog to walk me home.

"Who's that man who comes to pick you up?" one of the girls asked me during lunch. "Are you related?"

"Oh, he's just a guy who helped my family."

"He's so old," another girl said.

Sometimes, after work, Jan and I would walk to the marketplace, where the peasants had set up little booths with kerosene stoves, on which they cooked *pirogen* that we would eat as we walked around. Other times he would come home with me and sit in an armchair while he watched me do my homework or listened to amusing tidbits from the day's dossiers. Mrs. Axelrod would bring him a glass of tea. We spent Sundays walking, stopping at a café for a treat, before spending a few hours in his room.

We were still lovers but circumstances had changed and, with them, my feelings. I felt connected to Jan, I owed him a great debt, and we had been through life-changing experiences together, but I was more aware than ever of the great disparity in age, religion, and background. I had no one with whom to share my dilemma. My two best friends, Lotka and Zhenia, were dead. Shimek was dead. I felt isolated and alone.

Everybody in Czortkow knew about Jan and me, as they had in Skala; it was something of a scandal that he had saved me, that he was a "Jewish uncle," that he wasn't working — he was afraid to work for the Russians and kept a low profile — but devoted much of his time to watching out for me, as he had when we were under the boot of the Germans.

One sunny Sunday, as Jan and I were climbing a deserted hill, he told me that his sister had written him a letter reporting what people in Skala were saying about a Polish fellow from Czortkow named Stephan. The case had caused an uproar reverberating all the way back to Skala.

Stephan was already married when he fell in love during the war with a Jewish girl, a cosmetician who had studied in Vienna. Stephan had saved her and her younger sister's lives.

After the Liberation, Stephan had wanted to leave his wife — being Catholics, they could not divorce — and live with his lover. But she fell in love with a Russian officer and married him instead.

Stephan went to her apartment and hanged himself there.

Jan said there was talk about prosecuting her.

I began to shiver. For a moment I felt I was back in the chill dark of the hiding place. Jan sat down on a rock and motioned to me to sit beside him.

"I suppose your sister thinks the woman deserves to be killed."

"Her death will not bring Stephan back," he said. He chafed his hand up and down my arm to warm me up. "Her Russian general is a powerful man. I doubt anything will happen to her."

Jan draped his jacket around my shoulders.

"Why did your sister write to you about this?"

"Back in Skala," he said, "people who heard the story made fun of me, saying it would soon be my turn to be abandoned by my Jewish lover."

Neither of us spoke for a while. The stone I sat on was rapidly losing the heat of the afternoon sun. I got up to go. Jan insisted I keep his jacket around me.

"My sister," he said, "ended her letter with the words, 'When are you going to hang yourself?'"

•   •   •   •   •

I returned to Skala when I received word that my mother had pneumonia. When I reached her bedside, it was clear that agitation over my father's death, rather than disease, was making her ill.

"They say Jan did it."

"Who says that?"

"Everyone. People. Jan murdered your father."

"Do you believe it?"

"Yes, and you should too. We're too naive," she said. "You don't understand the depths of Ukrainian barbarity."

Were these only feverish ravings or a deliberate effort to drive a wedge between Jan and me? She liked Jan, I knew, but not for me. It astounded me that, when Jan came to visit, my mother treated him as one of the family. Yet she suspected him of murder.

"He lived near the Jewish cemetery," she said. "He could have axed the body to pieces and buried them in one of the graves. The dogs wouldn't scratch there like in a yard."

When I got back to Czortkow, I dreamt that my father's body had been buried and that I was compelled to find his grave. In the dream I searched cemeteries, scrambling over broken stones and ransacking graves, expecting Jan to help me, but I always woke up before he arrived.

One day, when I came home late after being delayed at work, I found Jan in tears and Mrs. Axelrod patting his hand. She cast a somber look in my direction. I could see she was upset.

After Jan left, she told me that he had blurted out his love for me and his fear that we would be parted. "He says you think he murdered your father. Is that true?"

I was angry with Jan for involving Mrs. Axelrod in our private life.

"It doesn't matter what I think. My father is dead. Jan saved my family, and I am grateful," I told her stiffly.

The next day, after work, I told Jan I wanted to go to his room. Usually I sat on the bed, but today I chose the wooden chair.

"You shouldn't have told Mrs. Axelrod about us."

I wanted him to look at me when I talked, but he concentrated on a spot on the wall.

"My aunt and uncle want me to come to live with them in Lvov." Aunt Sophia was urging me to finish high school in Lvov. She regretted that her schooling had been cut off early. She had been a good student and spoke Polish, Russian, Ukrainian, German, and Hebrew, and had a sophisticated command of Yiddish; she said she wanted me to have a good education. But her real motive, obviously, was to end my affair with Jan.

That got his attention. He looked up quickly.

"Are you going?"

Another departure, another gamble. Saying good-bye to each other while in hiding and now daily at the door was as much a part of us as clasping hands. Missing him had become a habit. Yet often, while reading or walking alone, I felt exhilarated in a way that didn't occur when Jan and I were together.

The idea of going to live in a big city frightened me, and yet the chance to meet new people beckoned. I thought of Lvov as a lake into which I could stick my toe, then watch the ripples fan out. True, I might fall in and drown, but on the other hand I might learn to swim.

"The school is better in Lvov," I said. "And my mother wouldn't have to pay toward my upkeep."

I had expected him to advise me not to go. But suddenly he was all plans.

"My cousin Elena in Lvov has a spare room I could live in, and jobs are much easier to find there. I'll follow you in a month or so," he said. I found his single-minded enthusiasm irritating. Here I was trying to distance myself from him and he wouldn't take the hint.

"You know," he said, "I care for you more than ever."

He got up and, tugging gently on my hand, tried to draw me toward the bed.

"I have homework to do for tomorrow," I said.

He wrote down his cousin's address in Lvov in case I needed anything. I watched him adjust his collar and jacket. I noticed, as I had thousands of times, how the dexterity of his hands triumphed over the loss of two fingers. The touch of those hands had become as familiar as my own, and at that moment I longed for them to stroke me. We kissed as if we had already decided to part forever. We both cried.

The following Sunday I managed to arrange for a place in an army truck going to Lvov.

Riding in the cab of the truck, I remembered the rides to and from the high school in Borszczów, squeezed under a lap robe between Russian soldiers, and how their busy paws had tried to pry a space between my knees. Those ordeals with the Russians had angered me to curses and tears, but I hadn't felt in my gut the fear of rape, as I did now.

The other passenger, a high-ranking Soviet officer, had offered me the window seat, but I declined. I decided that sitting in the middle, with the sober-faced driver to my left, might serve as a deterrent to the officer on my right. Of course, there was always the possibility that they were in cahoots and would take me to a deserted cul-de-sac. But the glum-faced officer made certain to leave several inches of space between us and, after a formal greeting, he ignored me.

Several hours later, coming out of a daze, I saw that the truck was stopping in a fairly large town. Empty barrels and litter in the square were evidence that a fair had been held there earlier in the day. Apologizing for the delay, the officer told me to get out of the truck and follow him. He took me to the back of an inn and instructed me to help an old woman who was filling up pails of water from a kettle.

I followed her to an inner room. Lit candles stood like sentinels around the nude body of a dead man lying on the table.

"An officer," she said. "The third one in two weeks." Although the sight of the inert body upset me, it was the agonized face that disturbed me most. The man, no older than Jan, had died in great pain.

"The Banderowtzi," she told me. "Like hawks," she said, flapping her arms to show how they swooped in from the forest to catch their prey.

The woman directed me to imitate her, dipping a rag in the pail and washing the corpse. We dressed him in a freshly laundered uniform, affixed his medals, and rouged his face. Then Russian soldiers laid the body in an open casket and carried it the long way around the market-place to the cemetery. A violinist, following the entourage of soldiers, played a funeral march by Chopin that would reverberate in my ears for years to come.

I stood between the driver and the officer, watching soldiers roll a large stone into position to mark the grave. Two others had already been planted nearby. The townspeople stood close to their houses in silence.

Back in the truck after the burial, the officer took out a bottle of vodka and offered me a sip. I took it, hoping that food would be offered too. It wasn't. When we got to Lvov the officer instructed the driver to take me to my uncle and aunt's door. After I jumped down from the truck, the driver, whistling the Chopin melody, executed a screeching U-turn so that, as I stood there, I could receive the officer's correct, un-smiling salute.

❖ 35 ❖

I had wanted to go to Lvov to test myself — to be independent, stand on my own, make my own way. I lived with Aunt Sophia and Uncle Zygmunt and Dolek in an apartment they shared with a few other survivors. The three of them slept in one room and I slept in another, sharing a bed with another woman.

Business occupied my uncle at all hours. He always brought home in his small portmanteau something to eat, to wear, or to put on a shelf, some object that was "better than money."

The late-winter cold of Lvov mocked my pleasure in wearing the now worn sandals Jan had given me, and my skin turned a mottled red and blue under my short-sleeved dress and thin jacket. Aunt Sophia presented me with a decent coat. My uncle traded a pound of butter for a pair of heavy, peach-colored stockings. Dolek had two wool caps and offered to let me wear one.

Still, I felt like an outsider. Often, when I came home from school at two or three in the afternoon, there would be leftovers from dinner for me to eat. I'm sure my aunt didn't mean to neglect me, but I felt almost like a stranger.

Mornings at school were followed, as in Czortkow, by afternoons working at an army office. For once I knew the latest war news. When we heard that the Germans had finally been pushed out of Warsaw, we danced among the desks.

In Lvov I had neither school friends — the few Jewish students were very guarded — nor an escort from work. It exhilarated me at twilight to strike out on my own down unfamiliar streets and trust my sense of direction to land me, eventually, back at my aunt and uncle's apartment building. Yet it was a sad time for me. I felt lonely. I missed my mother and my brother. And I missed Jan.

One evening, Uncle Zygmunt's nephew arrived from Skala to have supper with us. At first he was quiet, shooting quick glances at me as he ate his soup. He was about four years older than I, with heavy black hair and the insistent shadow of a beard under his bone-white skin. As we ate dessert, my aunt beckoned my uncle and Dolek out of the room.

The fellow told me he had lived through the war by remaining, day after day, one hayloft ahead of the Germans and Ukrainians. As he related his stories, I marveled at his luck.

"Luck, yes — and this," he said, tapping his forehead. He invited me to see a movie with him.

We saw a Russian picture with lots of galloping horses. As we stepped out of the cinema lobby, he suggested, "Why don't you come to my room for tea?"

"Thank you, I can't — I have school tomorrow," I told him politely.

He took my elbow. "Don't be a baby," he said, and steered me in the opposite direction from where I lived. I pulled out of his grip and walked away. He cut me off.

"You think you're too good for me." He looked as if he were about to spit at me. "You had a goy. Why not me?"

The next morning my aunt set a bowl of porridge in front of me. "Did you have a good time last night?"

"I enjoyed the movie," I said, "but why did you tell him about Jan and me?"

My aunt sat down facing me.

"Everybody knows. If he hadn't heard it from me, he would have heard it from someone else. Did you like him?"

I got up and gathered my books for school.

"Do you want to marry a goy who left school after the eighth grade? You can't tear yourself away from him?"

She gestured for me to sit down.

"I'm saying this for your own good. Jan saved your life, your parents' and Arthur's lives. So thank him. Finished. Do you have to marry

224

him?" Her voice softened as she saw my defiance turning to tears. "Why do you think I brought you to Lvov?"

"Look," I said, inching toward the door, "I wouldn't marry Zygmunt's nephew even if he were the king of England."

She called after me as I ran down the stairs: "A murderer! You want to marry the man who killed your father!"

Her words echoed in my head. She said them not as a question but as fact. What proof did she have? She wanted make me revile the hand that had saved me over and over again, a hand schooled in tenderness, a hand missing some fingers, a broad and calloused hand with a deep palm that fed me water when I was dying of thirst. "Every time he touches you with that hand," she was saying, "think of your father. Think," she was saying, "of who you are."

So I tried to give Zygmunt's nephew another chance. But I knew for certain that he would never win me over when he said, "I like you, but I wouldn't want to take your mother and brother with us."

• • • • •

The day Jan's blue-eyed, blond cousin Elena came to the apartment to invite me to her house — Jan was expected soon — I told my aunt that I would not be home for dinner. After work, bearing a can of preserved meat I had received from an admirer at the office, I knocked on Elena's door and surveyed the yard while I waited.

Elena and her husband owned a comfortable house with a big garden and a gazebo covered by grape vines. As I stood there, I looked forward to the warm weather when Jan and I would drink lemonade in the arbor, or Jan would repair some household object for Elena, and I ... I pictured my books spread on the table as I did my homework.

Elena opened the door. I was expecting that she would want me to help prepare a party to welcome Jan, but her sorrowful face alarmed me.

"No, nothing has happened to Jan," she said. She placed me in a chair and sat down next to me. "Not to him but ..." She couldn't speak for a minute. Finally, after I comforted her for her undisclosed grief, she said, "Your mother, it's your mother."

"What? What happened to my mother? Is she hurt?"

"She's dead. She was killed in the forest."

I fainted. As I came to I felt a pain in my side where I had bumped my hip on the table as I fell. Elena was applying a wet rag to my temple.

Elena's husband came in, followed by Jan, who rushed over to me. I began to cry, and he took me in his arms and rocked me.

"What happened?" I asked. "Tell me what happened."

Jan looked puzzled. Elena explained that I had fainted from the shock of hearing that my mother was dead.

"She's alive," he said. "I went to see her before I left and she gave me these for you." He handed me a pair of worn but warm slippers.

He saw that I didn't believe him.

"It was a mix-up." This was his story:

Once a month my mother traveled by wagon to the marketplace in Czortkow to sell tobacco leaves which she had bought from farmers. The rich soil of the Ukraine was perfect for tobacco culture. Merchants would dry the leaves, grind them up, and sell the tobacco to cigarette makers.

One morning the previous week, as my mother was getting ready to leave the house, Arthur began to cry and begged her not to go. She protested that they would have nothing to eat if she didn't go, but he made such a fuss that she stayed to calm him. Then, an hour or two later, she went to the spot where she usually managed to get a seat in a market-bound wagon. Her regular wagon had already left. She waited a while and was about to give up and go home when a farmer who was late for market agreed to let her ride with him.

When they arrived in the square in Czortkow, an agitated woman made the sign of the cross and said, "What, you're not dead?" The Banderowtzi had waylaid the first wagon, the one my mother usually rode in, killing the two Jewish women passengers, plundering their

226

goods, and letting the others go.

When he finished his story, Jan hesitated. "That's it," he said. I could tell by his face there was more, and I insisted he tell me the rest.

"They sliced off the women's tongues and gouged out their eyes."

"Why did they think it was my mother?"

"One of the dead women was named Gottesfeld," he said. I knew the woman, one of "the other Gottesfelds."

Elena came over to me with a pillow to support my back.

"I'm so sorry," she said. "When I heard 'Mrs. Gottesfeld,' I thought..."

For days I couldn't shake off the shock. I wrote to my mother asking if Arthur had been told she was dead. Yes, she wrote back, but he was all right. When she had returned and walked into the room, he had told her she should regard him as her savior and be grateful to him for the rest of her life because he had made her miss the first wagon.

❖ 36 ❖

During that spring of 1945 in Lvov, as the war drew to an end, my aunt arranged Sunday teas and produced a string of eligible men for me to meet. It irked me to be expected to encourage these marriage-hungry men.

Jan was not welcome at my aunt and uncle's home. He had moved in with Elena and we met several times a week, but he was still under pressure to pay court to the Skala girl he had wooed as a cover when he was accused of being a "Jewish uncle."

Some Sunday mornings I told my aunt I was going to a girlfriend's house to study but took my schoolbooks to Elena's. Though I didn't return until nine or ten at night, she never asked what I had done that day. I would certainly not have told her that I had dinner at the home of Elena and her husband and then spent a few hours with Jan outdoors or in his room. She didn't even know he was in Lvov until my mother mentioned it in a letter.

I had been planning to bring my mother and Arthur to Lvov as well. There were rumors afloat that the Jews of Skala and the surrounding area were going to be shipped off to Siberia. Aunt Sophia, Zygmunt, and Dolek had other plans — they were intending to work their way west to Paris, their first station being Cracow.

One evening as we were finishing supper, Aunt Sophia asked me, "Why don't you come to Cracow with us?"

"I can't leave school now! I only have a few months left until I finish the last term and get my diploma."

She had obviously thought about this. "You can finish there," she said.

"When I next visit Skala I'll ask my mother if she and Arthur want to go to Cracow."

"Not your mother and Arthur," my uncle said, "just you."

"I'm going back to Skala," I said. I took my plate and fork and put them in the sink. "Thanks for your offer. But I prefer being with my mother and brother even if it means going to Siberia. I belong with them."

I ran to my room. Dolek came in. "What's wrong?" he asked as I cried into my pillow.

"Nothing. I'm going back to Skala. I'm crying because I'm so happy."

Jan wasn't bothered by the news that my aunt and uncle were going to Cracow and I was returning to Skala.

"After Easter," he said, "you can come back here and finish school. I'll find a room for you in a house near Elena's."

"I'm not coming back to Lvov," I said. " I'm staying with my mother and Arthur." It meant I would be one semester short of graduating from high school, but I felt I had no choice.

He shrugged. "Then I'll move back to Czortkow," he said.

Back in Skala, I found my mother despondent because there was no matza available for the Passover holiday. Nevertheless, she showed how pleased she was to have me home by declining my offer to scrub the floor. "Sit," she said, "and read a book." Then after a minute she said, "Well, on second thought, if you could patch this sheet," and she held up a tattered length of fabric. "See if you can mend this so you won't have to sleep on the bare mattress."

The pair of heavy irons borrowed from a neighbor stood heating on the stove for ages before the drop of water I used to test them sizzled into steam. That meant they were hot enough to conquer the wrinkles in the coarse fabric. The steamed-linen smell from the crazily patched sheet I was ironing blended with the smell of stewing onions. I wandered to the window and saw Jan coming up the street. When Arthur saw Jan he jumped up, ran out to him, and held his hand as they walked to the door.

My mother sat Jan down and insisted he try a plate of her "chicken" soup, which merited its name only by virtue of a few chicken feet that had strayed through it. Jan pronounced it first class. I had to admit that my mother was an expert counterfeiter.

We speculated on how long it would take the Allies to defeat the Japanese. My mother said he must come tomorrow to eat the carrots he had brought, which she would add to the remaining soup.

This cozy family scene was heartwarming, but questions nagged at me. Supposing we had been able to make a Passover seder, and Jan and I had been married. Would Jan participate? Or would my mother banish him from the house? Son-in-law or not, I could not picture a non-Jew at our seder.

On the other hand, I had long witnessed Jan's presence in our family — my father's and Jan's heads bent over a plan for a hideout, Jan carrying my mother up the ladder in his barn, Arthur riding Jan's shoulders — all these and a thousand other scenes. The trouble was that these pictures were filed in a big box called "the war." Where did this box belong now?

None of us could bear to speak of my father. Our boat was continuing to float downstream, but its rudder had fallen to the bottom of the river. How were we supposed to steer without it?

• • • • •

Jan invited me to Easter dinner at his cousin Irena's house. His mother and sister would not be there.

"I'm surprised you agreed to go," my mother said.

"Why?"

"If the girl he's supposed to be courting finds out he invited you instead of her, there'll be trouble."

"Don't worry," I said. "Jan wouldn't invite me if it wasn't all right."

She stopped working for a moment. I looked at her and saw a gaunt-faced woman who had no use for her old headache bands, a woman determined to survive with her children and make sure they could look forward to a decent life.

"Watch yourself," she said. "Watch yourself when you go there."

Irena's small house was very clean, with whitewashed walls and a table large enough to seat the many guests. All were blond but Irena, who had black braids. The men were mostly heavily muscled except for Irena's shoemaker husband, who was short and skinny. The women wore blouses and jackets embroidered in the folk style.

I marveled at the variety of food on the heaping platters. The men, as they ate the soup, hunched down to it with the concentration of peasants just in from working the fields. I watched one woman probe her mouth with her fingers and pull a string of meat out from between her teeth.

"Don't you like blood pudding?" Jan's cousin asked.

I assured her I did and pretended to spoon it up with pleasure. But I could not bring myself to eat the blood pudding nor the pigs' feet.

They joked and gossiped. This was obviously a family whose members liked each other. Everyone tossed back glass after glass of vodka except for Jan, who had never been a drinker, and me. The frequent swigs of vodka contributed to the air of conviviality.

Jan had seated me next to him and kept one arm around my shoulders protectively until he had to cut his meat. When he replaced his arm, I wriggled to indicate that he should remove it. He ignored my hint. He was saying, "This is my girl" to these people who meant so much to him, as he had often done when my life had been in jeopardy. He seemed to be making a statement to his family that I was his real girlfriend, rather than the Ukrainian woman he was still officially courting. Still, I didn't like his showing that he owned me to people I didn't know, and I felt uncomfortable.

Jan became so engrossed in an anecdote he was telling that he removed his arm from my shoulders, and I pushed my chair back to escape the radiating heat from the stoked bodies. Several hours later, during which the eating and drinking never abated, and parochial anecdotes and references to family stories swirled around me, I dozed off in my chair.

"Do you want me to take you home?" Jan asked.

"We must bore her," someone said.

"No," another relative answered. "She passed out." Laughter erupted.

I told Jan I felt fine and that he needn't walk me home. Stepping briskly along the streets, I wondered what they were trying to tell me by the pressure of their handshakes as we said good-bye.

❖ 37 ❖

Of the fifty Jews who had trickled back to Skala, some were conscripted by the Russians and some, like Aunt Sophia's family, migrated west. About thirty of us were left. One day in May, when the Banderowtzi killed a Jew walking on the street, we could no longer ignore the signal that it was time to depart.

Skala, along with most of the area which had been Galicia in Austria-Hungary before World War I, was slated by the postwar treaties to become part of the Soviet Ukraine. The Polish government-in-exile and the Soviet government had signed an agreement to permit non-Ukrainians — ethnic Poles and Jews — to leave for Poland. Skala's Jews decided to go together to the recently liberated section of western Poland called Upper Silesia. The Russians agreed to provide a train for us.

Ulanowski, who was Polish, also decided to leave for Silesia with his wife and two sons. So did Moizesevich. He was Armenian, but his wife, whom he had married before the war, was Polish, the widow of a major in the Polish army. Sidor could have left as well, but not Marynka, who was a Ukrainian, and he chose to stay behind with her. Jan, of course, was not eligible to leave but said he would try to get false Polish papers and join us in Silesia.

We had a few weeks to convert the goods and provisions we had managed to amass, in the year since Liberation, into foodstuffs that could be carried in a pack. Since we had very little — several pots, an old table and chairs, two beds, a large zinc washtub, and a few articles of clothing — conversion was not difficult. In fact, my mother enjoyed reselling the items for which she had bargained so skillfully.

She baked crackers and loaves of bread, which she dried, and hunted in the market for flour, sugar and a good supply of kasha, which she cooked in big pots on the stove. She rendered fat and packed it into crocks sealed with wax. She also made and sealed jars of jam. All these foods were designed to last.

My mother's memories of hunger and starvation made her feel entitled to do anything necessary, short of the seriously criminal, to feed her family. She came home one day with a container of walnuts. "They were sitting on a window sill as I passed," she said. "Such a shame to let them dry up."

"Whose window sill?"

"Who knows? I don't know who lives there now. It was once a Jewish home." Her shrug said, "Let them come for me — my children must eat."

"How are we going to carry it all?" I asked.

"We'll carry it," she said. "If we don't have food to eat, it'll be us they'll have to carry."

Day after day I debated whether I should go to Jan's cousin Irena to leave word for him that we were going, or should simply leave and write him later. He hadn't come to see me, written, or even sent a message since Easter.

A few days before our scheduled departure, Sidor dropped in to bring us some bread. He asked about Jan.

"I haven't seen him for a while," I said.

He paused in the middle of fitting a cardboard insole into Arthur's shoe, and gave me a long look. "Is he getting married?"

"I don't know," I said.

Sidor understood. At least with him I didn't have to pretend not to care.

Sidor promised to come by with some vodka before we'd leave. "You'll take it with you," he said. "It's as good as money."

My mother gave him our large zinc washtub. I could see that he didn't want it but was too polite to refuse.

"Do you expect me to carry it home on my head?" he asked.

"Marynka will want it," my mother insisted.

"If you say so," Sidor acquiesced. "I'll come in my wagon next time.

I have a strong new horse I want you to see."

As Sidor closed the door behind him, my mother burst into tears. "We have nothing to give him."

I couldn't keep my own tears back. After all the promises to Sidor and Marynka, we were giving them a washtub! And riches from Paris? We had no way to know whether Aunt Esther and her family were even still alive.

"Tonight we'll dig again," I said to my mother as I brought her a glass of water. "Perhaps last time I was still too weak and didn't dig deep enough."

One dark night, soon after we had come out of hiding, my mother and I had gone back to the yard behind our old house to dig for the silver utensils my father had buried there. But we hadn't found even a trace of one.

My mother brightened at my suggestion. "Yes. I'm sure Papa buried six silver schnapps glasses near the big tree."

We set out at three in the morning. A quarter-moon shed more light than I would have liked, since it was a clear night. The people who had taken over our house could beat or shoot us for trespassing. I didn't care.

I carried a pick in a sack so no light would glint off the blade. My mother brought along a pot lid to use as a trowel. We worked until the sky paled with first light. My mother, too exhausted to continue, sat down on a pile of earth.

"It's no use," she said. "Someone was here before us."

I shoveled dirt back into the last hole. We had nothing with which to pay Sidor. He had never asked for payment, but even a sack full of silver objects couldn't begin to compensate him for what he had done to save us.

It was too bad, in any case. Marynka would have liked the silver schnapps glasses. Under my breath I cursed the thief who had stolen them.

• • • • •

235

Early in the morning, two days later, I slipped out of the house before anyone else was awake. Irena had brought a message from Jan the day before: he wanted me to meet him in her garden at eleven.

As I pulled the door shut behind me, I felt the kind of May warmth that erases the last vestiges of winter chill and presages blue skies for the approaching summer.

Soon I would be leaving Skala for good, and I wanted to take a farewell tour of all my old haunts. My first stop was the Hebrew school, now an empty shell, and its library, which had been totally ransacked. The Germans had taken away whatever the Russians had left behind — all the books were gone. On the road to the count's estate, now bejeweled with late-spring flowers, along the same route I had walked to deliver sweaters to the estate manager, the turmoil of feelings that used to attack me hovered over me like a dark cloud.

The cloud darkened when I climbed up to the Turkish Tower, as I had often done before the war with Lotka, Zhenia, or Izio. My two best friends were dead, Shimek was dead, and I hadn't seen Izio since the Liberation.

As I sat surveying the stones of the fort and the newly green countryside, an overflow of tears diverted me from even these losses to a question that came often. Why me? Why had I been spared? Kicking stones on the path back down, always easier to descend than to climb up, I marveled that the road had not altered, that the flowers still grew in profuse clumps, that the duplicitous landscape revealed no hint of what had happened here during the last four years.

Passing the public park, the bandstand where I had often listened to military marches, and the Cukernia café where Grandfather Azriel used to buy me treats, I ended up at the railroad station where the same grandly mustachioed stationmaster, who had been on duty for as long as I could remember, still presided. He was standing on the platform, brandishing the same red flag he had always used to signal approaching trains, but now I saw in his signal a different message than I had as a young girl. I used to think it meant, "Stop, stop in Skala, the best place in the world!" Now, as an express train rushed through, I thought he must be saying, "Go, pass Skala by, keep moving, go west."

I walked back through town to the central square, hastening to pass the houses of former classmates from the Polish school. On my last day in Skala, I didn't want to run into any of them. Too often since the Liberation I had heard their incredulous and disappointed words, "So you've come back!"

Skala seemed like a ghost town. The houses on the main avenue where we had lived were deserted, their doors and windows gone. They seemed to totter, uprooted from the ground. In the debris of one house, I found a small, badly torn book, the only evidence that people had once lived there. I slipped it into my pocket and walked on.

When I got to Irena's, Jan was waiting for me in the gazebo.

Jumping up, he rushed toward me and kissed me and held me, and during that time in his arms I thought, "Yes, it's all right, we're together, nothing has changed."

He held my hand as Irena brought us bread, cheese and strawberries. He said he had moved permanently to Czortkow and was working as a day laborer, doing carpentry or digging ditches, whatever he could get. "Sometimes, when I look up from the muck I'm standing in and see a high school girl pass with books in her arms, I remember our afternoon walks."

"Remember that time when I forgot my books behind a rock and we had to walk back all those kilometers to get them?"

"Yes, and you looked behind the wrong rock and started to cry because they weren't there."

We laughed and he stroked my hand. "The Banderowtzi could have found us there, and that would have been it," I said.

"Not for us. We lead charmed lives." Jan leaned back on the wooden bench. "I'm going with that girl." He looked at me as if by looking deep into my eyes he could discover how I felt. "I go to see her, but it doesn't mean anything."

I nodded.

"I'm not getting married. I promise you that. Not till the war is over."

I wondered, "Does he mean to her or to me?" but I decided it didn't matter today, not on this fine spring day.

He said, "Silesia is so ugly, and everything reeks of coal dust, even the grass. You have to guard against tuberculosis." He put his arms around me again and began to cry. His warm tears soaked my neck and collar. For a while I managed to hold back, and then I cried too. We would never see each other again, that's what today's sunshine was about: a distraction, a screen so that I would not be able to look at the loneliness ahead. I felt I was leaving part of myself behind.

The flint floor of the gazebo served as our couch, a reminder that our love had often had to make do in harsh places and live stubbornly in stony ground.

Jan stopped to cut an early rose for me when we walked around the garden, talking about the budding trees. He led me back to the gazebo and drew a folded velvet cloth from an inside jacket pocket and put it in my hand. It held something hard, a gold ring, a plain band of gold.

He kissed me and put it on my finger. He looked into my eyes with that intensity of his, a wordlessness that spoke of too many words, and then he turned and walked away.

❖ 38 ❖

I looked for Jan at the station the day we left. I knew it was a working day and that Czortkow was forty-five kilometers away, but still I half expected him to come see me off.

The commotion of departure from our birthplace, from the dead we were leaving there, required us to keep an attentive eye on the bundles at our feet. The Russians had sent roofless cattle cars, not passenger cars with seats.

"Maybe they will bring us luck," someone said. We had heard confirmed stories of the Banderowtzi stopping passenger trains, dragging Jews out and shooting them.

Just as I began to load our things into the train, Irena tapped me on the shoulder.

"Jan is sorry that he can't come himself but he sent you a going-away present." She put a small box in my hand. I didn't know what to say. She shook my hand hard and left.

I walked around the corner of the stationhouse to open Jan's gift in private. The box itself was covered in prettily patterned, faded paper. Inside it were five gold coins, a small fortune. I decided that I would keep them and use them only as a last resort, to save us from mortal danger. It reassured me to have some money in case of an emergency.

We hadn't been told where in Silesia we were headed, only that the trip need not take more than a day. It lasted for four weeks. The train had wheels but they hardly ever turned. Most of the time we were shunted off on a siding so that trains with higher priority could use the tracks. After rolling along for fifteen minutes one day, we would sit derailed in an adjoining field for the next three. Once, after many days' travel without making much progress, we stopped briefly at a station where everyone fought to get to the water basin and the rain barrel. Several times we heard horses' hooves when the train had ground to a halt, and I was sure the Banderowtzi were coming for us.

Some people ran away, saying it was a doomed train. Others fell sick, and a few died. My mother's cache of food saved our lives on that four-week journey.

One day in the fourth week, my mother fell into a fit of crying and rebuffed my efforts to comfort her. She crawled around on her hands and knees, sweeping the straw on the floor from side to side. She refused to tell me what she was looking for.

Finally she stopped and slumped, motionless, on the floor. Looking at her, I saw what I must have looked like. Her hair stuck together in clumps and the blotched skin of her face reminded me of the dirt in Sidor's hen yard. Our clothes were filthy and had hardened from dried perspiration.

She spoke slowly: "I lost it. I'll never forgive myself. How could I lose it?" And she began to search the straw again.

Finally she told me what "it" was: Jan's gold ring. I had given it to her to wear because it fit her finger, and because her own wedding band had been traded away ages ago, and because it reminded her of my father.

"When did you lose the ring?" I asked.

"I'm not sure. It got stuck on this hook when the train lurched forward. Maybe it slipped off when I pulled my finger off the hook."

I was upset. "You could have lost a finger."

Then she came up with another theory: "Maybe it slipped off when I was putting preserves on the bread. Then it must be over here." She searched some more.

I tried to hold her. "Ma, forget the ring. We don't need it. It doesn't matter." She pushed me away.

I blamed myself for not having worn it around my neck on a string. I had been conflicted over the ring, which was probably why I was so eager to give it to my mother when she asked me for it. I felt uncomfortable about the ring from the start, not knowing where it came from, or whose it had been. Jan did not tell me where he had gotten the ring, and it hadn't occurred to me to inquire, but, when my mother asked, I saw immediately that she suspected that it was stolen goods: a Jewish ring, perhaps, taken from the finger of a dead German or Ukrainian, maybe from a hacked-off finger like those we had seen on the battlefield. Whether Jan had himself taken it off a corpse or had merely bought it from someone else who had — it came to the same thing. I regretted not giving the ring back right there in the gazebo. It was the May weather that had befuddled me.

Neither did I know what the ring symbolized for Jan. When he gave it to me I had not realized that the ring was a wedding band, and that Jan was implying something by putting it on my finger. According to old folk beliefs and medieval Christian practice in Eastern Europe, a man could marry a woman simply by saying "I marry thee" and putting a ring on her finger. No witnesses were required, as they were in Jewish marriage ceremonies.

My mother's voice shook me out of my reverie. "Jan gave you the ring for all of us. With it we could have bought papers and gone to Paris. Now we have nothing."

I hadn't shown my mother the five gold coins. Now I gave them to her. They eased her upset, but every once in a while she again reproached herself for losing the ring.

The train stopped. As usual, we were in the middle of nowhere. Someone said, "I smell coal." Indeed, we were finally in coal country, which meant we must be nearing our destination.

"After everyone gets out, I'm going through the straw one stalk at a time," my mother said. "I have a feeling it's still in this car."

But I knew the ring was gone forever. Gone with our house, our beautiful candlesticks, the ring we had given Derewienko, the buried schnapps glasses and tea holders, the shimmering silk dresses and Parisian suits. Gone with the life we'd had before the war. Gone with the aunts and uncles, the cousins, the friends. Of everyone and everything we'd had in Skala, only Jan remained. And now I had lost his ring.

I told myself that losing it didn't mean that Jan was lost too. The rose he had given me in the garden — that I still had. I had pressed it into the small, torn book I had found on my last walk through Skala.

We arrived at the barracks of the DP camp in Bytom with the little book, a sack with what little was left of the food we had taken on the train, Grandfather Azriel's old coat, and a comb that could make no headway through our tangled hair. And the five gold coins.

VIII

Displaced Persons in Bytom

Age 20–21: August–December 1945

❖ 39 ❖

J an had warned me that Bytom would be bleak, but I was still unprepared for the black skin on every house, every street, and even on the children playing in the coal-smutted alleys. The black grass in the park didn't discourage the pigeons, who were a shade lighter. There weren't many of them, and they were never offered food. There was none to spare.

There was little for sale in the shops other than glass objects emblazoned with the Bytom insignia in black, red, and gold: a man with a pickaxe chipping at a wall of coal and, joined to it, a German eagle ascendant. Bytom had been part of Germany before and during the war.

The DP camp consisted of wooden barracks with large dormitory halls. Day after day, people lay motionless on their cots, small islands of despair and sorrow marooned by exhaustion, by malnutrition, and by illness. Some committed suicide. Others — including the families of Ulanowski and Moizesevich with whom we shared advice and information in the camp — left as soon as they could get away.

My mother, a tireless provider in Skala, was disoriented by the trip, the camp, and the unfamiliar people, and contented herself with monitoring Arthur and talking to other survivors.

It was tempting to give in to this lassitude, and keeping busy was the only antidote. I followed up on the leads my mother heard from the grapevine as to where to apply for myriad necessities, from soap to exit visas. My fluency in German came in handy for my daily trading activities. Once a week I stood in line at the offices of the Joint Distribution Committee for our food package, setting aside the bare minimum we needed for ourselves and bartering the rest. If there was flour I converted some of it into fat, tinned meat into bread, and so on. We supplemented our meager diet with the remains of the food we had brought with us from Skala.

A letter arrived from Aunt Sophia in Cracow. She had finally heard from Aunt Esther in Paris. All the members of our family were alive. They had, by some miracle, received my father's postcard, sent before the aktsia. On his coded advice, instead of reporting for deportation to Poland, they had fled to Vichy, and later went into hiding when the Germans took over "unoccupied" France. The postcard had saved the lives of my Paris aunts, uncles, and cousins, Esther wrote. They had all survived the war.

Aunt Sophia added that she had told Aunt Esther where we were and that she, Uncle Zygmunt, and Dolek were leaving for Salzburg in Austria.

When we had arrived in Bytom, a letter from Jan had been waiting. The battered envelope had made the journey in half the time it had taken us. No word from us for so long had worried him.

I knew I should answer Jan's letter. This refrain would nag at me as I trudged across Bytom on some errand but I promptly forgot about it whenever I returned to the camp. I kept the past — Jan and Skala and all that had happened in the last three years — wrapped up and slung over my shoulder, carried on my back where I didn't have to look at it. It was still vivid in my mind, but it was of no use to me in Bytom.

•　•　•　•　•

The first priority was to find us a place to live. At the market, an old woman speaking very poor Polish asked if I would be interested in exchanging an occasional bag of flour for a room in a rundown worker's neighborhood. The fourth-floor walkup apartment had no electricity and one toilet in the hall for the tenants of the entire landing. I tripped on the rutted linoleum as I entered, but I took it.

When my mother, Arthur, and I arrived there, we found we would be sharing the place not only with its tenant, Miss Klampt, but with her six cats as well. Miss Klampt looked like an old maid out of a French movie — ageless and sexless.

"With you I can speak German," she said to me. Now that Silesia was part of Poland, she was afraid to speak German in public and her Polish was terrible. But our real value as her tenants was the weekly Joint package, stretching now to feed four humans plus the cats — all of whom were starving.

Her regret that she had not been rescued by marriage did not extend to her childlessness. "Cats are not as great a burden," she explained. Miss Klampt slept in the kitchen with the cats, and we had a little room overlooking a dingy courtyard, full of clouds of black dust whenever I stuck my head out the window to get a breath of air. Earlier in the year, while in hiding, I would have done anything for that privilege, but I didn't find this thought very helpful. My mother reverted to her old cleaning mania and her headaches.

Arthur was pleased with the cats. He had one friend who came over to visit but he was not permitted to play with the children in the courtyard. He spent most of his time at the window, watching them. My mother made a cover for the window sill to protect his forearm, but coal motes flew into his eyes and mouth. "Everything tastes sooty," he said.

Miss Klampt was an excellent seamstress but fabric was still unobtainable.

"Why don't I sew you a new outfit, so you can attract a husband who will solve all your problems?" she offered. So Miss Klampt made me a suit out of Grandfather Azriel's shiny black coat that my mother had not had the heart to barter away back in Skala.

Clothing was scarce, and I decided to exchange food items from Joint packages for clothes at the market in Breslau. One day I managed to hitch a ride to Breslau among the crates of machinery on the back of a Russian truck. At the market I bartered for a housedress for my mother, pants that could be cut down for Arthur, a man's jacket to sell, and some men's tricot shirts. Late in the day, dressed in everything I had bought, I wangled a ride back to Bytom in a truck carrying five Russian soldiers. My bizarre ensemble did nothing to discourage each one in turn from sitting next to me and kneading his hands over my body, which was insulated from sensation by the many layers of fabric. Eventually vodka, heat, and rocking on the bumpy roads put them to sleep. Another near miss.

It turned out to be a profitable trip. In the market in Bytom, my mother got more than a week's worth of food for the man's jacket and shirts. I kept one knitted tricot shirt, which Miss Klampt dyed light blue and made into a blouse for me. It looked smart with my glossy black suit, and Miss Klampt predicted I would now have my pick of beaus.

• • • • •

Winter was coming and I felt desperate. We had no money for coal or warm clothes for Arthur and there were no jobs available. I looked forward to snow, for a white cloud to cover the blackness of Bytom, but I knew my sandals would be even more useless in the snow than they were in the rain.

Arthur would go out early in the morning to stand on the long bread line, clutching ration stamps and money, but he often came back empty-handed. "No more bread," he would say with a shrug. Then he would go sit by the window and not move for the rest of the day.

I couldn't afford to buy the medicine my mother needed for her bronchitis. I nursed her as best I could, but her spirit appeared more damaged than her body. When she insisted that she had to go to a spa to recover, I saw that she had retreated into a prewar world of her own.

Miss Klampt, afraid she would catch my mother's illness, threatened to evict us.

Aunt Sophia and Uncle Zygmunt, writing from Salzburg, promised to send help when they got to Paris, but we heard nothing from them all that autumn.

Finally, I broke down and answered Jan's letter, writing how much I missed him. The minute I mailed the letter, I started to feel anxious. Did I really want to see him again? I didn't know — one day I missed him, and the next day I wanted to move on to new horizons. He had been the first man in my life, he was my security. He had saved my life, but did that mean I owed him mine? Was I supposed to give up my dream of studying medicine in Paris to become instead a Ukrainian housewife, cooking blood pudding and pigs' feet and hosting Easter dinners where everybody got drunk? We were so different; how could we be happy together? How could I be happy with him? I felt guilty for even asking myself this question.

Each day I wished my letter had gotten lost in the mail, and yet I ran to the mailbox to see if his reply had come. His letter finally arrived one morning when my mother's fever had returned and we only had enough bread to last for two more meals.

The letter carrier, who knew me by now, handed me two envelopes. I opened the one with the French stamps first and found, folded into Aunt Esther's letter, a fifty-dollar bill. Now we could go to Paris.

Jan's letter described the steps he was taking to get false Polish papers so he could join me in Bytom. So far, the papers hadn't come through.

"I know you want me as much as I want you," he wrote, "but I don't know if you'll have me." I groped for a seat on the stairs.

I thought of all the times he had held me through the night as I trembled with fear, how he took care of me when I was so sick, how we had shared our secrets in his barn and in our bed of straw in Sidor's attic. I thought of how gentle he was with me when we made love — how we had known each other for a year before he touched me, how I loved his rough and bony hands caressing me as the sun poured in. "You're so beautiful," he had said. I thought of how he had cried when he gave me the rose from his cousin's garden, an early rose of spring. I knew that no one else would ever love me in quite the way that Jan did.

My feelings for him — impossible to untangle from my deep gratitude — weighed down one side of the scale. And then, on the other side, I saw the image of a baby, my baby, the child I would have with Jan if we married, a baby with the face of my father — and a cross hanging from his neck.

How could I allow myself to have children with Jan knowing that they would not be raised as Jews? How could I betray my promise to my father, made when we were hiding in the chicken coop, that my children would read Shakespeare and go to Hebrew school?

Even assuming that Jan would be able to get false Polish papers, which was next to impossible, if Jan came to Bytom and began a life here, and I stayed with him, we would never get out of Poland. Nor could I return to Skala to live with him there, a lone Jew among Ukrainians who hated and had murdered my people. We would never be able to leave either place, we would never go to Paris or anywhere else. We and our children would live out our lives and die in this land of death.

How could I condemn my children to grow up in Poland or the Ukraine, the graveyard for millions of Jews? Not even a graveyard, for there were no graves. The Jews had been burned to ashes, and the ashes had turned to dust which permeated the air we breathed and the water we drank, as all-pervasive as the coal dust of Bytom.

I saw myself holding a baby to my breast, and my breast and the baby were black with the ashes of our murdered relatives. Black milk came out of my breast. I heard my baby coughing like Wolf and Malcia's daughter when she was ill with diphtheria in the hiding place during the aktsia. I saw Jan holding our baby and crying as the child went stiff in his arms and broke in two like a dry twig, then turned to dust which joined the ashes already suffusing the air and the water.

I went inside to sit on the bed next to my mother and cooled her brow with a wet cloth. In my mind I watched the scale seesaw up and down, back and forth, one end descending and the other rising. I felt paralyzed with anxiety and terror.

• • • • •

Arthur tapped me on the shoulder, jolting me out of my trance.

"Get up," he said. A man I had never seen before stood at the door. I was still clutching the two letters.

He introduced himself. "My name is Israel; I'm a good friend of your parents from Skala. For old times' sake and because you're such a beautiful girl, I'm going to do it for nothing."

"Do what?"

"Send you a nice man who wants to marry you."

The next morning, when my mother's fever went down a little, I told her of the matchmaker's visit.

"It won't cost anything," she said. "The husband pays anyway."

"But I don't want to get married."

"With nothing in the house to eat, you can afford to say no?" At least her mind wasn't wandering.

I told her about the letter and the fifty dollars we had received from Aunt Esther. She closed her eyes and turned away.

I found a man who could arrange three places on an illegal transport to Paris. I gave him the fifty dollars and promised we would be ready to leave on short notice. In the meantime, I thought I would humor my mother. I stopped at Israel's place and left a message that he could send the "nice man" to visit me some evening.

When I came home from my frantic outing, jubilant that we were due to leave within a few days, I found my mother delirious. She needed medicine and nourishment just then, not a train journey. I ran to get the fifty dollars back.

"Too late," the man said, "but I'll apply it toward a future transport."

Israel the matchmaker sent three men in rapid succession, and for each visit my mother insisted on getting dressed up, despite her persistent low-grade fever. I went to the movies with one, for a stroll with another, and to tea with the third. I answered their questions with restrained gestures and few words. All three proposed.

I picked the one who had taken me to the movies.

His name was Joseph. He was handsome — blond and slim, a year older than I, and religiously observant. He prayed every morning, ate only kosher food, and observed the Sabbath.

Joseph was sweet and gentle, and had a quality of innocence that appealed to me. He reminded me of a fawn who needed someone to protect and care for him; indeed, he had lived like an animal for the two years he was in hiding underground, and had almost forgotten how to speak.

He was originally from a little shtetl next to Skala — our grandparents probably knew each other. Joseph's mother had died when he was eight years old. His father, a descendant of the famous Rabbi Yom Tov Lippmann Heller, was a wheat dealer who, like Grandfather Jakob, had lost everything during the Depression.

After Joseph's sister had made aliyah in the mid-1930s, his father had followed. He had left Joseph with a married sister, hoping to have all the children join him later. The outbreak of the war made this impossible.

After the Liberation, Joseph ran away when he got word that the Ukrainians were looking for him because he knew what stolen property had belonged to Jews in the shtetl. He fled from city to city, first to Czernowitz, from there to Bucharest, and then to Budapest.

The youngest and only survivor among his siblings in Europe, Joseph had nobody and was very lonely. Learning that an old friend of his family had survived and was living in Bytom, he decided to find him. The old friend, a fervent Zionist, had been a lawyer before 1939 and, coincidentally, had been one of my teachers at the Russian high school in Borszczów. Joseph told him that he was lonely and wanted to get married. The friend sent Israel the matchmaker to see him, and Israel introduced Joseph to three girls. He hadn't liked the first two. I was the third.

When Joseph asked people about me, he was told that I was a nice girl, intelligent, educated, and from a fine family, but that I'd had an affair with a goy.

"If you tell me that you're a virgin," he said to me, "I'll buy you the finest Persian lamb coat."

I told him, "You can save yourself the coat." He said nothing more about it. He never asked me about Jan, not then and not ever, and I respected him for this.

Two days after we met, Joseph proposed to me. He promised to give me a wonderful life, to provide well for me, and he swore I could study medicine and become a doctor. He promised to help me take care of my mother and my brother. It was very important to me that my mother, Arthur and I stay together.

I told my mother I liked Joseph and that I was going to marry him.

"Are you crazy?" she said. "You know him for two days and you tell me you want to marry him? Your father courted me for five years; you want to get married after two days?"

But those were different times.

We were officially engaged a week after we met. Having lost both my father and Jan, I needed a man by my side as quickly as possible, so we were to marry at once. I remembered my father saying that if I survived, this was all that mattered. His wish had come true.

At the engagement party, my mother sat on Miss Klampt's sofa with her arm around Arthur, whose new shoes, a gift from my fiancé, tapped a tune on the floor. It irked me that money was being spent on a party when we didn't have enough for basic necessities.

"It's wasted money," I told my mother.

"I paid for it and I think it's worth it," she answered.

"You? How?"

She shrugged. "I used the gold coins."

Jan's coins! The coins were supposed to be our last resort, to be used only in case of mortal danger. My mother had concluded that all that was behind us now because I was getting married and my husband would take care of us. I thought of a gold necklace I had once seen around the neck of a Bytom woman whose sooty face and neck dripped sweat and bathed the necklace in it, and how the gold had looked as drab as lead. Perhaps my mother was right.

Jan wasn't in the room, but I felt his hand entwined with mine, as it had been so many times when we walked or sat or lay in the dark. I felt his right hand, a large hand which easily accommodated mine, and I remembered the feel of the callus on the ridge below the fingers. The callus had felt strange to me at first because the men and boys I knew, my father and Shimek, had soft hands, whereas Jan's were strong and bony. I remembered his left hand and the way I used to grasp its three fingers, my hand making up for the two missing digits, our hands an entity, a sufficiency of holding, a melding — like a marriage.

Now Jan's gold was paving the road to my marriage with a stranger.

Jan's gold flowed down our gullets and those of our guests, and the herring and chicken and cake his gold had bought tasted and smelled foreign to me, as if strange oils and spices had been used in their preparation. The schnapps, too, had the flavor of a fruit I had never eaten.

As the guests whom my mother had scraped together — anyone with even a remote connection to Skala — gave toast after toast to a fruitful union and a long life, Jan's coins filled our stomachs with manna and I tried to feel happy.

In a corner of the room, Jan's last letter lay unanswered, pressed between the pages of the torn little book, alongside the rose he had given me in Skala on our last day together.

And I rose to stand beside my bridegroom Joseph and accept our guests' blessings for a long, happy, and fruitful life together.

Epilogue (2004)

Joseph and I married in January 1946 and lived as nomads for nearly fifteen years. First we lived in Budapest, but we left because we were afraid to live under the Russians. We wanted to go to Paris, where I still had family and still dreamed I would go to medical school, but there was no guarantee we would be able to stay in France. Displaced foreigners had to report every four weeks to the prefecture, fill out forms, and hope for residency papers.

We lived in Munich and Vienna, among the very people who had collaborated with or sanctioned the murder of Jews and the destruction of Jewish life in Europe. Reminders of our recent past — a knock on the door, a barking dog, a uniformed policeman — all triggered irrational fears of impending danger. We lived in West Berlin, but the wall dividing the city and the proximity of Russian soldiers were a constant source of anxiety, so we moved to Holland. We were dispossessed, belonging nowhere.

Right after the war we wanted to go to Palestine, but the British had severely restricted the flow of Jewish settlers. Later, when we went to see Joseph's father in Israel, he said to Joseph, "*Mein sin*, things are not good here now. Life is hard. Go to America." But the United States had strict immigration quotas, and prospects for a grant of residency were remote.

Joseph worked very hard after the war. He was a natural business-man and a wonderful provider. He had little schooling but a good *kopf* and an infallible instinct. Everything he touched turned to gold. Joseph was a lover of beauty, and he became an expert in German porcelain. Together we collected all the beautiful pieces that have filled my home ever since.

Joseph and I were both deeply scarred by our wartime experiences, and we spoke often about our struggles for survival. "A variation on a theme," he said of his wartime experiences, "just a variation on a theme." I was determined to be a good Jewish wife and for a long time did not permit myself even to think about Jan and my past. I wanted a clean slate, to forget everything that had happened. Joseph's refusal to ask about Jan was a gesture of love and respect that endured.

In those early years after the war, we were both angry at God. We kept a Jewish home but, for a long time, were in spiritual turmoil, our belief deeply shaken. Joseph came from the more Orthodox family and his crisis of faith was, if anything, greater than mine. My father's values had been those of the *Haskalah* (Jewish Enlightenment) and I was raised in an environment that emphasized learning and culture above all else, including faith. But, for both of us, it took many years for our faith and trust in God to be restored.

Our first child was born in 1946 in a Munich hospital. I was still severely underweight and emotionally traumatized. The circumstances surrounding her birth were among my most frightening postwar experiences. I refused to surrender my baby to the German nurses because of scenes this evoked from my past — infants snatched from their mothers' arms and shot or beaten to death.

We named our daughter Miriam Wasserman, after my grandmother. Our son Benjamin, named for my father, was born in Berlin in 1957.

Jacqueline, named after Joseph's father Chaim, was born in 1959 in New York City, where I traveled to seek the expert medical attention — and hands I could trust — of American doctors. We hoped, as well, that having a child born in the United States would help us obtain permission to return there as permanent residents.

My trip to New York had reunited me with my mother and Arthur, who had lived there since 1951. My great-uncle David, my grandmother's brother, had left a successful business in Vienna, just after the *Anschluss,* and settled in New York. Selling women's blouses out of a tiny downtown shop, he had worked for years to arrange immigration visas for all of us. When the first two had come through, my mother and Arthur had sailed for New York from Germany in 1951. My mother remarried a few years after arriving in the United States and lived in New York until her death in 1982 at age 82. Arthur continues to make his home in Manhattan.

With David's help, visas for Joseph, the children and me were approved shortly after Jacqueline's birth. We arrived in New York, this time to stay, on February 1, 1960 and took our first apartment in Washington Square. Surrounded by other German-speaking immigrants, we began building "normal" lives for ourselves and our children.

Miriam grew up to share my love of art and now runs a gallery in London. Benjamin is a successful New York attorney. And Jackie, who fulfilled my dream of becoming a doctor, practices psychiatry in Los Angeles. I have eight beautiful grandchildren, whose kindness and caring for those in need are a reflection of their parents. My children, grandchildren, and brand new great-grandchild are a constant source of happiness and pride in my life. I write this not long after attending the *bris* (circumcision ceremony) of my first great-grandson, a joy beyond words for any great-grandmother, but especially for a Holocaust survivor.

● ● ● ● ●

I never got to Paris to study medicine but, once we settled in New York, I was as hungry for learning as I had ever been, and more. New

York offered a world of educational opportunities, and Joseph was generously supportive of my studies. I took courses in art history at Columbia University, where my passion was Northern Renaissance painting — the Dutch and Flemish masters of the fifteenth and sixteenth centuries. I pursued my interests in philosophy, psychology, and literature at the New School for Social Research, receiving B.A. and M.A. degrees in psychology.

I was searching for answers. My father would have been proud of my intellectual pursuits, and I often felt his presence in the room as I studied, nodding his approval. Yet what I needed more than anything was some explanation for the evil that had occurred. How are ordinary men transformed into killing machines? Why against the Jews? Why had some of us survived and not others? Where was God? I read Primo Levi inside and out, and Albert Camus, and of course Elie Wiesel. I learned that Elie had problems with God, too, and was comforted to know I was not the only one.

The answer is that there are no answers. I came to accept that.

Disturbing thoughts still possessed me. I was living with a secret, with fear and guilt, and the mystery of my father's death. I had my first session with a psychoanalyst in January 1969, thinking it would be a good way to start the new year. Two years of therapy passed before I even mustered the courage to tell my therapist what I had witnessed during the war, and when I finally brought myself to speak it was without a trace of emotion. I had a deep and abiding fear that, if I exposed myself, somehow I would come to harm.

Yet gradually my faith returned. The birth of my children and the experience of watching them grow, knowing that my quandaries were shared with great writers and thinkers, the work of psychoanalysis, and the healing balm of time all led me to the realization that it is easier to believe than not. I must have survived for some purpose — fate, divine justice, I don't know exactly what. I was not spared because I was so smart or so good. We had love and hope, but we also had luck, or karma, or it was *bashert* — meant to be. We were able to pick ourselves up by the bootstraps and piece a life together, however troubled.

Synagogue was for us a place of meditation and remembrance, a vestige of the life we knew as children. Joseph and I were successful in many ways, and we did the best we could for our children. We gave them good educations, and they in turn educated *their* children, who are caring, loving human beings. What better answers can one find?

Joseph died in 1986 at the age of 63. In my grief and loneliness, and amid all my memories of our years together, I gave silent thanks for his long life and mine. To have survived the unspeakable and lived long enough to see our grandchildren reach their teen years, enjoying the safety, comforts, and full range of choices we never had, is a profound blessing.

I realized too that the survivor population, myself included, was advancing in age. Many of us were in our sixties, seventies or beyond, and it was essential to record our memories. Historical and analytical studies of the Holocaust had proliferated, establishing a vital factual record. Yet I knew it was the personal testimonies that gave a human face to the cruelty of the perpetrators, the suffering of the victims, and the courage of the rescuers.

And so I resolved to tell my story. I knew that there would never be "closure" for me, much as I wanted it, but I felt a memoir would be important for my children and grandchildren and for posterity. I had always felt ambivalent about recounting my experiences to Miriam, Benjamin, and Jackie. I wanted to but didn't want to. I had told them some things, but had confused them. They knew more than I realized — children have a way of knowing — but not in full context. This is what brought me to write a book, to give them the whole story in chronological sequence. I felt it was important for them to know why I, as their mother, hadn't always done what they might have expected of me, and why I had done things in certain ways. I wanted them to know me better and know the truth about what had happened.

Piecing together my story really began in the sessions with my psychoanalyst. Dredging up the memories was painful and frightening, so I resisted for a long time. Finally the dam broke and I was flooded with memories. The stream of memories continues to this day. Capturing them on paper, from beginning to end, took me three years of many sleepless nights.

As I neared completion, I realized how important it was to deliver my testimony directly to young people, gentile and Jew, privileged and needy. Forged by my passage from darkness into light, freed by facing my memories, I have since stood before student audiences and shared the lessons I learned about good and evil, redemption and renewal, the victory of life over death. This would be my testimony, my personal contribution toward putting a human face on what had happened.

• • • • •

My debt of gratitude to those who saved me, along with my mother and brother, can never be repaid. I made many attempts to contact Sidor, writing to him directly and through the Skala town hall, police headquarters, and general post office. He disappeared behind the Iron Curtain sometime in the 1950s and our efforts proved fruitless.

As the years passed, as I struggled to make sense of it all, Sidor's selflessness and courage grew ever brighter as a beacon of faith. He had not only saved my life. His example renewed my belief in the human capacity for kindness and decency in the face of the worst depravity and the gravest risks. Without the example of Sidor and the others who refused to stand by and do nothing, we would have only the lessons of hatred, brutality, and mass hysteria to teach our children. My greatest expression of thanks would be to share his faith and testify to his courage.

Quite unexpectedly in 1995, after the fall of the Soviet Union, through the efforts of a cousin who maintained contacts in the Ukraine, I learned that Sidor's daughter Hania was living in Skala and that Sidor, Marynka, and Jan were all dead. My cousin gave me Hania's address and I wrote to her immediately that I wanted to meet, to which she agreed.

I began to consider the most appropriate place for our reunion. I had no desire to return to Skala — my memories were too vivid. There was no reason to go, not even graves to visit. My grandparents were in an unmarked mass grave, my uncles and aunts somewhere in the forest, and my father — who knows? There were no Jews left in Skala and few traces of life as I had known it. Except for Hania, only ghosts remained.

It came to me that we should meet at Yad Vashem, the Holocaust Heroes' and Martyrs' Remembrance in Jerusalem, where we should honor Sidor. I applied to have the title conferred on him of "Righteous Among the Nations," joining 19,000 others who had been recognized for risking their lives to save Jews during the Holocaust. The petition was approved several months later.

In October 1997, Hania and her son Boris flew from Kiev to Israel for our reunion. Arthur and I were reunited with the last surviving member of the family that had saved us. We were surrounded by family — Jacqueline, Benjamin, his wife Beth, and their three children — close friends, and a swarm of media. Our meeting fell on Succos, the fifty-fifth anniversary of that first horrible aktsia in Skala on my eighteenth birthday, in which half the Jews of the village were slaughtered.

I took one look at Hania as she emerged from the runway, and I burst into tears. Though a woman in her early sixties, she had the same blond hair and dark eyes that I remembered from her childhood. Her features and expression were Sidor's. We held each other and pressed our foreheads together, tears streaming down our faces.

We talked for hours during the time we had together, mostly about Sidor and our lives after the war. She remembered very little about the most desperate times, having been only six to eight years old. She and Arthur did not remember each other at all. She remembered my beautiful black hair, "Like a Chinese," she said. Most of all she remembered the fear, the hunger, and the fighting between her parents. She remembered not being allowed to go to school due to her parents' worry that she would say something that might give us away. She remembered when the Gestapo came to look for us. And she remembered that Ukrainian neighbors made fun of her after the war, calling her a "little Jewish kid" for having helped save us. Now she was a nurse with a husband and two children, living in a small house on the edge of town. She said that the fear had never gone away.

Hania also had a brother, born after the war. Sidor spent several years in a Siberian jail for stealing vodka from the distillery where he worked and selling it on the black market. He had done the same thing to help feed us and his family, and I had been anxious about the risk he was taking even then. Hania said nothing about her mother. She knew it was a subject better left alone.

And what of Jan?

Sidor and Jan had stayed in close contact for several years. Jan married the girl he had dated as a cover for his relationship with me. She brought a daughter into the marriage. Sometime thereafter, Jan was deported by the Soviets to the gulag, accused of being either a Ukrainian partisan or a Nazi collaborator, Hania didn't know which. After ten years in the Siberian gulag, he returned to Skala a broken man, hobbling on a cane. He managed to build a beautiful new home, at least by Skala's standards, but lived there only a short time before someone denounced him for having stolen money from Jews. The police found a small amount of gold under the floorboards of his house and told him to pack his things — they would be coming back for him the next day. When the police returned in the morning, they found him hanging.

• • • • •

Izydor (Sidor) Sokolowski was enshrined as a Righteous Among the Nations at Yad Vashem on October 21, 1997.

The ceremony began with a rekindling of the eternal flame, the laying of a wreath in Sidor's honor, and a blessing for the dead at the Hall of Remembrance. At the Garden of the Righteous, Hania Irena Sidorovna was bestowed a medal and certificate in honor of her father. His name was inscribed on the memorial wall with the names of all the others known to have provided safe haven to Jews in peril. Hania, too, was recognized for her role in helping to save us. Though only a child at the time, her intuition and cooperation in guarding the secret of our presence had made her a full partner in our rescue.

The shelter provided by Hania's family, that cramped space squeezed between a barn wall and the false back of a chicken coop, was our only protection from the hostile human wilderness that had surrounded us. We had uncommon luck, to be sure, but we had survived on the love, hope, and determination that we shared in that cold, dark, lice-infested refuge — a sanctuary afforded by an ordinary man who could neither read nor write but who stood alone among his neighbors, at risk of death, in resisting evil.

When it was my turn to speak, I fumbled for words that would express our gratitude for Hania's role in securing our safety, for the courage of her father, whom my entire family considers a patriarch, and for their enduring example. "The Shoah showed us not only the worst of which human beings are capable, but also the best — and that was your father. I believe a person's good deeds do not end with their departure from this world, but continue to live on in future generations and institutions."

• • • • •

My relationship with Jan and the accusations that he had killed my father had colored my whole life — as a Jewish woman, a wife, and a mother. At first I refused to think about it. Then I was consumed with ambivalence and guilt and uncertainty: how could anyone possibly make sense of this, resolve the apparent contradictions? In therapy I worked hard on this issue for years, afraid of the truth but needing answers as a matter of my own identity — to know *who I was*. Finally, I could no longer escape the conclusion that the accusations were true. I knew it in my heart, my mind and my soul. Jan's story didn't fit. Perhaps I had seen it in his eyes or heard it in his voice when I confronted him. Perhaps my father, in the heady atmosphere of the liberation, broached the subject of how he would repay our family's debt to Jan but told Jan he would not allow me to marry him. It was never clear what happened. No one ever had any factual information or concrete evidence. But something must have gone very wrong, and I was, and remain to this day, firmly convinced that Jan killed my father.

How can I explain my love for a Ukrainian militiaman who ended up killing my father? Or my own coveting of a piece of bread that would feed my starving brother? Would I have risked my life and the lives of my children to save four people who were condemned to death anyway? Can I find forgiveness in my heart? Could it all happen again?

As I go about the business of my daily life, as I take joy in the lives of my children and grandchildren, painful questions still gnaw inside me. Survivors of the Holocaust bear scars that are theirs alone and endure nightmares that others cannot fathom. As witnesses to the darkness in the human psyche, we know that it is vital to remember, but remembering is not enough.

We can no longer afford the luxury of ambivalence. The sickening plumes of smoke on September 11, 2001 and the people running terror-stricken through the streets were a vivid reminder for me, and I felt a kinship with those whose loved ones were lost. We cannot assume that the world has learned the Holocaust's lesson about the human capacity for evil. Unless we stand up for what is right and take action against those motivated by hatred, violence, and intolerance, we will be condemned to our past.

I speak to groups of American students. I tell them my experience of the Holocaust and the lessons I have learned about the preciousness of life and the importance of fighting to defend it. I hope in this way to follow Sidor's example and to contribute my part toward bringing out the best, and resisting the worst, in human nature.

• • • • •

Having seen this best and worst in human nature and destiny, I decided many years ago to make a commitment to *tikkun olam*, my own modest attempts to make the world a better place. My involvements today reflect my past and those of my family and my people. In Skala, many Jews suffered from great poverty but received no help from the Polish government. We always took care of our own, from the cradle to the grave. I have taken to heart the precept that I should help in areas that are important to me to the extent that I can.

My involvement with the Shaare Zedek Medical Center in Jerusalem is in the Jewish tradition of caring for people who need help. The Center treats those in pain with the utmost dignity and respect.

I support the YIVO Institute for Jewish Research because the unique and wonderful Yiddish language remains close to my heart. It was the language of my home when I was a young girl. Our community's rich Yiddish culture was an integral part of our family life. My father and uncle were both Yiddishists, and I have always admired Yiddish writers and their vibrant depictions of Jewish life.

The unique experience of women interests me greatly. When I was growing up, girls were not expected to study — except the domestic arts of cooking, sewing, and knitting — but my scholarly father, as I have described in this book, always encouraged me to learn both secular and Jewish topics. Several years ago, Bar Ilan University approached me to get involved with the Center for the Study of Women in Judaism. Today, I am proud to have the Center bear my name.

Although the mantra of Holocaust education is "Never Again," we have to wonder who is listening. The world continues to see far too much hatred, rape, murder, and violence. Miklat, Shelter From Abuse is a unique organization in Israel that assists religious women and children who are victims of domestic violence. Many of the women come from insular communities where they have received little formal education. Miklat protects these women and their children from abusive spouses while empowering them to rebuild their lives. Miklat also manages shelters for teenagers who have had to leave their families due to intolerable abuse. All of these shelters provide warm, stable, and supportive environments where the residents learn to engage in responsible, fulfilling relationships.

Before Joseph and I arrived in the United States in 1960, we wandered around Europe. One positive outcome of this nomadic existence was the opportunity it afforded me to visit many of the world's premier art museums. I am a lifelong lover of art and always dreamed of a world-class Jewish museum to stand proudly with its secular counterparts. When I arrived in New York, The Jewish Museum was still a relatively small institution. I wanted very much to get involved and, even though I was a recent immigrant, the Museum welcomed me with open arms and trained me as a docent. I felt so accepted into the Museum community that I vowed to help them in every way I could. I am now a life trustee of The Jewish Museum and am extremely proud of how it has grown and flourished over the years.

The Museum of Jewish Heritage: A Living Memorial to the Holocaust, where I also serve as a trustee, does a fantastic job of conveying the history of our people to a broad audience. Its programs and exhibits advancing Holocaust education are essential resources for students and educators. The Museum is helping current and future generations take to heart the message, "Never Again."

The cultivation of Jewish leadership lies in Jewish education. Even in Europe, no matter how poor Jews were, we always believed that education must be cultivated and perpetuated. Yeshiva University, the first institution of its kind to offer an intensive Judaic studies program intertwined with an accredited secular curriculum, is producing leaders who will ensure our Jewish future. The knowledge that Y.U., and particularly its women's division, Stern College, imparts to its students about how to live as a Jew in the modern world empowers them to carry on the traditions of our faith.

Involvement in all these causes is one way I have sought to give my life meaning and purpose, and has made me feel blessed indeed.

• • • • •

Inscribed in the Hall of Remembrance at the United States Holocaust Museum in Washington, D.C. is an inscription from the Book of Deuteronomy:

> *I call heaven and earth as witness! Before you, I have placed life and death, the blessing and the curse.*
>
> *You must choose life, so that you and your descendants will survive.*

F.G.H.
New York City
December 2004

Ceremony honoring Sidor at Yad Vashem, the Holocaust Heroes' and Martyrs' Remembrance in Jerusalem, October 21, 1997. Izydor (Sidor) Sokolowski was enshrined as a Righteous Among the Nations. (L to R:) Arthur, Fanya, Hania's son Boris, Hania Sidorovna, Avner Shalev, Chairman, Yad Vashem.

(L to R) Hania, Arthur, and Fanya at Yad Vashem, 1997.

Hania Sidorovna holding Sidor's Award as Righteous Among the Nations. (L to R) Fanya, Hania, and Arthur at Yad Vashem, 1997.

Fanya joined by Prof. Melvin Bukiet, Sarah Lawrence College and Prof. Froma Zeitlin of Princeton University.

Fanya with two of the many groups of wonderful high school students she has addressed.

Dedication of the Department of Pediatric Cardiology, 1994. Shaare Zedek Medical Center, Jerusalem. The department was a gift from Fanya's family.

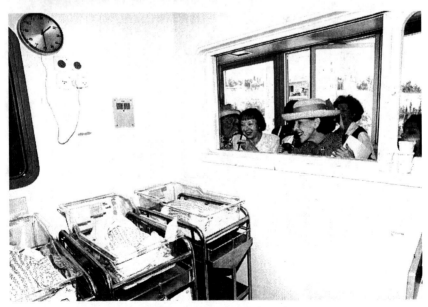

Visiting the Nursery at Shaare Zedek Medical Center in Jerusalem.

269

Graduation Ceremony at which Fanya accepted an Honorary Doctorate from Bar Ilan University. Fanya is standing with Brig. Gen. (Ret.) Yehuda Halevy, Executive Vice President of Bar Ilan University.

Fanya at Bar Ilan University

Fanya Gottesfeld-Heller Center for the Study of Women in Judaism, Bar Ilan University, Faculty of Jewish Studies

"The Triumph of the Spirit" This photo was taken at the Jewish Museum as part of "The Triumph of the Spirit" photo series on Holocaust survivors.

Fanya with Elie and Marian Wiesel

Fanya with John Cardinal O'Connor, Archbishop of New York, and David Altshuler, former Director of the Museum of Jewish Heritage

Fanya with Manhattan District Attorney Robert M. Morgenthau, Chairman of the Museum of Jewish Heritage.

273

Fanya receiving Honorary Doctorate from Yeshiva University. Presenting the degree is Judith S. Kaye, Chief Judge of the State of New York, who received an honorary degree from Y.U. in 1993.

Yeshiva University graduation where Fanya received her Honorary Doctorate. (L to R:) Judith S. Kaye, Chief Judge of the State of New York, Rabbi Dr. Norman Lamm, then President of Yeshiva University, Fanya.

Yeshiva University dinner. (L to R:) Edgar Bronfman, Senator Bob Dole, Rabbi Dr. Norman Lamm.

Fanya with renowned scholar Rabbi Adin Steinsaltz

275

About the Author

Fanya Gottesfeld Heller

As a Holocaust survivor, Fanya Gottesfeld Heller's personal mission is to teach others about the dangers of intolerance and the lessons she has learned about the triumph of life over death. Since the first edition of her book was published, Mrs. Heller has traveled throughout England, Israel, and the United States, sharing her wartime experiences with audiences of all ages — Jews and non-Jews at inner-city and suburban high schools, Ivy League universities and community colleges, museums, government agencies, corporations and service organizations. Her candor about her coming-of-age experience during the Holocaust has enabled her to connect with people of all ethnicities and backgrounds, especially those who have themselves experienced discrimination.

Mrs. Heller has been recognized by the Social Security Administration for her efforts and, in 1998, she received the Louis E. Yavner Citizen Award from the Regents of the University of the State of New York in recognition of her contributions to Holocaust education.

Professor Froma Zeitlin introduced Mrs. Heller with the following comments when she spoke at the Princeton University Center for Jewish Life in 1995:

I first met Fanya through her book. One afternoon, I idly picked it up and started to read — and I read and read and read until I had finished it. I was struck immediately by the voice that told the story. Of the innumerable memoirs of Holocaust experience I have read, Fanya's story was different. It was the voice — the voice of recovered memory — that so captured my attention. It had charm and honesty, an intensity of feeling, both innocent and self-aware, that gripped me. I decided that I wanted to share the book with the students in my Holocaust course, and that I would invite her to come and share with us in turn.

So long ago, so vividly present still in memory are those events that tore a great gash in Western consciousness and conscience. This wound to the spirit remains and eludes healing. Fanya's story does not take place in Auschwitz; or in one of the better-known ghettoes like Warsaw or Vilna. It took place in a little town in Eastern Poland, once part of the Austro-Hungarian Empire, a town named Skala not far from Lvov, which was under Soviet rule between 1939-1941 until the Nazis came and the mayhem really began. An area largely Ukrainian, with some mixture of Poles as well, a town of only 1,500 Jews; a loving family surrounded by numerous relatives, a happy and pampered childhood, a promising adolescence with dreams of studying medicine in Paris.

Fanya brings this town to life in her memoir: the streets, the town square, the market, the surrounding countryside. And in recounting her story, she not only performs the work of memory for those who were slaughtered or shipped off to extermination at Belzec, she not only adds to the Yizkor Books, the remembrance books that were later compiled of these innumerable small towns and settlements. She also

277

brings her own unique experience, to be treasured as each survivor's story is treasured, should be treasured, for its own individuality in the struggle for survival, in the effort to preserve the spark of life amidst the ruins.

By all our conventional standards, Fanya's life story might be counted a success. But the past is always there as a haunting shadow — sometimes submerged, sometimes erupting to the surface — and if we, from the security of our safe and sheltered lives, are determined not to ignore the burden of that past, then it means attempting to close up the distance between then and now. It means listening to individual voices — a voice like Fanya Gottesfeld Heller's.

In addition to speaking about her experiences during the Holocaust, Mrs. Heller has many additional interests and philanthropic involvements. In Jerusalem, Shaare Zedek Medical Center's Fanya Gottesfeld Heller Floor houses the ER and other vital departments. Mrs. Heller serves on the board of Miklat, Shelter from Abuse — a shelter in Israel that addresses the unique needs of observant woman and their children who are caught in the vise of domestic violence. She is also a trustee of the Museum of Jewish Heritage: A Living Memorial to the Holocaust, which hosts the annual Fanya Gottesfeld Heller Symposium for educators to provide them with the tools in teaching the Holocaust to future generations. Bar Ilan University in Israel is home to the Fanya Gottesfeld Heller Center for the Study of Women in Judaism. Mrs. Heller is also involved in the work of the Jewish Museum and the YIVO Institute for Jewish Research and is active in supporting Yeshiva University.

More Letters of Appreciation

From educators...

"Never before have I seen an audience as engaged and responsive as yours was...I was deeply moved by your memoirs, and feel that your telling the truth contributes profoundly to dignifying the suffering of the victims and helping outsiders comprehend what happened."

— Dorothee von Huene Greenberg
Pace University, New York

"It is an extraordinary book. In addition to the obvious contribution that it makes to understanding the history of European Jewry during the Holocaust, it reveals an author who is honest, courageous, resolute, sensitive, and with a capacity for exemplary self-sacrificing devotion to family."

— Rabbi Dr. Sol Roth
Fifth Avenue Synagogue, New York.

"Your talk provided our students with an insightful and meaningful look into the most tragic of all periods of human history. The students were moved not only by your words, but also by your courage and strength."

— Antoinette Branscum and Margaret Burns
Saint Rose of Lima School, New York

From students...

"Hearing and seeing a survivor from the Holocaust is better than sitting in school and reading about it. The speech made me think about all the pain and suffering your family went through and made me realize that when I don't get what I want I shouldn't be sad, but rather appreciate the things I have and be happy I didn't have to go through the suffering you went through. Not only did you teach me a lesson on tolerance, but also on thankfulness; to be happy with the hand that God dealt me. You have put a new vision of the Holocaust into my life because of your stories."

— Andrea

WITHDRAWN

"As you told your tale, all of the movies and excerpts and bi-ographies we have read came back to me, and I began to feel the pain of these people... When I was younger, the man who lived in the apartment above my family was a Holocaust survi-vor...Now that I know about his past I want to send him a letter telling him how much he meant to me as a child and how I love him...Thank you for inspiring me."

— Sara

"It meant a great deal to actually listen to an account of the Holocaust, person to person, from a survivor who witnessed it all... In my class, we have gone in depth into the Holocaust through literature, films, and presentations. However, your story has further enhanced my knowledge regarding this subject and it is an experience I shall never forget."

— Maryse

"I enjoyed listening to you because you were like any other teen-ager with hopes and dreams, except you were not given a choice to pursue them...I am currently a senior in high school facing college decisions and I have my goals and dreams as well, but not having the chance to pursue them is unimaginable. Listening to your story gave me a better insight into the study of the Holocaust."

— Anita